Tax Guide 303

SIMPLIFYING YOUR ESTATE

by

Holmes F. Crouch
Tax Specialist

Published by

Allyear Tax Guides

20484 Glen Brae Drive
Saratoga, CA 95070

ISBN 0-944817-57-2

LCCN 99-72407

Printed in U.S.A.

Series 300
Retirees & Estates

Tax Guide 303

SIMPLIFYING YOUR ESTATE

For other titles in print, see page 224.

The author: **Holmes F. Crouch**
For more about the author, see page 221.

PREFACE

If you are a knowledge-seeking **taxpayer** looking for information, this book can be helpful to you. It is designed to be read — from cover to cover — in less than eight hours. Or, it can be "skim-read" in about 30 minutes.

Either way, you are treated to **tax knowledge** . . . ***beyond the ordinary***. The "beyond" is that which cannot be found in IRS publications, FedWorld on-line services, tax software programs, Internet chatrooms, or E-mail bulletins.

Taxpayers have different levels of interest in a selected subject. For this reason, this book starts with introductory fundamentals and progresses onward. You can verify the progression by chapter and section in the table of contents. In the text, "applicable law" is quoted in pertinent part. Key phrases and key tax forms are emphasized. Real-life examples are given . . . in down-to-earth style.

This book has 12 chapters. This number provides depth without cross-subject rambling. Each chapter starts with a head summary of meaningful information.

To aid in your skim-reading, informative diagrams and tables are placed strategically throughout the text. By leafing through page by page, reading the summaries and section headings, and glancing at the diagrams and tables, you can get a good handle on the matters covered.

Effort has been made to update and incorporate all of the latest tax law changes that are *significant* to the title subject. However, "beyond the ordinary" does not encompass every conceivable variant of fact and law that might give rise to protracted dispute and litigation. Consequently, if a particular statement or paragraph is crucial to your own specific case, you are urged to seek professional counseling. Otherwise, the information presented is general and is designed for a broad range of reader interests.

The Author

INTRODUCTION

IRS Form 706: Ever heard of it? Ever seen it? Ever held it? Ever filled one out?

Most probably not. It is a *death* tax return. Its short title is: ***U.S. Estate Tax Return***. Its full title is: ***U.S. Estate (and Generation-Skipping Transfer) Tax Return***. The form itself is 44 pages long . . . without attachments. Ordinarily, it is prepared after your death by your executor. Yet it is one of those rare forms that you can initiate on your own before death, to simplify your affairs while living, in preparation and planning for the inevitable.

Generally, Form 706 is required for gross estates exceeding $600,000 at time of death. This filing threshold increases each year until 2006. In that year (and thereafter), its filing is required when your gross estate exceeds $1,000,000 (1 million dollars).

If your gross estate exceeds the $600,000 to $1,000,000 thresholds, Form 706 can NOT be avoided by those exotic estate planning arrangements that you may have heard about, or may have been lured into. Living trusts, charitable remainder trusts, generation-skipping trusts, terminable interest trusts, annuity trusts, foreign trusts, and any other sophisticated arrangements that mesmerize you, do not circumvent Form 706. Furthermore, such arrangements do nothing — absolutely nothing — to simplify the preparation and filing of said form.

Of all those sales pitches about the magic of trusts, have you ever been told *anything* about Form 706? Anything significant at all? Have you been told about the probing questions into your during-life transfers for insufficient consideration, co-ownership of property with others, gifts in excess of $10,000, closely-held business interests, and trusts created for you by others? Have those promoters told you about the facts of life being resurrected at death? Have they? If not, go ask them now.

Ask them to explain ***powers of appointment***. Ask how you would answer and value the assets behind the question: *Did the decedent ever possess, exercise, or release any general powers of appointment?* ☐ *Yes* ☐ *No. If "Yes," you must complete and* *attach Schedule H* [and] *include "5 and 5" lapsing powers held by the decedent.*

Have those promoters forewarned you about the "safe deposit box" question on Schedule F of Form 706? The full text of this question reads:

> *Did the decedent at the time of death have, or have access to, a safe deposit box?* ☐ *Yes* ☐ *No. If "Yes," state location, and if held in joint names of decedent and another, state name and relationship of joint depositor. If any of the contents of the safe deposit box are omitted from the schedules in this return, explain fully why omitted.*

Particularly ask what the proposals for trusts will do about simplifying the nine asset schedules that comprise Form 706. Said schedules are titled—

A — Real Estate
B — Stocks and Bonds
C — Mortgages, Notes, and Cash
D — Insurance on Decedent's Life
E — Jointly Owned Property
F — Other Miscellaneous Property
G — Transfers During Decedent's Life
H — Powers of Appointment
I — Annuities

Do you have any idea at all how these schedules are filled out?

You *will* have more than an idea when you get through reading this book. After our whisking you through Form 706, you'll become that RARE PERSON who knows what "the system" does with his estate. Once you fill out the form, even in the most preliminary way, you will see opportunities for simplifying your affairs, not only for daily living, but also for expediting the transfer of your assets to others upon your demise.

CONTENTS

Chapter **Page**

Chapter		Page

1

YOUR "GROSS ESTATE"

Your Gross Estate Will Be Form 706 Probed For: (A) Real Estate, (B) Stocks & Bonds, (C) Notes & Cash, (D) Life Insurance, (E) Joint Property, (F) Other Property, (G) Gifts & Transfers, (H) Trust Powers, And (I) Annuities. These "9 Asset Schedules" Define Your Gross Estate ANYWHERE IN THE WORLD! Very Little Property Of Value Or Rights To The Enjoyment Of Such Property Escape The Formidable Corralling Process Of The 44-Page Death Tax Return. Knowing What Is Required On Form 706 Is The NECESSARY PRELUDE For Simplifying Your Affairs While Alive.

Over our years of working and living, raising a family and so forth, we accumulate assets and liabilities. The term "assets" refers to items of property and monetary holdings which are readily marketable to third-party (nonfamily) interests. The term "liabilities" refers to those obligations of debt — more than 30 days old — that are owed to third-party interests. Taken together, your assets less your liabilities constitute your "net worth." More specifically, however, the IRS focus is on your *Gross Estate*. The magnitude of such estate sets the stage for a whole raft of probings into your financial and property affairs, after death.

One's gross estate changes over the course of time. After the children are grown, the gross estate tends to accumulate more rapidly than it can be consumed. During the rapid buildup period, rarely does one take a serious snapshot of his or her estate . Even when occasional snapshots are made, they do not involve the detailed accounting nor the permanency, when you are no longer around to supervise and manage your own affairs.

When the end of life comes, you have what is then called: a *Transfer Estate*. This is that estate which is no longer being accumulated or consumed by yourself. It is that which is available — after expenses and debts — for transfer to heirs and others. Before the transfer is consummated, however, a federal transfer tax (otherwise known as an "estate tax" or "death tax") is imposed. This, then, becomes the ultimate defining moment of your gross estate.

In this introductory chapter, therefore, we want to familiarize you with what constitutes your gross estate . . . for death tax purposes. We also want to acquaint you with a rather formidable tax return — **Form 706**: ***U.S. Estate Tax Return*** — that you've probably never seen or thought about before. Rare indeed does a living person give serious thought to the disclosure requirements of Form 706. It is for this reason that we want to present to you an overview of it.

Transfer Tax Imposed

We want you to start off thinking in down-to-earth reality. A federal transfer tax **is** imposed. Whether you transfer a portion of your estate irrevocably during life, or transfer it all after death, a tax is imposed. Before said tax is determined, however, you are allowed certain deductions, exemptions, and credits. What is left after these allowances is subject to tax. It is a *transfer tax*. It is tax on the privilege of transferring money or property gratuitously, to successors who will use it for their own enjoyment.

We know, you've been led to believe that, perhaps, if you set up some kind of exotic-sounding trust, you can avoid taxes, avoid probate, avoid creditors, avoid complicating your estate, and avoid anything and everything that you don't like to do. You can succumb to such fantasies all you want. But you can't avoid the reality that a transfer tax *will be imposed*! The Internal Revenue Code (IRC) does not vanish into cyberspace simply because you are enthralled with the prospects of tax and other avoidances through various trusts and insurance arrangements.

IRC Section 2001(a): ***Imposition of Estate Tax***, says succinctly and forcefully—

> *A tax is hereby imposed on the* ***transfer*** *of the taxable estate of* ***every decedent*** *who is a citizen or resident of the United States.* [Emphasis added.]

IRC Section 2501(a)(1): ***Imposition of Gift Tax***, says also succinctly and forcefully—

> *A tax . . . is hereby imposed for each calendar year on the* ***transfer of property****, by gift during such calendar year by* ***any individual****, resident or nonresident.* [Emphasis added.]

IRC Section 2601: ***Imposition of Generation-Skipping Tax***, says tersely and succinctly—

> *A tax is hereby imposed on every generation-skipping transfer.*

A "generation-skipping transfer" is the transfer of property directly to grandchildren and great-grandchildren. The GST tax is *added onto* that imposed by Sections 2001 and 2501. So, the next time you attend one of those free wealth preservation seminars sponsored by legal, accounting, insurance, and financial firms, keep the above three citations in mind. Listen carefully to all of the selling points and advantages of the "estate planning" arrangements being proposed. At the opportune moment, pop the ugly question. Nervously . . . and politely, ask—

> *"If I have a 3 million dollar estate, will the arrangement you propose avoid the transfer tax imposed by Sections 2001, 2501, and 2601 of the Internal Revenue Code?"*

You'll become instantly unpopular with the seminar sponsor and his entourage of experts. Similarly with many of the attending guests. You may even be accused of being an IRS spy. Assure the accusers that you are not. You — like all the rest of the attendees — want to avoid as many taxes as you can. Then explain—

"I read a book by some tax guy who claims you can't avoid transfer taxes for estates in the one million dollar and upwards range. Is he wrong?"

Unified Exemption Amounts

Every taxable estate is allowed a specified exemption amount, depending on the year of transfer. The term "every estate" means just that. The term applies to every individual decedent and/or to every living individual. The exemption amount is a separate right of every individual, regardless of marital status. For a married couple, there are two exemption amounts: one for each spouse. There is no sharing or trade-off between spouses. Form 706, previously mentioned, is a **per individual decedent** tax return. There is no joint Form 706.

The basic tax law on point is Section 2010: ***Unified Credit Against Estate Tax***. Its subsection (a): ***General Rule***, reads—

> *A credit of the applicable credit amount* ***shall be allowed*** *to the estate of* ***every decedent*** *against the tax imposed by section 2001* [above]. [Emphasis added].

Similarly, Section 2505: ***Unified Credit Against Gift Tax***, applies. Its subsection (a): **General Rule**, reads—

> *There* ***shall be allowed*** *as a credit against the tax imposed by section 2501* [above] *for each calendar year an amount equal to—*
>
> > *(1) the applicable credit amount in effect under section 2010(c) for such calendar year,* ***reduced by***
> >
> > *(2) the sum of the amounts allowable as a credit to the* ***individual*** *under this section for all preceding calendar periods.* [Emphasis added.]

Note that the common term: ***Unified***, is used in Sections 2010 and 2505. This means that there is just **one** overall aggregate exemption amount. It can be used in full during life; or it can be used in full upon death; or any combination of life and death use is allowed. In other words, the unified concept enables the exemption amount to be cumulatively used until the statutory limit is reached.

The statutory limit on the exemption amount is prescribed in Section 2010(c): ***Applicable Credit Amount.*** In general terms, the exemption amount extends from $600,000 to $1,000,000 depending on the year of irrevocable transfer. Before any transfer tax applies, the statutory exemption amount is factored in. A tabulation of the specific amounts is presented in Figure 1.1. You might want to glance down the center column there, and pick the exemption threshold that would apply in your case.

Decedents Dying & Gifts Made During -	Exemption Amount	Equivalent Credit Against Tax
1997	$600,000	$192,800
1998	625,000	202,050
1999	650,000	211,300
2000 & 2001	675,000	220,550
2002 & 2003	700,000	229,800
2004	850,000	287,300
2005	950,000	326,300
2006 & after	1,000,000	345,800
Sec. 2010 - Unified Credit Against Estate Tax Subsec. (c) - Applicable Credit Amount		

Fig. 1.1 - Applicable Exemption Amounts for a Transfer Estate

The exemption amounts in Figure 1.1 are NOT contingent upon any professionally prepared "estate plan," exotic trust, or insurance arrangement. Whether you have some fancy plan or not, you are entitled to the statutory exemption amounts. Yet, most sponsors of wealth preservation seminars and their expert speakers *imply* — they don't come right out and say so — that the exemptions are the consequence of the particular arrangements that they propose. If you have this belief, you have been misled.

Particularly note in the section titles above, use of the term: ***Unified Credit Against . . . Tax.*** This term arises from computational technicalities involving mixed life/death use of the exemption amount. A tentative tax (at graduated rates from 18% up to 55%) is computed first. Then a "credit" corresponding to each exemption amount is applied. We posted in Figure 1.1 the equivalent credits for reducing the tax. We can tell you now that the rate structure begins phasing out the benefits of graduated rates and unified credits for taxable estates over $10,000,000 (10 million).

Gross Estate Defined

Regardless of your specific exemption amount, all estate matters and transfers during life have to be fully accounted for at time of death. This involves the process of establishing your gross estate: item-by-item, dollar-by-dollar. This itemization for transfer tax purposes is far more detailed than you ever imagined. Yet, it is the very first step in understanding what you need to do towards simplifying your estate for its transfer to others.

In the most succinct terms possible, your gross estate is defined by Section 2031(a): ***Gross Estate***; ***General***, as follows:

> *The value of the gross estate of the decedent shall be determined by including to the extent provided for in this part, the value at the time of his death of* ***all property, real or personal, tangible or intangible, wherever situated.*** [Emphasis added.]

This is an all-sweeping concept: *all property* (real, tangible, intangible, personal) *wherever situated.* The term "all property" means those property items which are marketable to third-party interests at arm's length value. The term "wherever situated" means anywhere in the world! Why, only at death, is such a concept imposed?

Answer: Upon death, one's gross estate is fixed. It cannot be further changed by the decedent who accumulated the estate. It is that moment of finality we all face.

Exactly, what does the Internal Revenue Code have to say about: "all property . . . wherever situated"? You really don't want us to enumerate and explain each of the 92 applicable sections (2001 through 2704), do you?

The simplest official response that we can present is ***Part 5 — Recapitulation***, of **Form 706**: ***U.S. Estate Tax Return***. Accordingly, we do so in Figure 1.2. You might want to take a moment to read down each of the nine Form 706 schedules listed. The title of each schedule (though abbreviated in some instances) gives you a bird's eye view of what is regarded as your gross estate at time of death.

Form 706	**U.S. Estate Tax Return**	
Part 5 - Recapitulation		
Schedule		Value at Death
	Gross Estate	
A	Real Estate	
B	Stocks & Bonds	
C	Mortgages, Notes, & Cash	
D	Insurance on Decedent's Life	
E	Jointly Owned Property	
F	Other Miscellaneous Property	
G	Transfers During Decedent's Life	
H	Powers of Appointment	
I	Annuities	

Fig. 1.2 - The 9 Gross Estate Schedules on Form 706

Each of the Figure 1.2 schedules is a comprehensive accounting document of its own. A few purely overview comments on each of these nine schedules are essential to "estate planning."

Schedule A — Real Estate

The ownership of land (and its appurtenances) is fundamental to any transferable estate. Land is real and fixed. Though its surface may be modified and improved, and buildings erected onto it, it generally is not capable of being consumed or destroyed. Except for defined subsurface mineral, gas, and water rights, one's ownership of land, technically, goes down to the center of the Earth.

At any rate, Schedule A of Form 706 requires a descriptive listing and the current market value of all parcels of land owned and used by the decedent. On this point, and for all gross estate schedules, Section 2033 is directly pertinent. The title of Section 2033 is: ***Property in Which Decedent Had an Interest.*** Its one sentence mandate is—

> *The value of the gross estate shall include the value of all property **to the extent of the*** [ownership] ***interest therein** of the decedent at the time of his death.* [Emphasis added.]

By its very nature, land and its appurtenances is subject to co-ownership and multiple ownership arrangements. This characteristic is more prevalent in real estate holdings than with other forms of a decedent's assets. Hence, the ownership aspects of the decedent must be identified in exact percentages of the total parcel, for proper entry on Schedule A. Generally, if the decedent owns 50% or more of a real estate item, that item is entered on Schedule A. If he owns less than 50%, the item is listed and described on other schedules, such as E, F, G, or H.

If a parcel of real estate is co-owned by the decedent and his spouse, the total professionally-appraised value of the property is entered on Schedule A. Immediately below said entry, an offsetting entry for the surviving spouse is made. Typically, such ownership is 50/50, though it could be non-50/50. For example, the offsetting entry could be—

> LESS 50% for spouse's interest < >

The official instructions to Schedule A of Form 706 say—

> *Describe the real estate in enough detail so that the IRS can easily locate it for inspection and valuation. For each parcel of real estate, report the* [geographic] *area and, if the parcel is improved, describe the improvements. For city or town property, report the street or number, ward, subdivision, block and lot, etc. For rural property, report the township, range, landmarks, etc.*

There is a crucial point being made by the above instructions. Of all your gross estate holdings, real estate is the principal target for "inspection and valuation" by the IRS. This is because, in most cases, real estate comprises the dominant dollar value item. For practical purposes, transfer tax rates for real estate *start* at 35% to 40%. Consequently, there is temptation to low value real estate rather than fair market value it. The IRS is fully aware of this temptation.

The more parcels and types of real property that a decedent has, naturally the more complicated his estate affairs will be. It is for this reason that we devote an entire chapter, namely Chapter 4: Culling Real Estate, to ways for simplifying one's real estate "estate."

Schedule B — Stocks, Bonds, Etc.

Officially, Schedule B of Form 706 is titled: ***Stocks and Bonds***. By so limiting the title, the implication is that nothing else goes on this schedule whatsoever. But what about mutual funds? And, what about other portfolio assets which are stock-and-bond-like in character? Ownership interests in real estate investment trusts, mortgage backed securities, limited partnership activities, mining exploration undertakings, oil and gas wells, foreign government securities, foreign corporate securities, and a host of other interests in stock and bond derivatives, certainly qualify for inclusion and listing on Schedule B.

For our purposes of identifying asset areas that can be simplified, we regard Schedule B as the repository for variable-unit-value assets of the decedent. More collectively, the items listed are intangibles known as *portfolio* assets. Said assets are "intangible" in that they are "pieces of paper" representing fractional interest in real and tangible property, and in entrepreneurial businesses.

The IRS is certainly not going to object if one lists on Schedule B every single variable-unit-value asset that a decedent has. In fact, no other schedule of Form 706 is so adaptable for such items. Furthermore, many estate holders have a very large portion of their wealth in Schedule B-type intangibles. In some, the extent of wealth in Schedule B exceeds that in Schedule A.

The official instructions to Schedule B are exceedingly detailed. Only to give you the flavor of these instructions, we cite just one of its 21 paragraphs, to wit:

> *List interest and dividends on each stock or bond separately. Indicate as a separate item dividends that have not been collected at death, but which are payable to the decedent or the estate because the decedent was a stockholder of record on the date of death. However, if the stock is being traded on an exchange and is selling ex-dividend on the date of the decedent's death, do not include the amount of the dividend as a separate item. Instead, add it to the ex-dividend quotation in determining the fair market value of the stock on the date of the decedent's death. Dividends declared on shares of stock before the death of the decedent but payable to stockholders of record* ***on a date after the decedent's death are not includible*** *in the gross estate.* [They are includible on Form 1041 which is an income tax return. Form 706 is a transfer tax return.] [Emphasis added.]

In many gross estate situations, the number of entries on Schedule B can range from 5 to 50 . . . to 150! In this event, one or more *Continuation Schedules* is necessary. For simplicity-focusing purposes, Schedule B is where most of the action lies. Accordingly, we have much more to tell you about Schedule B in upcoming Chapter 5: Slimming Portfolio Assets.

Schedule C — Mortgages, Notes, & Cash

Whereas Schedule B accommodates variable-unit-value assets, Schedule C accommodates fixed-value assets. That is, a Schedule C asset is fixed in terms of number of dollars. There is no $/unit, $/share, or $/contract to be concerned with. The only concern with fixed dollar assets is the effect of monetary inflation (over many years: five or more). However, for Schedule C listings, the effect of inflation is ignored. Account balance values are used.

As to the assets prescribed for Schedule C (Form 706), the instructions say—

List items on Schedule C in the following order:

- *mortgages,*
- *promissory notes,*
- *contracts to sell land,*
- *cash in possession, and*
- *cash in banks . . . and other financial organizations.*

The instructions go on to say—

List on Schedule C:

- *mortgages and notes* ***payable to*** *the decedent at time of death.*

Do not *list on Schedule C:*

- *mortgages and notes* ***payable by*** *the decedent at time of death. (If these are deductible, list them on Schedule K.)*

Mortgages payable **to** the decedent generally arise from self-financing of real estate sales, or from monies advanced in the form of second trust deeds secured by real property. A mortgage is an enforceable instrument which has a face value, an unpaid balance, rate of interest, and date of maturity. Seller-financed mortgages are especially attractive as a simplifying endeavor where there are multiple holdings of real estate. Mortgages can be reassigned to one or more of the decedent's heirs without the appraisal, title, and management complexities of real property itself.

Cash holdings in the form of promissory notes, land contracts, savings accounts, certificates of deposit, money market funds, and checking accounts often comprise a very significant portion of a decedent's estate. The liquidity of such assets makes them the ideal focus for serious estate-simplifying effort. We devote a full chapter to this aspect, namely: Chapter 10: Building Needed Liquidity.

Schedule D — Life Insurance

Officially, Schedule D (Form 706) is titled: ***Insurance on the Decedent's Life***. Said insurance is treated as an asset of the decedent. Before death, each life insurance policy, ordinarily, has a determinable cash value. At the instant of death, its cash value is substantially magnified. It is for this reason that the headnote instruction to Schedule D says, emphatically:

> *You must list **all** policies on the life of the decedent and attach a Form 712 for each policy.*

Form 712 is titled: **Life Insurance Statement**. It consists of two parts: (A) ***Decedent-Insured*** (32 lines), and (B) ***Living Insured*** (20 lines). The "statement" provides information on the face amount of the policy, amount of one sum proceeds, value of proceeds as of date of death (if not payable as one sum), name of beneficiaries, and name of the policy owner. Other instructions to Form 712 say—

> *If decedent is not owner, attach copy of* [insurance] *application. If policy has been assigned* [to other than the decedent or his estate], *attach a copy of the assignment.*

Schedule D is the direct consequence of IRC Section 2042: ***Proceeds of Life Insurance***. The gist of which is—

> *The value of the gross estate shall include the value of all property—*
>
> > *(1)* ***Receivable by the executor*** *. . . to the extent of the amount . . . as insurance under policies on the life of the decedent.*
> >
> > *(2)* ***Receivable by other beneficiaries*** *. . .* [if] *the decedent possessed at his death any of the incidents of ownership* [of the policy on his life], *exercisable either alone or in conjunction with any other person* [or entity].

To include or not include the proceeds of life insurance on Schedule D (Form 706) has been a controversy of long standing between the IRS and the insurance industry. This controversy arises because Irrevocable Life Insurance Trusts (ILITs) are marketed as being excludable from gross estates. The IRS has argued successfully that if proceeds from a life insurance trust are used to pay the estate tax, or any other taxes, debts, or charges against the decedent's estate, such proceeds **are** includible.

Schedules E & F — Other Property Items

Schedules E and F are titled, respectively: ***Jointly Owned Property***, and ***Other Miscellaneous Property Not Reportable Under Any Other Schedule***. Schedule E is arranged in two parts (jointly owned with spouse, and jointly owned with others), whereas Schedule F starts off with three probing Yes-No questions. Both Schedules E and F are regarded as catchalls for those assets that don't expressly qualify for inclusion on Schedules A, B, and C: real estate, stocks and bonds, and cash.

Part 1 of Schedule E: Qualified Joint Interests Held by Decedent and Spouse, overlaps with those items in Schedules A, B, and C. The term "qualified" spousal interests applies when an item is held as:

- Tenants by the entirety, or
- Joint tenants with right of survivorship

As such, once the spousal property assets are itemized and totaled, one-half (or 50%) is excluded from the decedent spouse's gross estate. If several significant assets are so held, listing them in Schedules A, B, and C, then subtracting 50%, is more convenient than listing them in Part 1 of Schedule E.

Part 2 of Schedule E directs attention to "all other" surviving co-tenants. The form is set up for listing separately the name, address, and percentage ownership of each co-tenant. For each property so identified (and full valued), the *inclusion percentage* of the decedent is stated and applied to the full value. Otherwise the instructions say—

> *If you believe that less than the full value of the entire property is includible in the gross estate for tax purposes, you must establish the right to include the smaller value by attaching*

> *proof of the extent, origin, and nature of the decedent's interest and the interest(s) of the decedent's co-tenant or co-tenants.*

Co-tenancy property tends to be that which is inherited, held in trust, acquired in joint ventures, shared in a partnership, or held for investment (such as rental real estate). Where there are multiple properties and multiple co-tenants, the result often is extreme complication when gross estating a decedent's Form 706. We address this matter in more detail in Chapter 6: Clarifying Co-Ownerships.

The headportion of Schedule F: ***Other Miscellaneous Property***, directs specific attention to—

- Articles of artistic or collectible value,
- Bonus or awards to other than decedent as a result of decedent's employment or death, and
- Access to a safe deposit box.

Below the Yes-No safe deposit box question, instructions say—

> *If any of the contents of the safe deposit box are omitted from the schedules in this return, explain fully why omitted.*

In other respects, Schedule F is a pure catchall for extraneous forms of assets which decedents and others are often unaware that they have. A listing of the types of items commonly involved is presented in Figure 1.3. The general idea behind Figure 1.3 is that nothing is to be omitted from Form 706 (if it has a value of $100 or more per item). We'll come back to Schedule F and related matters in Chapter 7: Purging Collectibles, Etc.

Schedule G — Transfers During Life

Without question, Form 706 is THE most exhaustive tax return ever prepared for an individual. No asset can be omitted if the decedent had even the remotest of ownership interest in, or strings attached to, during-life transfers. The instructions to Schedule G: ***Transfers During Decedent's Life***, make the point clear:

Sched. F	Other Miscellaneous Property	Form 706
1. Articles of artistic or collectible value	☐ Yes ☐ No	
2. Bonus or award to spouse or other	☐ Yes ☐ No	
3. Access to a safe deposit box	☐ Yes ☐ No	
Marital deduction property from predeceased spouse		
☐ Debts due decedent	☐ Proprietorship business(es)	☐ Insurance on life of another
● Partnership interests	● Closely-held corporations	
• Claims	• Judgments	• Farm machinery
• Refunds	• Trust funds	• Farm products
• Rights	• Automobiles	• Recreational vehicles
• Royalties	• Household goods	• Reversionary interests
• Leaseholds	• Personal effects	• Remainder interests

Fig. 1.3 - Range of Items Includible on Schedule F (706)

> *All transfers (other than outright transfers for full and adequate consideration and bona fide sales) made by the decedent* ***at any time during*** [his] ***life*** *must be reported on Schedule G regardless of whether you believe the transfers are subject to tax.* [Emphasis added.]

This instruction requires that the decedent's executor rummage back many years into the decedent's prior life. The rummaging process can be a frustrating experience.

Other instructions to Schedule G specify five specific types of transfers that must be included. These are—

> ***(1) Certain gift taxes*** *— Enter the total value of the gift taxes that were paid by the decedent or the estate on gifts made by the decedent or the decedent's spouse within three years before death.*
>
> ***(2) Other transfers within three years before death*** *— Include only the following:*
> *• any transfer by the decedent with respect to a life insurance policy within 3 years before death.*

- *any relinquishment or transfer of a power of appointment within 3 years before death, if the power would have been includible in the gross estate had the decedent continued to possess it until death.*
- *any transfer within 3 years before death of a retained life estate, reversionary interest, or power to revoke, etc., if the life estate, interest, or power would have been included in the gross estate had the decedent continued to possess it until death.*

(3) ***Transfer with retained life estates*** *— These are transfers in which the decedent retained the right to designate the person or persons who will possess or enjoy the transferred property, or the income from the transferred property if the transfer was made.*

(4) ***Transfers taking effect at death*** *— A transfer that takes effect at the decedent's death is one under which possession or enjoyment can be obtained only by surviving the decedent.*

(5) ***Revocable transfers*** *— These are transfers in which the enjoyment of the transferred property was subject at decedent's death to any change through the exercise of a power to alter, amend, revoke, or terminate.*

Not much can escape the asset probings of Schedule G. Special rules and tax forms apply when transferring items of value to family members, business associates (as in corporations or partnerships), into trust, or by other "insufficient consideration" means. Convincing documentation of the authenticity of the transfers must be attached.

Schedules H & I — Powers & Annuities

Schedules H and I are titled, respectively: ***Powers of Appointment***, and ***Annuities***. A "power of appointment" is the right of a decedent to enjoy all or part of the property of someone else which is in trust, under contract, or sequestered by insurance or other arrangement. An "annuity" is a contract for payments over a period of time referenced to the decedent's death. Any power or annuity exercisable in favor of the decedent **is included** in his estate. Instructions accompanying both schedules are explicit on this point.

Instructions to Schedule H say, in part—

> *Include in the gross estate: (1) The value of the property for which the decedent possessed a general power of appointment on his or her death; and (2) The value of property for which* [the decedent] *exercised or released the power before death by disposing of it in such a way that it would* [otherwise be treated] *. . . as a retained life estate, a transfer taking effect at death, or a revocable transfer.*
>
> *A power is* ***not*** *includible in the gross estate* ***if*** *the decedent* ***released the power completely*** *and the decedent held no interest in or control over the property.* [Emphasis added.]

Similarly, for Schedule I the instructions say, in part—

> *Include in the gross estate the value of any annuity that: (1) Is receivable by a beneficiary following the death of a decedent by reason of surviving the decedent; or (2) Is payable to the decedent . . . for life . . . or for any period that did not in fact end before the decedent's death.*
>
> *These rules apply to all types of annuities, including pension (profit-sharing, stock bonus) plans, individual retirement arrangements (IRAs), and purchased commercial annuities.*

It should be obvious by now that very little property of value, or rights to the enjoyment of such property, escapes the corralling arm of Form 706. No matter what you have accumulated or have tried to preserve during life, it is **all** resurrected at time of death.

Other Items on Form 706

Schedules A through I — the nine asset schedules — comprise the "heavy duty" items on Form 706. These schedules must be tackled and valued first. If the aggregate value of all of these schedules exceeds $600,000 to $1,000,000 corresponding to the years listed in Figure 1.1, Form 706 becomes a mandated filing. When this happens, other items on Form 706 must be addressed.

Preceding Schedule A (Real Estate), there is a series of entry spaces, questions, checkboxes, and requests for general information. These items are arranged as follows:

Part 1 — ***Decedent and Executor***
Part 2 — ***Tax Computation***
Part 3 — ***Elections by the Executor***
Part 4 — ***General Information***
Part 5 — ***Recapitulation*** [of Schedules A through I, and J through U]

Following Schedule I (Annuities), other schedules appear. These are:

J — ***Funeral and Administrative Expenses***
K — ***Debts of the Decedent***
L — ***Net Losses During Administration***
M — ***Bequests to Surviving Spouse***
O — ***Charitable Gifts and Bequests***
P — ***Credit for Foreign Death Taxes***
Q — ***Credit for Tax on Prior Transfers***
R — ***Generation-Skipping Transfer Tax***
T — ***Family-Owned Business Deduction***
U — ***Conservation Easement Exclusion***

(There are no Schedules N and S.) Schedules J, K, and L are expense deductions; Schedules M and O are bequest deductions; Schedules P and Q are credits against tax; and Schedules T and U, if applicable, provide additional reductions to your taxable estate.

The point that we are getting at is this. Unless you give serious thought ahead of time, the Form 706 process can be complicated, costly, and frustrating. With only a modest amount of forethought and dedication, Form 706 can be turned into an instructional and highly beneficial experience . . . while you are alive.

2

A FEW BAD EXAMPLES

Human Nature Is Such That Putting Off Until Death Is Preferable To Making Decisions While Alive. In Your Post-Mortem Estate "Bad Things" Can Happen. By Allowing Attorneys To Take Charge, Time Will Drag, Heirs Are Neglected, And Fees "Go Through The Roof." Blind Faith In Appointees With A Financial Interest In Your Estate Can Lead To DEATH BED SWITCHING, And The Shut-Out Of Your Heirs And Close Friends. Well-To-Do Heirs May Use Your Post-Mortem Estate As Their Own Private Tax Shelter. If Your Form 706 Includes Real Estate And Collectibles, The IRS May Intervene.

Lest you misinterpret the focus of ***Simplifying Your Estate***, we want to clarify certain matters early on. By "simplifying" we mean: doing your own thinking and decision-making while alive, with the objective of expediting and smoothing the transfer of your estate to deserving heirs. This objectivity is not a matter of high tax or low tax (or no tax). It is more a matter of formulating your estate in such a way that it becomes, virtually, a "no brainer" for your executor to follow through on. The underlying idea is not to overload your executor with things that you should have done, but didn't.

Face it! For a given taxable estate, whether simple or complex, your transfer tax will be the same. Therefore, isn't it better to know what the tax is within six months (for well organized estates) than within 36 months' time (for poorly organized estates)? If you really did a superb organizational job before death, your heirs could know within three months what the tax would be . . . and what each heir's share would be.

Good organization before death means less administrating after death. The less time spent on administrating (carrying out your wishes), the less the professional fees (for attorneys, accountants, appraisers, and clerical). Also, the simpler an estate, the less the aggravation and uncertainties with the IRS. In addition, there is less disharmony between designated heirs. When estate affairs are onerous and complex, heirs become disgruntled, the IRS becomes suspicious, and professionals become greedy.

Consequently, in this chapter, we want to exemplify **what not to do** when arranging your estate affairs. We all learn by the mistakes of others (and, sometimes, by mistakes of our own). For such learning, we present selected true-to-life (and true-to-death) variants of what not to do. First, we present the actual case itself (from the author's own repertoire of cases), then we critique the case on how it might have been handled differently. We'll present five bad examples and five critiques.

Small Estate: No Executor

In our first example, the decedent was a single man of modest means. He had never been married and, therefore, had no children. He had an older brother and older sister, both of whom had predeceased him. He lived in a rented apartment most of his adult life. He was frugal and was able to save reasonably for his old age and retirement. He was in his first year of early retirement when he had a fatal stroke.

His estate consisted of 5 CDs (Certificates of Deposit at $50,000 each) plus $10,000 in a checking/savings account. Other than a 5-year-old car and a recently purchased TV, his tangible and personal possessions for transfer tax purposes were negligible. Altogether, his gross estate was valued at $262,500 (including the car and TV).

The decedent was in his apartment when he had his stroke. Apparently, he slipped and fell, hitting his head against the corner of the title in his kitchen. After three days of not responding to phone calls and door knocks, the landlady called the police. She and the policeman together entered the apartment. They found the decedent slumped on the floor with a battered and bloodied head. The policeman called the coroner who pronounced him dead. The coroner immediately took charge of the body.

Not knowing who else to contact, the landlady called the local bar association. The bar association recommended several local attorneys who handled small probate estates. One was selected who agreed to get promptly on the case.

The next day, the selected attorney appeared on the scene. He began searching through the personal papers and effects of the decedent. He was looking for a will or other testamentary documentation, such as an insurance policy or other handwritten notes, identifying family members or intended heirs. No will or life insurance could be found. The attorney did find a list of about 25 names and phone numbers of various persons.

Over the next several weeks, after calling every listed phone number and others, the attorney located six near relatives: three nephews and three nieces. With this information, the attorney petitioned the probate court to be appointed as the decedent's personal representative. This gave the attorney full legal authority to administer and settle the estate . . . at his sole discretion.

Some *two years* later, the estate was settled. The unpaid debts amounted to $2,160. The accounting fees were $850; the cleaning and hauling costs were $400; the clerical and filing costs came to $130; the legal costs and fees came to $198,960. Yes: $198,960! These administration costs left exactly $60,000 to be distributed (transferred) to the six heirs . . . at $10,000 each. There was no transfer tax inasmuch as the estate was fully exempt under the allowable credit amount (in Figure 1.1).

Critique No. 1

What is bad about the above example? It was certainly a simple estate: three assets only (CDs, bank account, and car/TV).

The obvious first mistake was having no will. Without a will, one is unable to appoint his own executor to administer the estate. A will is the simplest possible legally recognized testamentary document. It need not be prepared by an attorney. It can be handwritten, typewritten, or word processed (on a computer) by the testator, and either witnessed or notarized.

Having no will means that the "legal system" takes charge and takes over. Attorneys and their self-serving system of laws are not known for promptness of effort, frugality of costs, responsiveness to heirs, nor accountability for acts. In the truest sense, the legal system condones "grave robbing" . . . legally. In the example above, the attorney fees amounted to 75% of the decedent's gross estate ($198,960 ÷ $262,500). The heirs received less than 25%.

The second mistake in the example above is not so obvious. The decedent, even for his own convenience, did not organize his personal papers and place them in one location. His financial records, personal phone contacts, and other vital statistics of his life were scattered around in his apartment. They were in drawers, on shelves, in boxes, and a few were on table tops where the decedent was last working on them. The very minimum that any prospective decedent can do is to collect his estate matters in one location. Attach handwritten instructions on what to do: "In Case of Emergency."

Yes, records and papers collected in one place can be found by thieves and robbers. Fortunately, these searchers move around hastily looking for money (green paper), credit cards, tangible items convertible to cash, and, of course, drugs and guns. Fortunately, also, young thugs are vulnerable to decoying techniques. That is, put some green paper cash in plain sight where robbers can find it. Also, put your prescription drugs in one location for easy finding. Otherwise, put your credit cards in your wallet or purse, and let the thieves pick up and carry away any tangible items that they can. If you are robbed shortly before your death, your executor does not have to include in your estate the stolen items.

Joint Trust: No Thought

In our second example, the decedent spouse was a cancer victim. The elderly couple had been married 60 years when the wife died. They were ordinary working people with a high school education. They never talked about a will and never thought about what their estate was worth. They had two married children: a son and a daughter. There was an implied understanding that the son and daughter would inherit everything, equally.

One day, the son suggested to his father that he see an attorney about drawing up some kind of trust for his parents. The son had no idea what his parents' estate was worth. The parents' house was paid off; all bills were paid when presented, including medical bills not covered by insurance or Medicare. There was no debt of any kind over 30 days' due.

The attorney drew up a 50-page *joint* living trust "estate plan." It was a combined will-trust document whereby everything (including household furniture and furnishings, old cars, garden equipment, and whatever collectibles there were) went into a family trust. Numerous contingency and hypothetical clauses were included in the trust instrument, depending on which spouse deceased first. Upon the first spouse's death. all joint assets were to be separated into "his" and "her" trusts after the trustee figured out the best way to take advantage of the exemption allowance for each decedent. The designated trustee was the surviving spouse. The son and daughter were named as successor co-trustees.

When the mother died, a preliminary review by the son's tax preparer indicated that Form 706: U.S. Estate Tax Return, would be required. The father had never heard of a Form 706 before; he became stressed, bewildered, and confused. The father's tax accountant had never prepared a Form 706. The attorney who prepared the trust instrument was not interested in taking on the chore. Thereupon, the son took the matter to his tax preparer.

The gross estate turned out to be $1,663,300. This consisted of the following marketable assets: personal residence $750,000; stocks and bonds $635,000; promissory notes $215,000; bank accounts $44,800; and tangible items of value $18,500 (total = $1,663,300).

Approximately $200,000 of the promissory notes turned out to be uncollectible (though the attorney who prepared the trust instrument was hired to take legal action). Other administrative expenses (including memorial services, debt payoffs, appraisal fees, and tax preparer fees) approximated $8,300. The decedent's transfer tax was about $30,000. This left a joint transferable estate of

$1,425,000. One-half belonged to the surviving spouse, leaving $712,500 belonging to the deceased spouse's trust.

For his own gamesmanship and preoccupation, the surviving spouse wanted the entire $635,000 in stocks and bonds assigned to his account. This meant that $700,000 of the $750,000 residence was assigned to the deceased spouse's trust (Trust A). Additionally, $12,500 in cash had to be assigned to Trust A from the joint bank account (to total $712,500). As a result, the residence had to be retitled as Tenants-in-Common: 93.33% belonging to Trust A and 6.67% belonging to the surviving spouse (for subsequent assignment to Trust B). Technically, the joint living trust had not been legally activated before death. That is, no "Exhibit A" had been executed. Nevertheless, probate was not sought.

Critique No. 2

What is bad about the above example? After all, the spouses had a joint living trust, didn't they? And, don't trusts take care of and simplify everything?

Several mistakes were made. But they were all covered over by the son's tax preparer with the help of the father's attorney. And since only two very cooperative successor co-trustees were involved, no beneficiary complained about what was done.

First off, the 50-page joint trust document had no legal binding effect. To properly avoid the probate process, all property intended for Trust A (for the first decedent spouse) should have been re-titled in the name of the trust. Normally, this is done via an "Exhibit A" attachment to the trust instrument. This was **not** done. It wasn't done until after the fact: after preparing Form 706. The Form 706 required that a trust obtain a Tax ID number and describe with specificity the amount and nature of property transferred to it.

The second mistake was the intended creation of a "joint trust" arrangement for elderly (in their 80s) and unsophisticated trustors. The 50 pages of legal gobbledygook were never actually read, much less understood, by the trustors. Preparing a testamentary document as a joint instrument lacks everyday reality. No two human minds act and think alike, despite many years of marriage. Instead of one joint trust, there should have been two separate spousal trusts: A and B. After the death of one spouse, the surviving spouse has the freedom of choice and timing in his (or her) own right.

The third mistake was the bypassing of an ordinary will: one for each spouse. The two wills could have been mirror images of each other, if so desired. A will permits direct bequests to adult children, thereby serving the same tax function as a living trust. Liquid assets, or those convertible to liquid form, could be so transferred up to the allowable exemption amount. Furthermore, the *marital deduction* could be directed in the first decedent spouse's will. The exemption amount plus this one deduction alone could eliminate all transfer tax on the first decedent's estate. Afterwards, the surviving spouse could commence a program of lifetime gifts (at $10,000 per donee per year) to further simplify and reduce the transfer tax (if any) on the surviving spouse's residual estate.

There was also a fourth mistake. The spouses, even though it was known that the wife was dying of cancer, never sat down with their two adult children to discuss — and think through — their estate affairs. For example, legal action on the $200,000 in uncollectible promissory notes should have been started while the wife was alive. The $635,000 in stocks, bonds, and mutual funds could have been reduced from the 35 or so different accounts to 10 or fewer. Having fewer accounts to retitle after death makes the transition process much simpler, and transfer time more expedient.

U.S. Executrix: Foreign Heirs

In our third example, the decedent was a bachelor man who died of leukemia at the age of 52. Leukemia is a disease of the blood-forming tissue whereby the white blood cell count becomes extraordinarily high . . . and potentially fatal. The most common cause for leukemia is frequent or prolonged exposure to nuclear radiation. Such was the case with this decedent. He was a nuclear physicist who was born, educated, and advance degreed in France. He was employed by a U.S. international company and became a U.S. citizen more than 25 years prior to his death. He was survived by a brother (a multi-millionaire Swiss attorney) and two sisters (each of whom had married into European wealth).

While employed, the decedent became a close friend of a comparable age U.S. couple with two small children. He became the "adopted uncle" of those two children. He and the U.S. family went on frequent private boat trips together. In his will, he appointed the children's mother as his executrix and directed that upon his demise a $30,000 educational trust be established for each "nephew" and "niece." He also directed that his appointed executrix (an energetic, educated woman) be entitled to the full statutory executor fee. After all taxes and expenses were paid, his residual transferable estate would go to his brother and two sisters equally. These three heirs were all foreign citizens.

The decedent's gross estate totaled $2,068,000 (approximately). This consisted of his residence ($450,000), a private yacht ($250,000), a yacht moorage ($100,000), mutual funds ($625,000), life insurance ($500,000), art collection ($75,000) and bank accounts ($68,000). After deductions, expenses, and the exemption allowance, his transfer tax (federal and state) was $315,000.

Within four months after the decedent's death, the executrix had completed and filed Form 706, probated the estate (a nonattorney executor *can* probate legally), and began assigning the residual estate to the three foreign heirs. Accomplishing so much in such a short time for a $2,000,000 estate is unheard of in the legal profession.

The decedent's brother (the millionaire Swiss attorney) became highly skeptical. He engaged a U.S. law firm to re-examine Form 706, the probate proceedings, and the entire accounting records maintained by the executrix. The U.S. law firm made incessant demands on the executrix for all of her documents. Its attorneys began threatening to have her relieved of her duties and have her $35,000 executrix fee invalidated. During the law firm's discovery and intimidation processes, the executrix received from the IRS a form letter: ***Acceptance of Estate Tax Return*** (Form 706). She showed this to the attacking attorneys. Their jaws literally dropped. The IRS had closed the case within the statutory filing time (nine months after a decedent's death) . . . another unheard of feat (in the legal profession).

What next did the attorneys do?

They demanded that the executrix reopen the case by filing an amended Form 706. They wanted her to claim an additional

$100,00 as their legal fees and seek a refund thereon. The executrix engaged her own attorney who defended her refusal to reopen the case.

Critique No. 3

What is bad about the above example? The decedent had a valid will, properly witnessed. The executrix took on the probate proceedings properly. So, what was done wrong?

Nothing, really. In hindsight, though, several things could have been done differently.

First, when the decedent had his will prepared, he had already been diagnosed for possible leukemia. He knew the potential seriousness of the disease. Several of his nuclear co-workers had died of it. As an act of prudence, therefore, he could have established the educational trusts for his U.S. friends' two children while he was alive. He loved those children as dearly as if they had been his own. Had he established the trusts while alive, he could have made exclusionary transfers to them yearly, augmented by direct bequests at time of death.

Secondly, he could have added a special paragraph in his will warning the executrix of possible interventions and difficulties with his attorney brother. The decedent and his brother never got along well. The decedent regarded his attorney brother as too aggressive and greedy. As the executrix later discovered, the brother had instructed the U.S. law firm to prepare misconduct charges against her. The complaint was that she paid the $315,000 U.S. transfer tax prematurely. Said amount, the brother claimed, could have been invested for 12 to 18 months (via extension of time for filing Form 706), thereby generating more U.S. income from the decedent's estate.

After the decedent's estate was closed for U.S. tax and probate purposes, the brother (the Swiss attorney) wanted the decedent's residence, yacht, yacht mooring, and all residual liquid assets placed in a U.S. trust having foreign beneficiaries. The brother arranged with the US. law firm to do this. This was the brother's prerogative after the estate was settled. The obvious motivation for this was to avoid, or to at least minimize, Swiss taxation on himself and his sisters. Insisting that the executrix do this as part of her duties in administering the will was improper.

Major Death Bed Change

In our fourth example, the decedent was an 84-year-old widow. She had no children and no siblings. Her predeceased husband, a small-business owner, left her financially well off. She died of natural causes within six months after selling her home and moving into a church-sponsored retirement community.

Before selling her home, she had a will prepared which she reviewed periodically. She directed that her entire portfolio of stocks and bonds (consisting of 22 different accounts) go to the Welfare Fund of her local church for needy ministers and missionaries. Additionally, she directed that all five bank accounts and her five limited partnerships be liquidated and distributed in specified percentage amounts to 25 close friends and cousins. She appointed her two dearest close friends as her executrix and successor executrix, respectively. She had known these two appointees for nearly 50 years. The decedent and her appointees were school teachers together.

Periodically, the decedent would review her will with her tax preparer. He had prepared her (and her husband's) returns for nearly 20 years. At each review, he urged that she significantly reduce the number of her portfolio accounts, liquidate the limited partnerships, and reduce her bank accounts to one, then place all liquid assets into one tax-exempt mutual fund of municipal bonds. Upon every urging, she responded that her financial counselor (a female stock broker) would take care of all this when she (the decedent) died. Upon death, the gross estate was valued at $2,285,000 (roughly).

Shortly after selling her home and moving into her church-sponsored retirement community, she had a stroke. This left her having difficulty walking and talking. She was bedridden and hospitalized intermittently. The financial counselor learned of this and immediately contacted an attorney friend (also a female). Together, the two counselors had the decedent revoke her existing will and authorize the creation of a Charitable Remainder Unitrust.

The decedent by this time could hardly see, hear, or write. Yet, she authorized the creation of the trust which shut out all 25 of her will-designated lifelong friends.

Simultaneously, with preparation of the 32-page trust instrument, the decedent (evidently) authorized her financial counselor to liquidate all assets except six specific stocks. The liquidation proceeds were used to purchase additional shares of the same six stocks. Altogether, the decedent, while barely alive, held 8,200 shares of oil company and utility stock. All 8,200 shares were listed properly in "Exhibit "A" to the trust instrument. This meant that all 8,200 shares in six different stocks were retitled in the name of the trust. About five days later, the decedent died.

Critique No. 4

What is bad about the above example? In a sense, it was a model of simplicity. Everything was quietly rearranged before the decedent died. The church got everything; lifelong friends and cousins were totally shut out. There was no Form 706 prepared; there was no transfer tax because the assets were all charitably donated; there was no probate (because the trust was legally executed just before death); and there was no accounting to anyone!

A model of simplicity it may have been. But this example is the classic *death bed switch*! The church attorney and the decedent's financial counselor took over. They were accountable to no one. The quiet rearrangement into a stock portfolio in the name of the church trust generated an estimated $186,800 in commissions for the financial counselor stock broker. The rearrangement also generated for the church attorney approximately $150,000 in legal fees. An additional $17,500 went to the female attorney who prepared the trust instrument. Stock brokerage commissions and church attorney fees were to continue until all 8,200 shares of stock had been sold and utilized for charitable purposes.

There was really nothing wrong with the 6-page will that predated the death bed trust. Though some probate would have been necessary for the noncharitable beneficiaries, the church attorney had been previously contacted for probate representation. The will-appointed executrix (a close and dear friend of the decedent for 50 years) was never notified of the death-bed switch. The intended executrix discovered the switch only after death, when inventorying the decedent's personal papers and effects. There, the executrix found a document by which the decedent (apparently) authorized that only the financial counselor would have access to financial records and assets of the decedent. This was a stunning rebuke to a lifelong friend and confidant.

The real wrong here was the decedent placing entirely too much confidence and faith in a smooth-talking business person who had ulterior financial motives in her estate. Signals to this effect were radiating for several years prior to death. Yet, the decedent steadfastly refused to believe what she was told could happen on her death bed.

Toughing It with the IRS

In our fifth (and final) example, the decedent was a 93-year-old widow (who was blind). Her husband predeceased her 12 years earlier. The decedent had a will and a living trust whose "Exhibit A" was amended, corrected, and changed several times. She was survived by two sons and a daughter. The daughter was the executor and trustee of the estate.

Initially, the gross estate totaled $712,000. It consisted of the decedent's residence, 50% interest in a commercial building, a 7.2% interest in a real estate partnership (valued at $5,626,000), 3 stock holdings, 5 bank accounts, 3 collectibles of value, a 15-year-old car, and sparse furniture and furnishings. The "Exhibit A" of the trust identified specific items and fractions thereof that were to go to each of the three heirs. The daughter, however, was to get all of the decedent's 7.2% interest in the real estate partnership.

Form 706 was prepared and filed with the IRS exactly three months and 10 days after the decedent died. The $28,000 transfer tax was paid at that time. Attached to Form 706 was a disclosure statement (Form 8275) explaining the 7.2% computation of the decedent's value of the real estate partnership. A minority interest *discount factor* of 25% was used. (Tax form instructions always require an explanation when an item is not self-explanatory on the face of the form itself.)

Exactly nine months *after* Form 706 was filed, the IRS hit the executor and the tax preparer with an audit demand letter. The lead-in sentence read:

> *Your Form 706 has been assigned to me for examination. Within the next couple of weeks, please mail the following records:*
>
> /s/ ____________________
>
> *Attorney, Estate Tax, IRS*

What followed was a 3-page, 15 paragraph, 1200 word examination list. Essentially, all records going back 12 years to the predeceased spouse's death (and Form 706) were sought.

To typify the audit detail the IRS attorney wanted, the 320-word paragraph (7) read in part—

> *Provide a room-by-room itemization of household and personal effects. All articles should be named specifically . . .; a separate value should be given for each article named. . . . If there are included among the household goods and personal effects articles* [such as] *jewelry, furs, silverware, paintings, etchings, engravings, antiques, books, statuary, vases, oriental rugs, guns, proprietary membership in a private club, or a coin or stamp collection, if of a total value in excess of $3,000, the appraisal of an expert or experts, under oath, must be provided.*

Upon reading this paragraph and the others (all of which were overwhelming in detail), the executor fired the tax preparer. She was unhappy with him because he sought only a 25% discount factor on the 7.2% partnership interest. She wanted a 50% discount factor. Accordingly, she took it upon herself to tangle with the IRS attorney on her own.

Eleven months and 10 days after the audit demand letter, the IRS assessed an additional transfer tax of $28,800. To this amount was added $2,830 in interest. The net effect was that the gross estate was *increased* by $78,000 (from $712,000 to $790,000). In a nutshell, Form 706 was filed in three months' time; yet, the IRS "screwed around" with it for 20 months!

Critique No. 5

What is bad about the above example?

Four things, actually. The most obvious is having the misfortune of being a selectee for audit by the IRS. Not only does settlement time drag on, but costs and taxes mount. What triggered the audit?

The audit was triggered by two particular items on the decedent's Form 706. The first trigger was the 7.2% ownership interest in a real estate family partnership valued at $5,626,000 listed in Schedule A (Real Estate). The second trigger was the listing on Schedule F (Other Miscellaneous Property) of three collectibles (gold watch, ivory chest, and crystal set) totaling more than $3,000. Once a Form 706 is selected for audit, the IRS goes gung-ho. It wants blood. Where real estate and collectibles are involved, it knows that the valuations thereof tend to be understated rather than market stated. In this particular case, the initial gross estate valuation was increased by only 11%. We know of cases where the IRS-assessed increases have been over 50%, and penalties imposed. No penalties were imposed in this case.

The second "bad thing" above is not so obvious as the IRS audit. It was the "Exhibit A" to the living trust. All three children were named, which is fine. Amending/changing/correcting said exhibit three times is also fine. The last amendment, as interpreted for Form 706 purposes, directed as follows:

Daughter: Item 3, Sch. A + 1/3 Item 1, Sch. A + 1/2 remainder
2nd Son: 1/3 Item 1, Sch. A + 1/2 remainder
1st Son: $10,000 + Item 4, Sch. F + 1/3 Item 1, Sch. A

A better way is to designate the assignment to heirs in *percentages* of the net transferable estate. In this particular case, the assignment percentages turned out to be:

Daughter: 60%)
2nd Son: 26%) 100%
1st Son: 14%)

By using percentages, when there is an adjustment in the gross estate, deductions, or tax, the adjustments apply across the board to all heirs.

The third "bad thing" was the decedent's retention of a 7.2% minority interest in a family-owned real estate partnership. The valuation of this interest was the source of much bickering with the IRS. The decedent should have had her share professionally appraised and transferred (either by gift or sale) before her death. It was the daughter who primarily objected to this. The daughter knew she would inherit her mother's interest at death. Other partners objected to the decedent selling her share to nonfamily members. Still, the decedent could have transferred it to her daughter before death, by filing Form 709: U.S. Gift Tax Return.

The fourth "bad thing" was the decedent's retention of collectibles exceeding $3,000 in total value. We have to ask the question: Why does a 93-year-old blind woman retain in her estate a $2,500 antique gold watch, a $1,750 imported ivory chest, and a $2,800 Waterford 12-place crystal set? These items should have been professionally appraised and gifted to the heirs, or to others, long before the decedent's demise.

The Common Denominator

Reflecting back on the five true life/death examples above, what do you perceive as the common denominator in all of them? Was it having or not having a will or a trust? Was it in preparing or not preparing Form 706 promptly? Or, was it having or not having an attorney engaged early in the decision making and transfer process?

No — None of the above.

The common denominator is the total absence of decision-making and action-taking while each decedent was alive. In each case, the decedent left it up to his/her appointees and/or professionals to make all decisions and take all actions post-mortem. At this stage, the tax and legal system takes over. At this stage, also, time, money, prudence, and simplicity are tossed out. Grave robbing is winked at. Deserving heirs are kept in limbo until the "system" is ready to recognize them. Such are the price and punishment that afflict every decedent who does not do during life what he or she could have done.

We summarize in Figure 2.1 the estate matter concerns that we have. They are subliminally presented; we hope you can sense them. If not, our concerns and ways for overcoming them will be more apparent in subsequent chapters. Whereas conventional wisdom focuses on estate contingencies post-mortem, our focus is on due diligence and prudent decision-making **before** the time clock of dementia (while alive) starts tolling.

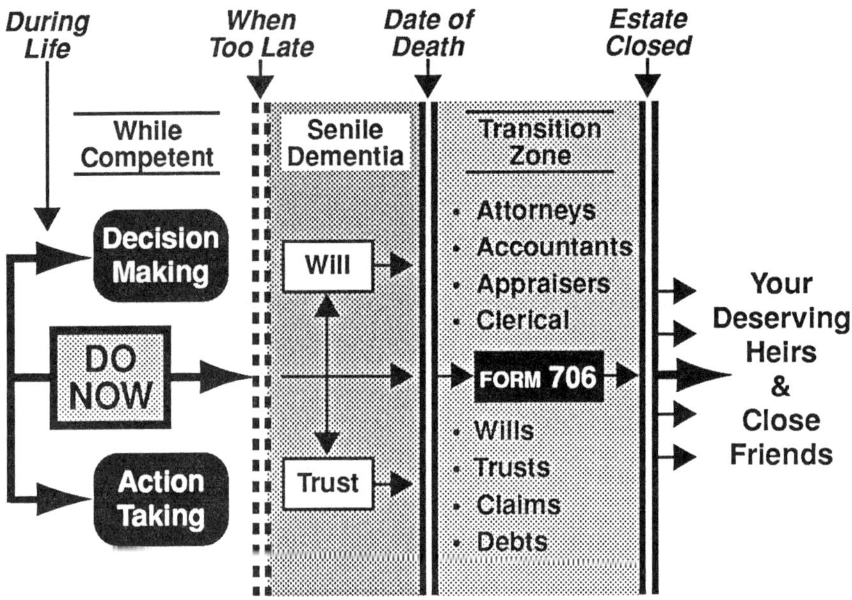

Fig. 2.1 - The Common Denominator of Human Life Change

More realistically, Figure 2.1 is a snapshot of basic human nature. It represents the procrastination problem we all have. No one likes to contemplate his or her own personal death. It is also a fact that few persons like to make hard decisions . . . when such decisions can so easily be postponed. When approaching the brink of making estate decisions, the general attitude is: "It's up to my heirs when I am gone. I can't think or worry about such matters now. Besides, I may live forever . . . or certainly for a long time. People are living longer these days, you know." And so it goes.

3

GOALS TO PURSUE

The Best Evidence Of Your Desire To Simplify Your Estate Is To Procure In Hand A Copy Of IRS Form 706. Skimming Through It (And Its Instructions) Will Trigger Self Thoughts On What To Do And What Not To Do. If Married, Each Spouse Has His AND Her Own Gross Estate. If Not 50/50, Clarify Ahead Of Time Each Spouse's Separate Property Interests, Then Discuss the MARITAL DEDUCTION-INCLUSION Rule. Once You Decide Which Heirs Or Which Trusts You Want Property Transferred To, Designate Your Assignments In Percentiles. Centralize Your Records For Ease Of Retrieval By Your Executor.

Very few noteworthy accomplishments are achieved during life without setting goals. Goals are especially important when tackling such a daunting subject as: ***Simplifying Your Estate . . . While Alive.*** There are two classes of goals: general and specific. A general goal points you in a *general direction.* Maybe you proceed in that direction without change; maybe you don't. More than likely, you'll redirect your direction as you gain experience along the way. And, still, you may not reach the directional end that you seek. Nevertheless, without some kind of directional goal, you wander, flounder, . . . and procrastinate. Floundering is what happens in most estate affairs.

Are *you* a flounderer or a goal setter?

If you are goal setter, here's an example of the kind of general goal that you might set. Say to yourself:

"Before senile dementia takes over my life, I want my gross estate formulated in such a way that—

(a) Its transfer to my heirs is a "no brainer" for my *designated* executor;
(b) IRS Form 706 can be prepared, filed, and the transfer tax paid within *6 months* of my demise; and
(c) My estate, except for my personal residence, is largely in *liquid form* or readily convertible thereto."

In contrast to a general goal, a specific goal targets a *specific category* of estate-likely assets. The objective is to inventory, appraise, rearrange, and reformulate the categorical assets for simplicity of identity, valuation, and transfer. Most of the subsequent chapters hereto focus on specific goals.

In this chapter, we want to focus on those general estate-simplifying goals which we think are laudable . . . and achievable. If you concur, what we present can be regarded as a self-guiding roadmap. Use the portions of it that appeal to you. If there are portions on which you want further guidance, please wait until after you've read any relevant chapters which follow. Then you may want specific professional guidance. We caution you, however, to keep professionals — especially attorneys — at bay as long as you possibly can. The legal profession despises simplicity with a passion. Complexity is its goal. You surely must already know why this is so.

Get Form 706 Now

Here's a little test of your resolve to make a decision and take some action while you can. It will cost you nothing other than a little time and a phone call. We want you to physically get into your hands a copy of Form 706 and its instructions. The form itself is 44 pages long; the instructions are 23 pages long. That's a total of 65 pages. You won't be able to get this number of tax form pages by downloading from the IRS's Internet Web Site. Your best bet is to phone for said copy. The anywhere-in-U.S. number is: **1-800-829-3676**. The hours are 7:30 a.m. to 5:30 p.m., your local time.

The correct full title of Form 706 is: ***United States Estate (and Generation-Skipping Transfer) Tax Return***. In Chapter 1, we referred to this form simply as: U.S. Estate (Transfer) Tax Return. We just want to make sure that you get the right form and its instructions. Ask for the latest revision of said form.

Don't worry. We don't expect you to fill out Form 706. We just want you to have it in your hands. Then, we want you to leaf through it, page by page, glancing at the headings and subheadings. We have previously cautioned you that it is a formidable form. You've probably never seen, or been told of, such a form before. This is your chance to one-upmanship those professionals who will take over when you are gone.

By your skimming and glancing through Form 706 and its instructions (the tax rate schedules are in the instructions), one of two things will happen. Either you will give up and say to yourself: "Let the professionals handle it when I am gone." Or, you may say to yourself: "Hmm! I think I can simplify things enough so that my executor can take charge. I'd rather my heirs get my money than the professionals."

All that we expect of you is a reasonable determination to change your status quo by earnestly wanting to simplify your estate affairs. If you already have a 35-to-50-page *living trust* tome, we ask that you review it to see if it assists you in any way towards the preparation of Form 706. Whether you have a trust or not, we have some useful guidelines for you.

Prepare Your Executor

No matter what you now do or don't do, Form 706 is the *central highway* through all of your estate affairs. Mandatorily, it starts at date of death and ends upon estate closure, as evidenced by an Acceptance Letter from the IRS. We think it should start sooner than the onset of any senility that may await you.

If your gross estate is more than $600,000, Form 706 is required. You have absolutely no choice in this matter. Your only choice is to prepare your executor for the tasks ahead. Perhaps your executor would relish the opportunity to procure Form 706 on your behalf.

No matter how you do it, you MUST APPOINT your own executor. Don't you dare let the legal system do it for you! Recall our "Small Estate: No Executor" example in Chapter 2. The simplest way is to make the appointment in your **own handwriting** (not by typewriter or computer). Date and sign a piece of nonletterhead paper which (in effect) says—

> *Upon my demise, I hereby appoint the following person or persons as my executor:*
>
> ______________________, *Executor*
> ______________________, *Successor Executor*
>
> *or,*
>
> ______________________, *Co-Executor*
> ______________________, *Co-Executor*

A better way is to make your appointment by means of a will, which is witnessed or notarized.

If you and/or your executor have a Form 706 in hand, you'll note that it is addressed to your executor only. It is *not* addressed to you as a prospective decedent. For example, there is a statement on its page 2 which says (boldly)—

> ***You must attach the death certificate.***

Obviously, you can't make such attachment on your own. Either your executor or a professional does it for you.

On page 2 of the Form 706 instructions, the subheading: ***Executor***, reads—

> *The term "executor" means the executor, personal representative, or administrator of the decedent's estate. If none of these is appointed, qualified, and acting in the United States, every person in actual or constructive possession of any property of the decedent is considered an executor and must file* [Form 706].

In the headportion of Form 706, the following information about your executor is required:

- Name of Executor
- Executor's address (also add phone number)
- Executor's Social Security Number

Just below this executor information block, a statement reads:

If decedent died testate [with will], *check here* ⟶ ☐ *and attach a certified copy of the will.*

Note carefully that this statement does **not** say: "Attach a copy of the trust, if any." It says: THE WILL. Consequently, we insist that, even if you have a trust or other nonwill arrangement, you have a will. Then make sure that your executor knows where your will is, among your personal papers. Better yet, provide your executor with a copy of your will.

Coordinate with Spouse

If you are married, your spouse has an estate in his or her own right. Form 706 is a **per decedent** tax return. It is NOT a joint husband and wife return. The head portion of the form asks only for the decedent's name, the decedent's social security number, the decedent's date of birth, and the decedent's date of death. Should both spouses die simultaneously in a common event, there is one Form 706 for spouse A and an entirely separate Form 706 for spouse B.

Since each spouse has a separate gross estate for Form 706 purposes, you should reach an agreement early on with your spouse as to which portion or items of the gross marital estate belong to each of you. If you have been married only once and are still married, the division of marital property is presumed generally to be 50/50. If you have been divorced and now remarried, the 50/50 division will most likely differ. Particularly so, if you have a prenuptial agreement with your present spouse. Also, the marital property division may be non-50/50 due to gifts and inheritances from parents and relatives. In addition, state law has some bearing on the division of property between spouses.

The trend throughout the U.S. is to allow the spouses to agree between themselves as to their marital division of property. No matter how acquired by each spouse, interspousal gifts are no longer transfer tax accountable. Prior to 1982, gifts to one's spouse in excess of $100,000 were transfer taxed . . . but no more [IRC Sec. 2523(a)]. Rather than leaving these matters to chance, it is recommended that if your division of marital property is non-50/50, you coordinate with your spouse the separation of estate items. You may use Figure 3.1 as a guide in this respect. Date and list each separate itemization, and each spouse sign each other's listing as an acknowledgment thereof.

Fig. 3.1 - Agreeing to the Separate Gross Estate of Each Spouse

In durable marriages without major gifts and inheritances from outside the marriage, the acceptance of a 50/50 division is increasingly common. If this is your intention, why not make title matters clear? Have all (or selected) recordable property titled as ***Joint Tenancy*** . . . with right of survivorship (WROS). The WROS titling does two things, namely: (1) it simplifies the marital division of property for Form 706 purposes at time of death; (2) it avoids probate of said property upon death of the first spouse. For modest marital estates — less than $3,000,000 — there is really no need for fancy trust arrangements. However, if one's spouse is likely to be incompetent, disabled, or spendthrift, then non-joint tenancy arrangements are preferable.

Discuss the Marital Deduction

Although Form 706 is not a joint spousal return, there is one feature that applies only to a decedent who is married at time of death. The special feature is the marital bequest deduction of Section 2056(a). This section is titled: ***Bequests, Etc., to Surviving Spouse; Allowance of Marital Deduction.*** With certain exceptions, the marital deduction is virtually unlimited in amount. This one deduction, plus your exemption amount, can totally reduce your transfer tax to zero. But, there's a catch. (Isn't there always?) Thus, you need to discuss this matter appropriately with your spouse.

The substance of Section 2056(a) reads—

> *The value of the taxable estate shall, except as limited by subsection (b), be determined* ***by deducting*** *from the value of the gross estate an amount equal to the value of any interest which passes or has passed from the decedent to his surviving spouse, but only* ***to the extent that*** *such interest* ***is included*** *in determining the value of the gross estate.* [Emphasis added.]

In other words, if the marital deduction is claimed, the property value so deducted must derive from one or more of your asset Schedules A through I of Form 706. Said deductible amount must be described and claimed on Schedule M: ***Bequests, Etc. to Surviving Spouse.*** Schedule M has its own separate instructions. There are technicalities with terminable interests, life estates, qualified trusts, etc. If these technicalities are applicable in your case, and are incomprehensible to you or to your spouse, seek professional counseling thereon.

The idea behind the marital deduction allowance is that, while it reduces your Form 706 tax, it increases correspondingly that of your spouse's Form 706. What you deduct, your surviving spouse must include. What is subsequently included, however, may be less than that which you deduct. Between your death and that of your spouse, the element of *consumption* takes place. Indeed, the very reason for the marital deduction is to allow you to provide adequately for your spouse. This is expected of you, should your spouse's portion of the marital gross estate be significantly less than yours.

There is still another coordination task that you should review with your spouse . . . and your executor. That is, you should establish some strategic apportionment between the marital deduction and your exemption allowance in Figure 1.1. It doesn't make sense to reduce your transfer tax to zero (which you could) by the marital deduction alone. If you did, you'd lose the benefit of your exemption allowance. Therefore, you should inform your spouse and instruct your executor to take advantage of *both* the marital deduction *and* your exemption allowance. Obviously, when your Form 706 is prepared you won't be around to strategize on your own. Because so, you must grant your executor sufficient discretionary authority to choose the best arrangement that he can. For some guidance in this regard, Figure 3.2 may be helpful.

Read the "Yes-No" Questions

On pages 2 and 3 of Form 706, there are 16 questions that must be answered "Yes," or answered "No." Leaving any question blank is construed by the IRS as being "Yes." Any "Yes" answer requires that a statement and explanation be attached. The 16 questions are directed to your executor: not to you. Nevertheless, you and your executor should read the questions together, and discuss those items that are relevant. Some of the questions are straightforward; some are tricky; some are highly technical; and some require research and the digging up of old records.

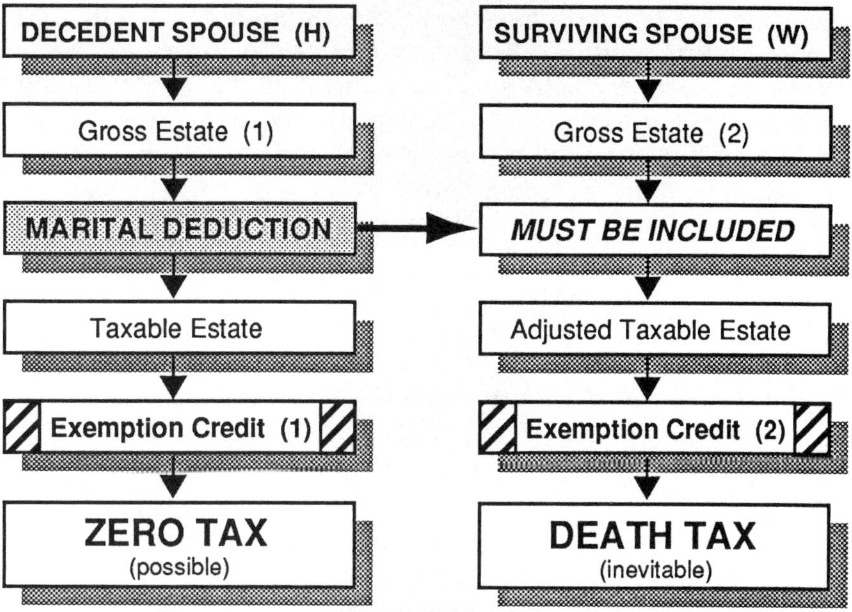

Fig. 3.2 - Effect of Marital Deduction on Surviving Spouse's Estate

For example, the very first question is the shortest and simplest of all. It reads—

Do you elect alternate valuation? ☐ *Yes,* ☐ *No.*

Your executor must fair market value all of your asset schedules (A through I) as of your date of death. In addition, he/she may elect to value those same assets at any dispositional time up to six months after date of death. Those assets not distributed, sold, exchanged, or otherwise disposed of at six months after death are valued on the six months' date [IRC Sec. 2032]. The idea behind this election is to allow your executor to decrease your gross estate for those assets which "waste away" or depreciate significantly after death.

Question 2 goes on to ask—

Do you elect special use valuation? ☐ *Yes,* ☐ *No.*

If "Yes," you must complete and attach Schedule A-1.

Schedule A-1 is titled: ***Section 2032A Valuation***. This IR Code section in turn is titled: ***Valuation of Certain Farm, Etc., Real Property***. Section 2032A applies to "qualified real estate" used by the decedent or a member of his family for five years or more during the 8-year period ending on the decedent's death. At least 50% or more of the decedent's gross estate must consist of said real property. If these conditions are met, the estate is allowed an additional deduction of $750,000. Obviously, if your estate does not consist of farmland or other real property, Schedule A-1 and Section 2032A would not apply.

A similar question is implied (not actually asked) regarding any family-owned business (other than real estate), to wit:

> *Do you elect the family-owned business deduction?*
>
> ☐ *Yes,* ☐ *No.*
>
> *If "Yes," you must complete and attach Schedule T.* [The attachment of Schedule T is a "deemed election."]

This implied question is the consequence of Section 2057: ***Family-Owned Business Interests***. For a "qualified business" (proprietorship, partnership, or corporation) owned by a decedent or a member of his family, each of whom has materially participated in the business for five years or more during the 8-year period ending on the decedent's death, a deduction up to $675,000 applies. This deduction is in addition to the regular exclusion amount that is allowed every decedent (as per Figure 1.1). However, the maximum amount of deduction plus exclusion cannot exceed $1,300,000 [Sec. 2057(a)(3)].

Rather than citing and explaining briefly all the other "Yes-No" questions, we present an edited version of them in Figure 3.3. Our listing gives you a quick idea of the kind of probing being done. Much better than Figure 3.3 is your actual reading of the official questions on Form 706.

Resurrect "Contemplation" Transfers

We realize that you realize that you won't be around to answer the Form 706 "Yes-No" questions. But your executor will have to

Estate of: ____________________	General Information		
	Please check the "yes" or "no" box for each question	Yes	No
1.	Does the gross estate contain any Sec. 2044 property?		
2.	Have Federal gift tax returns ever been filed?		
3.	Was any insurance on the decedent's life not included?		
4.	Did the decedent own any insurance on the life of another?		
5.	Did decedent own any property as a joint tenant with someone other than spouse?		
6.	Did decedent own any interest in a partnership or unincorporated business?		
7.	Did decedent make any transfers described in Sec. 2035, 2036, 2037, or 2038?		
8.	Were any trusts created by decedent during his/her lifetime?		
9.	Did decedent have any power, beneficial interest, or trusteeship in any trust not created by decedent?		
10.	Did decedent ever possess, excercise, or release any general power of appointment?		
11.	Was the marital deduction computed under Public Law 97-34?		
12.	Immediately before death, was decedent receiving an annuity?		
	If you answer "yes" to any question, you must attach additional information.		

Fig. 3.3 - "Probing Questions" on Form 706: General Information

answer them. Furthermore, he/she has to answer them . . . *Under penalties of perjury*. Any IRS penalties assessed detract from what your heirs will get. Under this kind of pressure, isn't it better that, while alive, you make it as easy for your executor as you can?

One way to do so is to resurrect what you may have done in the past, in contemplation of your death. The IRS is well aware that every human who has an estate of substance will do whatever he can to reduce the value of his gross estate reported on Form 706. As a result, a 3-year "presumption of contemplation" rule has emerged. The presumption is that **any** gratuitous transfer of property, rights to property, or use of money within three years of death is motivated strictly with transfer tax avoidance in mind. This may not be the actual case, but it is presumed to be so, nevertheless. You are held to the 3-year presumption, unless you adequately review your past and inform your executor appropriately.

Your first signal of the 3-year presumption is item 7 in Figure 3.3. Officially, the full question is—

> *Did the decedent make any transfer described in sections 2035, 2036, 2037, or 2038?* ☐ *Yes,* ☐ *No. If "Yes," you must complete and attach Schedule G.*

Schedule G is titled: ***Transfers During Decedent's Life***. We will expand on the contents of this schedule in Chapter 8: Compiling Prior Transfers.

More on Contemplations

What do those Sections 2035, 2036, 2037, and 2038 refer to? Instead of you (and/or your executor) rushing off to an attorney, we suggest that you go to your nearest public library (reference section) and ask for a copy of the Internal Revenue Code. Then look up those four sections yourself. Their titles are:

Sec. 2035 — ***Adjustments for Certain Gifts Made Within 3 Years of Decedent's Death.***
Sec. 2036 — ***Transfers With Retained Life Estate.***
Sec. 2037 — ***Transfers Taking Effect at Death.***
Sec. 2038 — ***Revocable Transfers.***

The Section 2035 title is misleading. It does not apply only to gifts. It applies to all forms of gratuitous transfers *by trust or otherwise*, or by relinquishment of a power *with respect to any property*. The value of all such transfers within three years of the decedent's death must be included in his gross estate. The title reference to "certain gifts" addresses the amount of gift tax (or other transfer tax) paid within the 3-year period. The rationale is that any such tax paid is a premature reduction of the gross estate. The amount paid out prematurely must be included back in.

The gross estate inclusions under Sections 2036, 2037, and 2038 are not specifically limited to three years. They apply to *any time made* during the decedent's life. They are, however, *coordinated with* Section 2035. Thus, for example, if you created a living trust 10 years before death, all property designated for such (revocable) trust is included in your gross estate.

The contemplation-of-death inclusion rule also applies to Sections 2034 (dower or curtesy interests), 2039 (annuities), 2040 (joint interests), 2041 (powers of appointment), 2042 (proceeds of life insurance), 2043 (transfers for insufficient consideration), and 2044 (marital deduction property). See Figure 3.4.

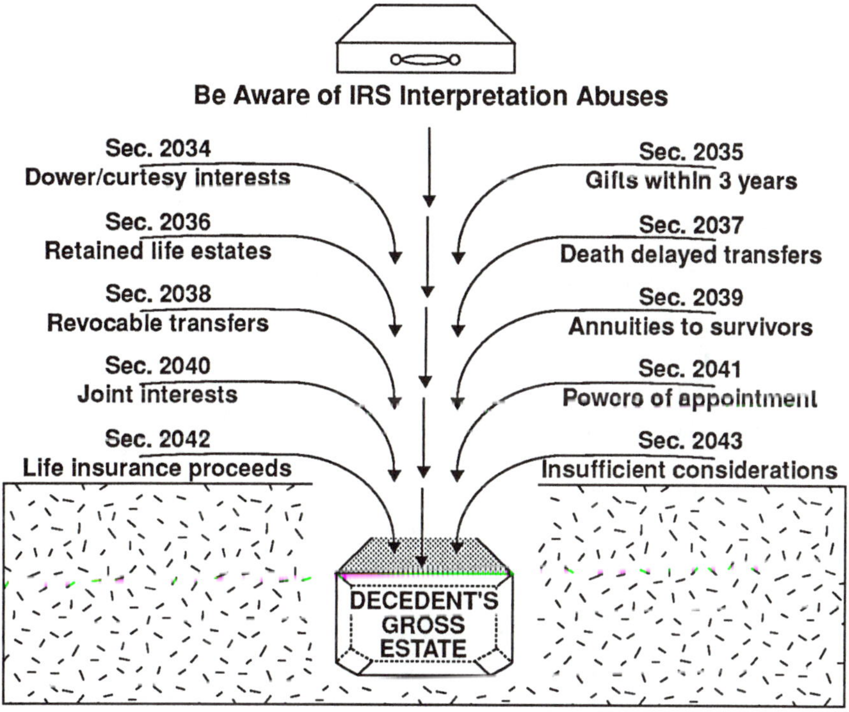

Fig. 3.4 - Ressurection at Death of "Prior Interest" Transfers

If the above sections do not expressly cover your specific contemplated arrangements, Section 2045: ***Prior Interests*** will. Its catchall provisions read—

Except as otherwise specifically provided by law, sections 2034 to 2042, inclusive, shall apply to the transfers, trusts, estates, interests, rights, powers, and relinquishment of powers, as severally enumerated and described therein, ***whenever made, created, arising, existing, exercised, or relinquished.*** [Emphasis added.]

It is the "whenever made" feature that can trap your executor. The tax penalties start at 20% of the nonincluded amounts due to ordinary negligence [IRC Sec. 6662]. The penalties can extend to 75% of the nonincluded amounts if willful attempt to avoid inclusion appears [IRC Sec. 6663]. Perhaps you should take the time now to go over with your executor *all* of your contemplative-of-death transfers . . . from "Day 1."

Percentile Your Distributable Estate

The term "distributable estate" pertains to the net portion of your gross estate that is available for distribution to your heirs and others. It is the "net" after diminution for expenses, debts, losses, and taxes. It is also the net after any marital bequest entered on Schedule M or any charitable bequest on Schedule O. Make it very clear that these bequests (if any) shall bear their prorata share of your total death tax. Otherwise, your heirs will bear the tax burden disproportionately.

All other heirs, including trusts (if any), should be designated as a percentage of your net distributable estate. This gives you the flexibility to change your mind at any time, up to the date of your demise. Percentile designation saves you the burden of having to designate specific property items or specific dollar amounts at a time when you have no precise knowledge of what your net distributable estate will be. Furthermore, percentiling allows your executor the discretion to distribute property *or* money to accommodate the stated preferences of each distributee.

In an oversimplified way, your net transferable/distributable estate is—

Your gross estate	$ ________
LESS	
• Expenses, debts, & losses	< ________ >
• The marital deduction	< ________ >

• Transfer tax (total) < >
EQUALS
Net amount distributable $

When you use percentile designations, whatever the total distributable amount of your estate turns out to be can be divided proportionately . . . and painlessly.

For example, you might designate your percentiles as—

Into trust	52%
Child 1	16%
Child 2	15%
Relative 1	10%
Relative 2	5%
Other	2%
	100%

You may want to assign only real estate to your trust, and money or property to all others. If so, make sure that the value of real estate (in this example) will appraise at *less than* 50% of your estimated distributable estate. Make up the difference with cash money.

Establish Liquidity Ratio

There's a truly major problem when real estate, stocks and bonds, mortgages and notes, jointly owned property, established businesses, and contemplative-of-death transfers constitute the lion's share of one's gross estate. The result is that many prospective decedents are "property rich and cash poor." Everything but a small amount of cash to pay monthly bills is tied up in some investment, some commitment, or some arrangement that is not readily convertible to cash. When such a person dies, where does the money come from to pay the estate administration expenses, the debts of the decedent, the transfer tax, and the necessary distribution proceeds?

Answer: It comes from the after-death forced sale of choice assets. When such assets are sold in an estate, rarely is the top dollar (valued in the gross estate) ever achieved. It takes anywhere from 90 days to 180 days, or more, to close some transactions.

Here's a typical situation: a true case. The prospective decedent, a widow, had three multiple-dwelling rental units. They were gross estate valued at—

Property A	—	$ 850,000
Property B	—	675,000
Property C	—	425,000
Total		$1,950,000

She had cash in the bank of about $20,000. She had nil other assets of value. The rental income was her sole source of livelihood, other than a modest amount of social security. After deductions, expenses, debts, etc., it was estimated that her transfer tax would come to approximately $500,000. Where is she going to get $500,000 with only $20,000 cash in the bank?

The answer is that she (or her executor) will have to sell either property A or property B. Yet, she had assigned all properties into trust for her children and grandchildren.

The long and short is that one must have an adequate liquidity pool within his/her estate, to settle the estate affairs without forced sales of any kind. In the example above, a target liquidity ratio would be 25% ($500,000 transfer tax ÷ $2,000,000 gross estate). We think 35% would be a more comfortable ratio (to allow for outstanding mortgages, debts, and claims). A 35% liquidity ratio means that 65% could be in illiquid assets such as a family business, family farm, or rental real estate.

Organize Your Records

If you pursue none of the suggestions above, the least you should do is organize your estate records for that inevitable day. Organize them for yourself, organize them for your executor . . . while you can. By "organize," we mean arranging them in a systematic and logical manner that makes it easy for your executor to initiate Form 706 within 90 days after your demise. By "organize," we also mean centralizing them in a designated place in your home where they can be found and retrieved easily. A depiction of what we have in mind is presented in Figure 3.5.

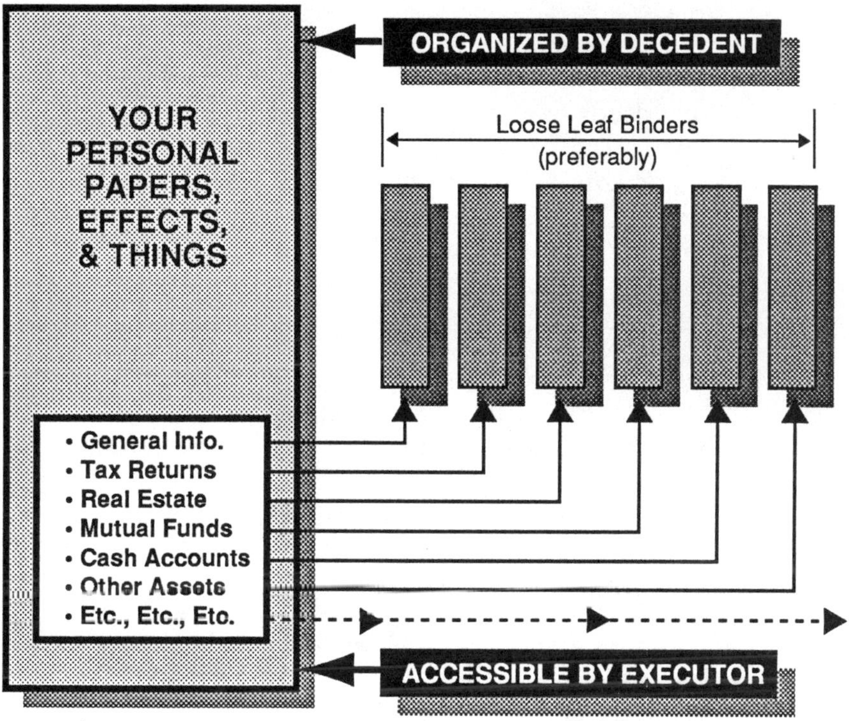

Fig. 3.5 - Setting Your Mind to Organizing Estate Records

As an organizer starter, we suggest that you consider the following separate filing arrangements:

1. General Information

   — birth certificate, military discharge, marriage certificate, divorce decree, educational diplomas, occupational status, retirement letter, prior transfers of property, etc.

2. Relevant Tax Returns

   — all gift tax returns (Forms 709); income tax returns (Forms 1040) and trust tax returns (Forms 1041) for the past three full calendar years; business tax returns (Forms 1065 and 1120/1120-S); Form 706 for predeceased spouse (if any).

3. Real Estate Holdings

— title deeds to real property on which you are named as owner, co-owner, or fractional owner; settlement statements and other documents when property was acquired; installment notes on property previously sold, for which full payment is not yet received.

4. Stocks, Bonds, & Mutual Funds

— latest end-of-year statements on each account in your name, and those identifying other co-owners (other than spouse); include documentation indicating the fractional ownership by others; also include Schedules K-1 for limited partnerships and subchapter S corporations.

5. Mortgages, Notes, & Cash

— end-of-year cash on hand; end-of-year bank statements, mortgage statements, CDs, T-Bills accounts, savings accounts, etc.

. . . and so on. Use the assets schedules (A through I) on Form 706 as a guideline, and combine items of a similar nature. Have a separate file for debts, credit cards, monthly utilities, and other creditors to whom you owe money.

For ease of organization and retrieval, we suggest using loose-leaf binders with dividers for each different set of records. Storing estate records in mailing-size envelopes, on computer discs, or in a safe deposit box, complicates retrieval and identifying tasks. The advantage of loose-leaf binders is that you are enticed to spread out your records into standard page-reading size of hard copy. Such records can be photocopied easily, for attachment to Form 706 as needed.

4

CULLING REAL ESTATE

With The Exception Of Your Personal Residence, Holding Multiple Real Estate Properties (5, 10, 15, 20, Etc.) Can Cause Multiple Complications At Time Of Death, AND 6 Months Later. Each Of The 2 Appraisals Requires 3 Pages Of Legal Documentation. For 15 Properties, For Example, 90 Pages Of Attachments To Schedule A (Form 706) Are Required. Simplifying These Affairs Means Culling Down The Number Of Properties WITHOUT Reducing The Total Gross Value Thereof. This Can Be Done Via An Orderly 5-Phase Culling Program, With The End Goal Of ONE MULTI-UNIT Rental Property.

For some prospective decedents, real estate gets into their blood. There, it becomes a life-long addiction as a means of amassing power and wealth, or at least for building a comfortable nest egg for retirement and old age. Rental real estate is especially addictive in this regard because it—

1. Generates income while being held.
2. Has significant tax shelter benefits.
3. Generally appreciates in value.

These addictive features make it difficult to ever dispose of real estate.

There is a common stance among those who have real estate in their blood. Even though one may point out to them the illiquidity of their estate when they die, they are deaf, blind, and immune to any suggestions to lighten up their holdings. Their bristling response is: "It's up to my children and heirs to worry about the illiquidity problem and the tax consequences when I go. This is the way I made my money; this is the way I'm going to pass it along." This *pass it along* attitude is quite typical of multiple-property ownership of real estate.

Aware of this attitude, it is with trepidation that we pose in this chapter ways to lighten the load. For this, our focus is not on disposing all real estate holdings, but on culling through them. The goal is to thin down the number of properties retained . . . to no more than three. One property that should always be retained to the very last is your personal residence. The most desirable properties for retention are multi-unit rentals (commercial or residential) in upscale locations. Other realty holdings such as undeveloped land, odd-shaped lots, farm land, low-income housing, and depleted resource property (cut timber land, abandoned mines, polluted-beach property) are the obvious first candidates for disposal. We offer some constructive culling ideas, if you really want to simplify your estate.

Canvass Your Children's Wants

Persons with extensive real estate holdings tend to think that real estate being in their blood is also in the blood of their children. This often is not the case. Property owners with more than one adult child may find that not all children have the same desire or financial savvy to inherit real property. In a family of up to five children, we can virtually guarantee that one, two, or three will *not* want your property holdings. They will want money or other arrangements instead.

Here's a typical, yet true example of what can happen after it is too late. The decedent was the surviving parent (father) of four adult children (three sons, one daughter). His gross estate was approximately $7,000,000 (7 million). Of this, $6,500,000 (approximately 92%) consisted of real estate holdings. All children were to share equally in the estate proceeds. The estate tax on Form

706 approximated $2,500,000, leaving about $1,000,000 potentially distributable to each child.

The oldest son was financially independent on his own. He had his own business and employed his youngest brother in that business. He did not want his share of his father's estate, but wanted to pass it on to his children. His youngest brother desperately wanted the money, as he had recently married and was buying a home (he had a new baby on the way).

The second son and oldest son never got along with each other. Each was in an entirely different occupation. The second son didn't want to be beholden to his financially independent brother. He wanted his $1,000,000 in cash, and he wanted it now! As executor, the oldest son objected. Thereupon, the second son sued the father's estate and was judgment awarded his full share. The attorney and accountant fees amounted to just over $250,000. This reduced the residual estate for the three nonsuing children to about $2,700,000 ($900,000 per heir). The lawsuit caused five years' delay in settling the estate. This caused an additional $600,000 in tax penalties and interest for filing and paying Form 706 late. This further reduced the residual estate for the three nonsuing children to $2,100,000 ($700,000 per heir).

The youngest son, seeing his share of his father's estate diminished by $300,000 ($1,000,000 – $700,000) began to get nervous and concerned. He hinted that he, too might sue the estate for his cash share. The older brother hinted back that the younger brother would be terminated from employment if the estate were sued a second time. In the end, the brother and sister agreed to buy the youngest brother out . . . at some unspecified time.

The example above points up the realities of passing on real estate to multiple children. There is a logical alternative. Canvass them before it is too late, as to their specific choices among your real estate holdings. Prudently feel them out. Which one wants property? Which one wants money? Which one wants to substitute other assets in lieu of his/her share of your real property? Of the children who want your real estate, do they want to own it separately or will they accept co-ownership with their siblings? These and other probing issues should be directed at your children.

Offer to Sell to Children

Canvassing the preferences of your children as above may not turn out to be particularly useful. Your children may not want to offend you, or may not want to appear covetous of your property. They may agree outwardly to accept anything you want to pass on to them, but inwardly they are planning to dispose of it after your demise.

There is a better way of ascertaining the attitude of your children towards real estate. Offer to sell it to them! Make the financial terms of your offer uniquely opportunistic. But make the terms legally enforceable. That is, go through all of the regular appraisal and escrow closing processes. If one or more of your children truly has real estate in his or her blood, an offer of sale is the quickest way to find out.

For example, suppose you have a duplex rental currently market valued at $300,000. You bought the property, or acquired it by exchange more than 20 years ago. It is now paid off and has no mortgage against it. You offer it to all of your children for 5% (or $15,000 down). You offer to take back a secured deed of trust note for $285,000. As part of the deal, offer whichever child wants to buy it (and take responsibility for it), a gift of $10,000 towards the down payment. Make sure that you make clear to the nonbuying children that you'll give each of them also a $10,000 cash gift. Money or property gifts up to $10,000 per donor, per donee, per year **are excludable** from your gross estate, and are **not taxable** to the donees thereof [IRS Sec. 2503(b)]. You've probably already heard about this $10,000 annual gifting rule, haven't you?

Suppose you die some five years after the one child bought the duplex for $300,000. Its value at time of your death is $400,000. Can't you sense what will happen? The nonbuying children are going to start squawking about the buying child getting a $100,000 inheritance advantage. To a certain degree, that's true. Furthermore, you pay no transfer tax on that $100,000. It's a good deal for you, and a good deal for the buying child.

Your nonbuying children need to be reminded that you offered the same deal to them, but they turned you down. They also need to be reminded that when you gave the $10,000 towards the buying child's down payment, you also gave each of them $10,000. What did they do with their $10,000? The buying child "invested" his $10,000 in a parcel of real estate. This is something you had hoped the other children would do, but didn't.

Had you sold the $300,000 rental duplex to your real estate minded child for $15,000 down, you'd be taking back a $285,000 mortgage note. Each year while alive, you would credit that child for $10,000 on principal each year, as part of your annual gift to him. This, together with the child's own payment on principal from his rental proceeds, could drive the balance on principal due down to around $200,000 in five years' time. If you died at that time, the $200,000 unpaid balance would go into your gross estate. This would be in lieu of it $400,000 value had you not sold it to your child. Upon your death, the buying child would inherit the $200,000 balance due note. The note would then be deemed paid in full. Although your other children may grumble about this, they had their chance.

Thus, truly, there are tax advantages both before and after death, when selling real estate to your children. We depict these advantages for you in Figure 4.1. Make sure, however, that there is a bona fide sale, and not a gift disguised as a sale. Also make sure that the transferee child understands Section 453(e): ***Second Dispositions by Related Persons*** of installment sale property. There is a 2-year prohibition against any resale.

Example of Culling Need

We know it is heresy to make the slightest hint or suggestion that you reduce the multiplicity of real estate holdings in contemplation of your demise. The idea of culling your properties goes against all the conventional wisdom that you have aspired to throughout life. The aspiring wisdom is that you never sell real estate. It is the ancient foundation of wealth and power. Exchange it, if you want, but never sell it. If your children don't want it, put it in a GST (generation-skipping) trust until some grandchild, great-grandchild, or great-great-grandchild somewhere down the line has inherited your savvy and wants to take charge. We are not faulting the wisdom. All we're saying is that you can simplify your estate

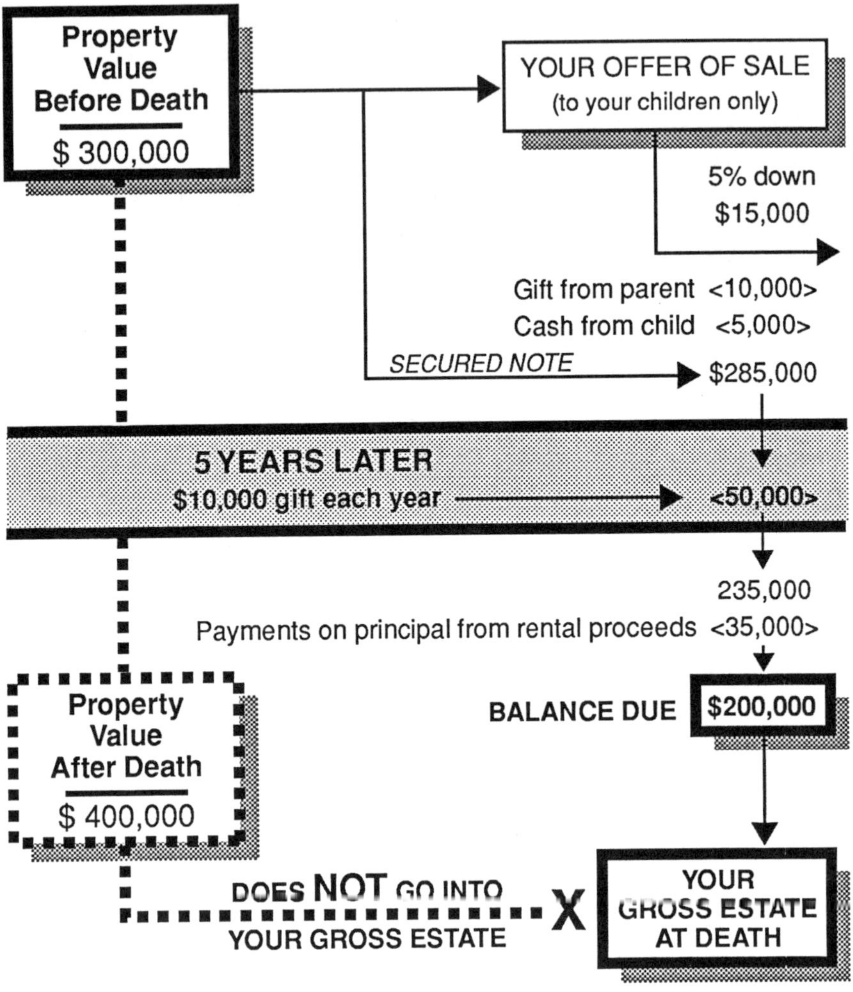

Fig. 4.1 - Tax Benefits When Selling Realty to Your Child

for passing it down the line by pursuing certain culling effort while alive. "Culling for the future," we call it.

Here's a true example of the need for culling. The decedent and his surviving spouse had 17 separate parcels of real estate. The properties were acquired during their 50 years of marriage. The decedent was a real estate broker, and, after the children became adults, the spouse, too, became a real estate broker. Real estate was truly in their blood. The thought of ever selling any of it was anathema.

All 17 properties co-owned by the decedent and his surviving spouse are listed in Figure 4.2. Be aware that the full appraisal value of each property listed is actually *two times* that amount shown. For listing clarity, we have subtracted the 50% belonging to the surviving spouse. Note that values at date of death and six months after date of death (alternate value) are also shown. The data was taken directly from Schedule A (Real Estate) of Form 706 that was timely filed with the IRS within nine months of the decedent's death. The data is NOT fictitious.

When a Form 706 Schedule A consists of several properties more than the decedent's personal residence, using the 6-month alternate value date is advisable. If the total alternate values turn out to be greater than the date-of-death total values, the higher values can be disregarded. This is the substance of Section 2032(c): ***Alternate Valuation Election Must Decrease Gross Estate and Estate Tax.*** As you can see in Figure 4.2, the alternate values decreased the gross estate by $236,000 (1,777,500 – 1,541,500). This incurred a tax saving of about $94,000 . . . no small piece of change.

For 17 properties valued on date of death and again six months later, there had to be 34 professional appraisals! For each appraisal, the latest recorded title deed to each property had to be resurrected. In addition, the latest zoning ordinances, environmental restrictions, and building codes had to be at hand. Also, each property had to be physically inspected, as some were over 30 years old. The result was a logjam of paperwork; a lot of physical scurrying around on the properties; and the inevitable differences of professional opinions as to the likely fair market value of each property.

Each appraisal required three legal-size document pages. Page 1 was a detailed description of the property (lot size, building size, type of construction, etc.). Page 2 was a side-by-side summary of three to five "comparable sales" in the neighborhood. Page 3 was a map plot showing access streets and roads and the official parcel numbers assigned by the local assessor. Four different appraisers were used. Altogether, there were **102** (34 x 3) **appraisal documents**! All had to be attached to the Schedule A of Form 706. Seeing this volume of attachments, the IRS accepted the values

Form 706	Estate of: ____________ SSN: ________		
	Schedule A - REAL ESTATE		
Item	Description	Alternate Value	Value at Death
1	Personal Residence	110,000	190,000
2	Adjacent Lot #1	81,250	90,000
3	Adjacent Lot #2	81,250	90,000
4	Adjacent Lot #3	37,500	40,000
5	Adjacent Lot #4	32,500	37,500
6	Business Office (Adjacent)	82,500	105,000
7	Rental Property (R-1)	90,000	90,000
8	Rental Property (R-1)	100,000	100,000
9	Rental Property (R-1)	115,000	165,000
10	Rental Property (R-1)	100,000	100,000
11	Rental Property (R-1)	105,000	105,000
12	Rental Property (R-1)	95,000	95,000
13	Rental Property (R-2)	104,000	120,000
14	Rental Property (R-2)	120,000	125,000
15	Rental Property (R-2)	120,000	125,000
16	Rental Property (R-2)	120,000	140,000
17	Unimproved Lot	47,500	60,000
	Addresses & parcel numbers omitted — **Total ▶**	**1,541,500**	**1,777,500**

Fig. 4.2 - Example (Abbreviated) of Properties Listed on Sch.A (Form 706)

shown in Figure 4.2. Still, there was a lot of work, a lot of organizing, a lot of time, and a lot of apprehension involved. Had prudent culling taken place before death, some of the agony by the surviving spouse and her children could have been reduced.

The "Never Sell" Plan

The decedent and his spouse had four children: 2 sons and 2 daughters. The decedent had his four young children in mind when he bought his personal residence. He also bought four adjacent lots. Contiguous to these lots, he bought another residence which he converted to a real estate office. His idea was to have his children and their spouses (and his grandchildren) in one contiguous family tract. Upon each child becoming an adult and married, each would be given a parcel of land on which to build his or her own home. This is the "plan" that jumps out at you in the first six items listed in Figure 4.2. At one end of the tract was the parents' residence; at the other end was a residence converted into a real estate office. In between were the four building lots: one for each child. The assumption was that at least one of the children (hopefully more) would become a real estate broker and take over the parents' real estate business.

Here's how things turned out after the death of the father. Only one child, the oldest (a daughter) became a real estate broker. The younger of the two sons was killed as a teenager in a hang glider accident. The other son was not married and had no interest in building a home. The youngest child (a daughter), though married with one infant child, didn't like any of the lots offered to her. She wanted the equivalent value in money to buy an existing home elsewhere. Thus, the older daughter (married) had her choice of the lots and indeed wanted one. Aware of this, the decedent's spouse offered the older daughter all four lots under very favorable financial terms. But she and her husband couldn't come up with enough money to make the minimal 5% down. The daughter decided to wait, and inherit all four lots from her mother.

In the meantime, the local planning commission deemed the lots to be vital public access to nearby coastal beaches. Also, the commission proclaimed the lots to be emergency fire and sewerage line easements, and public access lanes. The surrounding area had built up substantially since the lots were bought (some 40 years prior). The end result was that the four lots had become nonbuildable (for residential purposes) . . . and, therefore, virtually nonsaleable.

The rest of the decedent's "never sell" plan consisted of six single-family residential rentals and four duplex (two-family) residential rentals. All 14 of the dwelling unit rentals (6 x 1 + 4 x 2) were to go into a family estate trust. This intention created liquidity problems for paying the $350,000 transfer tax, and for raising money to remodel and upgrade the properties. None of the children wanted to be responsible for the properties in their present rundown condition. Furthermore, only half of the properties were to go into the decedent's trust. The other half belonged to the gross estate of the surviving spouse. Which half is which? You can't cut a residential building down the middle to make it decedent-trust acceptable. Adding to the dilemma is the fact that the 14 rental units were not of the same value.

Do Culling in 5 Phases

There's a moral to the above true life example. You cannot plan the lives of your children, nor the lives of your grandchildren, no matter how admirable your intentions may be. Human minds within the same family are not clones of each other. Each mind acts and thinks differently. The same is true of spouses: each acts and thinks differently.

Reality — other than hopes and dreams — requires that you start a culling plan at some appropriate time. The idea is not to diminish the total value of your real estate holdings. Instead, the goal is to reformulate your holdings in a manner that makes directing them into a trust both convenient and expedient. The culling/reformulation process **excludes** your personal residence.

Regardless of your children's likes and dislikes regarding the ownership of rental realty, they all have a nostalgic twinge for the family homestead. Particularly if one or more were raised therein. All individuals reflect back to their pre-adult years . . . with good memories and some bad. Consequently, the family residence is the one piece of property where you'll find easy consensus for co-ownership among your children. It is your one piece of property that is not eligible for culling. You dispose of it only if you intend to retire elsewhere, and need the proceeds for retirement living. Otherwise, retain it until you and your spouse have deceased. Bequeath it to your children equally. Then leave it up to them to live in it, rent it out, exchange it, or sell it.

Once you set aside your personal residence as a noncandidate for culling, treat all other holdings as full culling candidates. Do so in a logical and orderly manner. We suggest doing your culling in five distinct phases. This will give you time to think through your options, test the current market, and benefit by your one-at-a-time experiences. The five phases that we have in mind *exclude* the preculling phase to your children, which we've already discussed.

What are the five phases that we propose? They are as follows:

Phase 1 — Sell off all raw land.
- unless you have a binding commitment to build on it or develop it in some manner, sell it.

Phase 2 — Sell or gift low-income and poor quality property.
- gifting to a charitable organization while alive has tax advantages of its own.

Phase 3 — Sell one or more good quality single-unit rentals.
- sell to raise the necessary cash for acquiring one or two multi-unit rentals (of 4, 8, 16, etc. units).

Phase 4 — Exchange your duplex and triplex rentals into one or two multi-unit properties.
- multi-unit properties are more income self-sustaining, and are more attractive for ongoing professional management.

Phase 5 — Designate one multi-unit property for Trust A (for yourself) and a separate multi-unit property for Trust B (for your spouse).
- you have one property to be valued and transferred at death: not dozens.

Our rationale for each of these phases is presented below.

The end goal that you could be focusing towards is summarized in Figure 4.3. Note that your personal residence is not for culling. It will remain in your estate until death. Any property sold to your children will *not* be in your estate at time of death (as per Figure 4.1). This leaves just one target property (a multi-unit rental) for appraisal and its transfer designation. The value of this one property alone could equal or exceed the total value of *your share* of all other properties culled. In total value, you can retain just as much real

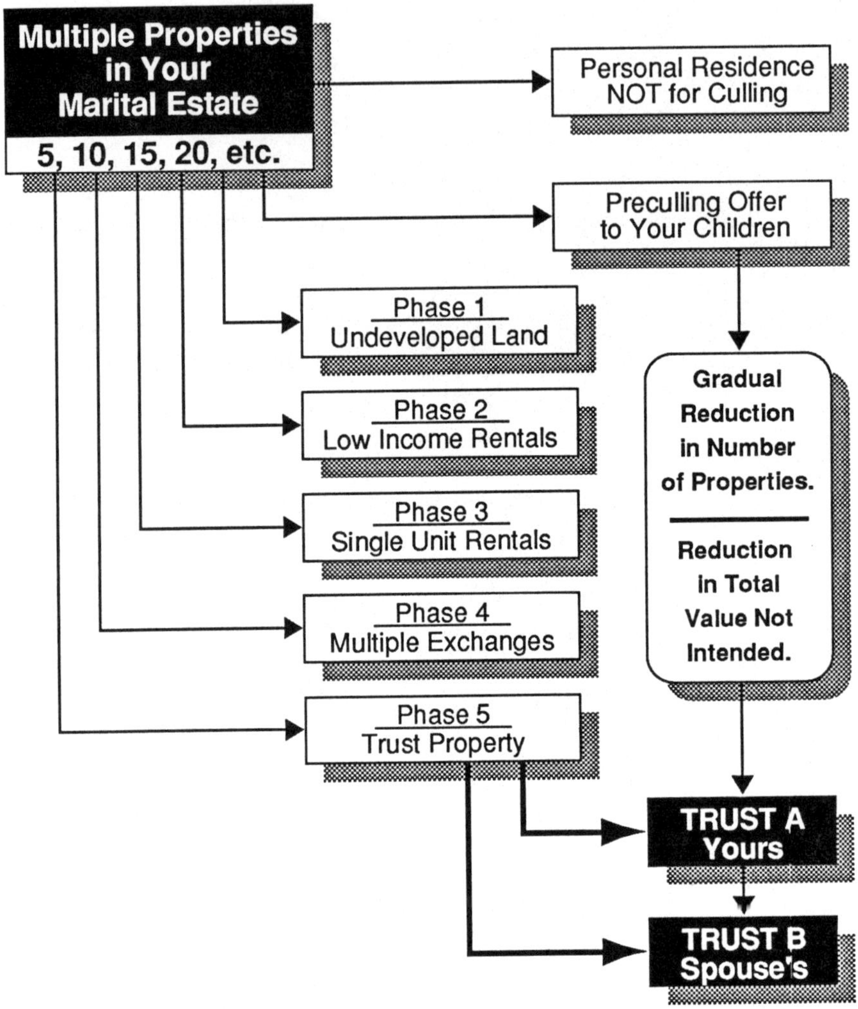

Fig. 4.3 - A "Culling Plan" for Multiple Property Holdings

estate as you want. By having one property instead of 5, 10, 15, or more, your Form 706 processing is much simplified.

Phase 1: Undeveloped Land

We have no qualms about your reasons for buying land which is bare, undeveloped, and possibly depleted (of its natural resources). Land is the fundamental ingredient of real estate holdings: residential, commercial, industrial, recreational, etc. Undeveloped land, however, does not produce significant current income. It is *income-producing* property that you want in your final estate. Not some parcel of land that you let some friend park a vehicle or two on, now and then.

Undeveloped land is a drag on your estate. Not only does it clutter your accounting affairs, it ties up money that could be used for acquiring quality income property. It also consumes money in the form of property taxes, weed abatement, trash control, trespassing notices, etc. Our position is: if you have land that you've been holding more than five years, get rid of it! Offer it for sale or auction it; even let it go for property taxes. Rarely can undeveloped land be sold for cash. No one else wants to tie up his money for an uncertain length of time, either. Installment sales are the only practical way to go.

In the example cited above, the decedent actually made two installment sales of land before he died. One such sale was a parcel of commercially zoned land near the heart of a growing community. His share of the sale was $250,000. At the time of death, his share of the installment note was paid down to $228,350. This is the amount that went into his gross estate. No professional appraisal was needed; no alternate valuation was involved. It was a Schedule C (Form 706) asset: Mortgages, Notes, and Cash.

His other before-death land sale was a small lot for $16,500. He gave an interest-only note which he had held for more than five years when he died. The fact that he accepted such a note (no payments on principal) attests to the fact that land is often difficult to sell. This note was included in his gross estate at its initial face amount of $16,500.

Item 17 in Figure 4.2 was also undeveloped land. It was included in the decedent's estate to the tune of $60,000. Its alternate value was appraised at $47,500: a 20% decline.

Phase 2: Low Income Rentals

Having low income rental property means one of two things, or both. One, the property is in such rundown condition that the only way to rent it at all is to charge below market rates. Two, the property is in good condition but is located in a deteriorating neighborhood. Crime, drugs, shootings, rapes, and kidnappings are occurring with increasing frequency. Rarely does low income property reverse course on its own.

Having low income property is often indicative of one's "never sell" philosophy. The property was acquired years and years ago: 30, 40, 50, or more. Its depreciation tax benefits have been used up. The acquisition mortgage is probably paid off or nil. Its basic structure is just so old that the cost of renovation and remodeling would not likely be recovered through rent increases. If it is in your estate at death, it is the most likely to decline in value after death. Such was the case for Item 9 in Figure 4.2. It declined 30% from its date-of-death value ($165,000) to its alternate value ($115,000) six months later.

Low income property is very difficult to sell. Yes, there are potential buyers out there; but, getting a mortgage from a financial institution is not assured. Selling said property on an installment sale is high risk. The risk is in collecting full monthly payments on the note. If the buyer defaults, you — or your heirs — are left with having to take the property back. When you do, its physical condition will be worse — often much worse — than when you sold it.

An alternative is to *gift* the property away. Donate it to a qualified religious, charitable, educational, homeless shelter, or other worthy organization where volunteers will fix it up and maintain it. By a "qualified" charitable entity, we mean one which is IRS-approved pursuant to Section 170(c): ***Charitable Contribution Defined.*** Preferably make the gift while alive. If not, set the designated property up such that there is no question about your donative intent after your demise. Either way, there are distinctive tax benefits for you.

Phase 3: Single Unit Rentals

Culling your property holdings in Phases 1 and 2 is not going to produce much of a cash pool. At best, it will rid your estate of clutter and problem property while you are in control. Even so, you still need a cash pool to acquire quality property in multi-unit form. How are you going to generate this cash pool? Assume that you have multiple property holdings along the lines of Figure 4.2

One way to raise money is to remortgage several of your existing properties to the hilt. Remortgaging can create additional property and financial problems. Each property has to be appraised and risk discounted by the mortgage company. Other property not being remortgaged will have to be pledged as security. If you had six single family rentals, for example (as in the Figure 4.2 case), it is doubtful that you could remortgage more than two or three of them at a given time. Your other low mortgage properties would be held hostage to your remortgaged properties.

Remortgaging is a good idea *when building up* your real estate holdings over a long period of time. It is not a good idea when culling down your holdings in contemplation of transferring your property holdings to heirs.

Why not consider selling one, two, or three of your multiple single family rentals? A single family unit is relatively easy to sell. It is also relatively easy for the buyer to get a high mortgage. Particularly if the buyer is married and both spouses are employed. In other words, sell for cash-out only. Don't sell under the installment method. Yes, there will be capital gain tax consequences to pay. So, use some of the cash money to pay the taxes. Whatever income taxes you pay before death are NOT resurrected in your gross estate after death. Your transfer taxes will be reduced correspondingly: a point to keep in mind.

We already know that our sell suggestion above will not sit well with you. We can hear you asking: "What about a Section 1031 exchange?" In response, we point out that our focus is on **simplifying** your estate: not on complicating it. We also point out the desirability of an *up*-exchange, for which you'll need a cash pool.

Phase 4: Multiple Property Exchanges

Phase 4 is a continuation of Phase 3, with a difference. Instead of seeking primarily a cash pool, you are seeking primarily a reduction in the number of properties that you are holding. For this effort, Section 1031 exchanging **is** the way to go. Chances are, though, one exchange alone will not do it. Phase 4, therefore, contemplates several sequential exchanges. Furthermore, Phase 4 contemplates no payment of taxes, because in each exchange you'll be exchanging UP in property value. You'll be tapping into your cash pool for the up-value differences.

Suppose you had 10 rental properties as in Figure 4.2: six single units and four duplex units. If you'd sold three properties in Phase 3, you'd have seven properties left. Suppose you wanted to exchange these seven properties for one multi-unit rental complex in an upscale metropolitan area? How many exchanges would be required?

A 1-to-1 exchange would get you nowhere. You start with seven properties and would still have seven properties at the end of seven exchanges. You have to think in terms of 2-to-1 and 3-to-1 exchanges. If you can do better than 3-to-1 in a single exchange, go to it. Otherwise, pursue a combination of 2- and 3-to-1 exchanges.

Three 2-to-1 exchanges would reduce your property holdings to four (7–1–1–1). Three 3-to-1 exchanges would reduce your holdings to 1 (7–2–2–2). Or, you could make two 2-to-1 exchanges (7–1–1=5) *plus* two 3-to-1 exchanges (5–2–2=1) to get down to a single multi-unit rental property. The number of exchanges you need to make will depend, obviously, on the number of properties you start with, and on the number of properties you want to end up with. Making more than two exchanges in a given year is not advised: too many financial complications. Therefore, plan your Phase 4 exchanges over a period of several years.

Exchanges are ideal when you want to *up-exchange*, which is what Phase 4 is all about. To engage in an up-exchange (where the value of the property acquired is greater than the property conveyed), you need cash and/or other boot. You need the cash and/or boot to equalize the equities (value minus debt) among the properties involved. The term "boot" is property which is not like-kind to those properties being exchanged. To clarify some of the fine points of exchanges that you may have overlooked in the past, we present in Figure 4.4 an illustrative example of "equity balancing." After negotiating this phase of an exchange, let your tax accountant do the rest of the exchange computations for you.

Step 1	EQUITY BALANCE WITH "BOOT"			
	Properties Conveyed			Property Z Received
Item	A	B	Total	
FMV *	$130,000	$170,000	$300,000	$365,000
Mortgage Debt	<100,000>	<150,000>	<250,000>	<285,000>
Actual Equity	30,000	20,000	50,000	80,000
Boot Required				
• Cash	4,700	5,300	10,000	——
• Other	——	20,000	20,000	——
Balanced Equity	34,700 ●	45,300 ■	80,000	80,000

* FMV = Fair Market Value; "Other" at Fair Market Value

● = 130/300 x $80,000 = 34,700; ■ = 170/340 x $80,000 = 45,300

Fig. 4.4 - Illustrative "Equity Balancing" for Up-Exchange

Phase 5: Trust Designated Property

Every avid owner of real estate wants to memorialize his achievements made during life. Having built up a substantial estate of realty holdings, he wants to leave some sort of monument for his heirs to see. This is a natural human desire. For satisfying this memorial desire, a trust arrangement has definite merit. Particularly so, if your real estate monument is significant in value . . . say, over $1,000,000 (1 million).

The problem with most trust arrangements is that the property transfer paragraphs are far too generalized. Everything that is not specifically bequeathed elsewhere goes into the trust: all the "pots and pans" (junk real estate) as it were. This is the lazy person's way of creating a trust: assign everything; let the trustee sort things out after the decedent's death. If you have gone through the culling phases above, or intend to, you'll be focusing now on one or more specific items of property that you want in your trust. You want to be most remembered for your organization, expertise, and good judgment in real estate matters. Such focusing is what Phase 5 is all about.

First off, our position is that you want **one** parcel of quality, multi-unit rental property assigned to your trust. Such property could be a 16-unit apartment building; an 8-unit shopping center; a

24-unit light industrial complex; a 1000 acre farm; a boat marina with 30 docks and slips; or any other property that can be described on a single title deed and given a single parcel number by the local assessor. Thus, the whole idea of Phase 5 is to define and acquire your final property holding for your monument-to-be. Then you spend your active phase-out years improving and sharpening-up your memorial property.

There is just one concern with our little scenario. If you are married, does your spouse go along with what you want to be your memorial property? If so, which 50% (or other fraction) is yours, and which 50% (or other fraction) is your spouse's? If the two of you do not agree, your Phase 5 culling should be confined strictly to your own share of the gross marital property holdings. Either way, you need to think in terms of "Trust A" for yourself, and "Trust B" for your spouse. In this manner, each spouse can separately direct the final rearrangement of property holdings as he or she sees fit.

When your Phase 5 effort is complete, and you have perfected your monument, you will have accomplished two major objectives. One, you have "bitten the bullet" and thereby have greatly simplified your transferable real estate. Two, you have assigned income-producing property which is self-sustaining and, thereby, potentially self-perpetuating. With these two accomplishments, you should be proud of the monument that you leave behind.

5

SLIMMING PORTFOLIO ASSETS

Having Multiple Separate Items Of Paper Assets — 10, 20, 30, 60, Or More — Can Be Exhilarating While Alive . . . And Debilitating After Death. Debilitating Because Each Has To Be Described In 6 Ways On Schedule B (Form 706), UNIT VALUED At Its Market Selling Price, And Share Extended To Whole Dollar Amounts. When No Market Exists, Liquidation Computations Are Required. Tax Exempt Bonds, Foreign Securities, And Domestic Stock Of "No Value" Are Includible In Your Estate. Electing The "Alternate Date" For Valuation Adds Further Complication. Slimming Requires Pre-death Sales And Reportings On Schedule D (Form 1040).

The term "portfolio assets" refers specifically to your holding of variable unit-value securities. The securities are "pieces of paper" representing fractional ownership interests in underlying physical items, such as real estate, corporate enterprises, government activities, natural resources, commodities, and other products of commerce: national and international. Your ownership interests in these items are designated as shares, units, contracts, ounces, barrels, tons, or whatever. Since you are holding paper instead of a chunk of the physical item itself, you own an *intangible* asset. Multiple such ownerships constitute your "portfolio."

One of the truly attractive features of portfolio assets is that one can amass a quite substantial amount of wealth in pieces of paper alone. Over a lifetime of portfolio accumulations, one can amass in his estate $1,000,000 (1 million dollars), 10 million dollars, 100 million . . . even more. Any such amount can be evidenced by 100 different security issues, or by one security issue alone. The greater the number of security issues outstanding at time of death, the more complicated Form 706 becomes. All portfolio assets are listed and valued on Schedule B of Form 706: ***Stocks and Bonds.***

Stocks, bonds, mutual funds, commodity contracts, and various derivatives thereof are bought and sold daily on stock exchanges, on commodity exchanges, and through mutual fund accounts. As a result, portfolio assets can vary in unit price hourly, daily, weekly, or even by the minute, if there is breaking news (good or bad) in the financial markets. This volatility of unit price makes valuing these assets at time of death quite complicated. Although you cannot plan precisely for your date and hour of death, you can take action beforehand to greatly simplify estate matters.

Accordingly, in this chapter we want to focus on techniques and arrangements for slimming down the number of different pieces of paper or accounts in your portfolio. Once we explain the detailed descriptions and valuation procedures necessary for preparing Schedule B (Form 706), we think you'll see some merit to your thinking ahead while alive. Unlike that of real estate (Schedule A/ Form 706), you get ample signals and warnings where the complications lie, when you prepare annually your Form 1040. We'll tell you now that if you are a portfolio activist — buying/selling/trading/exchanging on a daily, weekly, or monthly basis — your year of death Form 1040 is one way the IRS has for establishing the validity of that which your executor lists on Schedule B.

The "Unit Value" Problem

As we pointed out in Chapter 1, there are nine asset schedules that attach to Form 706. All of these schedules require that the value of each listed item be valued ***at date of death***. This is mandatory. Additionally, all schedules *permit* an alternate valuation date within six months of date of death for assets actually sold, and *at* six months after date of death for assets not sold. Schedule B, however, is unique among the nine schedules. In addition to the date of death and alternate date values, the **unit value** must be stated for each date . . . for each item listed.

We've already hinted — as if you didn't already know — that stocks, bonds, and other securities experience value changes by the hour: even within the hour in some cases. They certainly change from day to day. This is evident by differences in published high, low, and closing values on any regular trading day. This daily change in unit value raises the question: If a decedent died on a weekend or on a holiday, when the security and commodity markets are closed, which unit value do you use?

For the answer, we have to look to IRS Regulation 20.2031-2(b): ***Valuation of Stocks and Bonds; Based on selling prices.*** This regulation reads in part—

> *In general, if there is a market for stocks or bonds, or a stock exchange, in an over-the-counter market, or otherwise,* ***the mean between*** *the highest and lowest quoted selling prices on the valuation date is the fair market value per share or bond. If there were no sales on the valuation date but there were sales on dates within a reasonable period both before and after the valuation date, the fair market value is determined by taking* ***a weighted average of the means*** *between the highest and lowest sales on the nearest date before and the nearest date after the valuation date. The average is to be* ***weighted inversely*** *by the respective number of* ***trading days*** *between the selling dates and the valuation date.* [Emphasis added.]

Note that this regulation requires the mean value (midpoint) between the highest and lowest value on a designated trading date. This raises the immediate question: Where does one get such values? If the trading date happens to coincide with the valuation date sought, and the security item is published in financial journals or in the business section of general circulation media, use the midpoint of the published high and low, and let it go at that. Keep a copy of the published data for Schedule B backup.

If the valuation date sought occurs when the security markets are closed, the nearest trading dates before and after must be researched. This is where your stock broker, commodity broker, or investment broker can be materially assistive. The value question for Form 706 purposes is a frequent request to brokerage firms dealing in publicly traded securities. You give your broker the name of the issuer of the security, its type and grade, and the valuation date (or dates) that you want. Request a written statement from him on his firm's letterhead. The IRS rarely questions a brokerage firm's values, if the firm is licensed and if the stock or bond is traded publicly (called: *listed securities*).

What If No Market

Not all assets listed on Schedule B are publicly traded securities. Many are "unlisted," "restricted," "private," or "inactive." Most such items are stock shares in closely held corporations, family businesses, and small-issue enterprises where there is just a handful of shareholders. These limited issuances of stock are generally exempt from security registration laws. As such, there is no market where daily quotations can be obtained. And rarely are there any "comparable sales" which can be used a guide. Now, what?

This is a tough one. You're not going to get any sympathy or help from the IRS. Its suspicion is that you'll undervalue the stock. Its instructions to Schedule B regarding unlisted stock read in part—

> *Send with the schedule complete financial and other data used to determine value, including balance sheets (particularly the one nearest to the valuation date) and statements of the net earnings or operating results and dividends paid for each of the 5 years immediately before the valuation date.*

This is a tall order. You (before death) or your executor (after death) has to compute the value of the private stock as though it were being offered for public registration. That is, you need to use such information as: (1) liquidity ratio (current assets to current liabilities), (2) book value and market value of primary assets, (3) working capital, (4) long-term indebtedness, (5) retained earnings, (6) net worth, (7) voting power of stock if more than one class, (8) history of dividend payments, and (9) ownership preference to assets in the event of liquidation. It is not a matter of computing a reasonable value. Nor is it a matter of referencing some fixed, prior, buy-sell agreement between the principals of the enterprise. It is a matter of computing the *selling price* value . . . in a fair (public) market.

The valuation method most acceptable to the IRS is conducting a *liquidity analysis* of the corporate entity. That is, the corporation is treated as being liquidated for the best immediate cash that can be raised. All salable assets are market valued, all indebtedness is paid off, and a residual net worth is established. Dividing this net worth by the number of shares outstanding gives the value per share. There is no discounting for minority interests, as all stock is treated as being sold simultaneously.

Of all unit value amounts entered on Schedule B, the correctness of the amount for a close corporation is highly controversial. If the number of shares times the unit value exceeds $1,000,000 (1 million), count on the IRS to challenge you in court. If the extended value is $100,000 or less, your entry would probably be accepted. If more than $100,000 but less than $1,000,000 (extended value), you'd better do your homework carefully.

For its instructional benefit, a summary of the principles above is presented in Figure 5.1.

Converting Fractions to Cents

Unit values of publicly traded stock are posted in dollars and fractions of dollars. The fractions used are 1/2, 1/4, 1/8, 1/16, 1/32, and 1/64. For example, a stock quoted at $4^{9}/16$ is the price equivalent of $4.56 (9/16 = 0.5625 dollars, or 56 cents). Similarly, a stock quoted at $34^{37}/64$ is the price equivalent of $34.58 (37/64 = 0.5781 dollars, or 58 cents). All three of the major U.S. stock exchanges (NYSE, NASDAQ, and AMEX) quote selling prices in fractions of a dollar, instead of cents. As you can surmise on your own, this practice adds awkwardness when applying the unit price to the number of shares, and entering the total value result for each stock in the decedent's estate.

Question: When entering the unit value on Schedule B, do you use the dollars and fractions amount or the dollars and cents amount? The IRS really doesn't care. Its only concern is that you

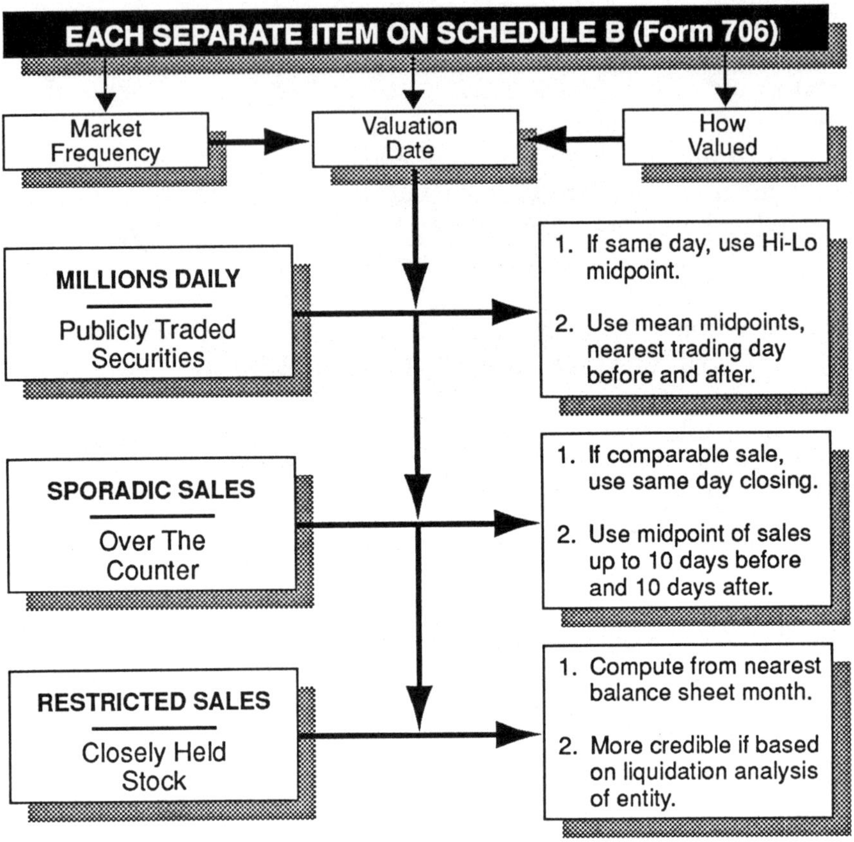

Fig. 5.1 - Establishing "Unit Value" (Selling Price) of Portfolio Assets

enter *whole dollar amounts* in the "at death" column (and in the "alternate date" column, if used). In the extended value columns, the IRS doesn't want to see dollars and fractions (1,896^{9}/16 for example) or dollars and cents (1,896.56). Its computers will go berserk! Instead of $1,896 and 9/16 hundredths (one thousand eight hundred ninety six), it will read the amount as $1,896,916 (one million, eight hundred ninety six thousand, nine hundred sixteen). It will read the $1,896.56 amount as $189,656 (one hundred eighty nine thousand, six hundred fifty six). See how you are exposing yourself to computer errors?

For a few stock issues traded publicly, using fractions in the unit value column of Schedule B is not too distracting. The benefit is that you can match more directly the published values in the financial media. But if you have 15 — or 150 — different stock issues, it is awkward and inconvenient to convert the fractions into whole dollar amounts.

For illustration purposes, Figure 5.2 is an actual Schedule B for a true decedent. Let's take item 7 and run it through: 134 shares of Image Entertainment, Inc. at $4^{9}/16$ per share equals 611 in whole dollars (134 sh x 4.56/sh = 611.04). Take item 11 and run it through: 80 shares Pacific Telesis at $34^{37}/64$ per share equals 2,766 in whole dollars (80 sh x 34.58/sh = 2766.40). The item 11 entry in Figure 5.2 is 2,769 — off a few dollars. Perhaps you can find other items "off a few dollars"? Figure 5.2 shows only 16 different stocks: total valued at $201,695. What would you do if you had 64 different stocks (another true case)?

Listing 64 different stocks on Schedule B requires *continuation sheets*. Each Schedule B can handle between 20 and 25 separate stock listings. For 64 stock listings, you would need two continuation sheets. The total of the two sheets is brought forward to a line at the bottom of Schedule B. Said line reads—

Total from continuation schedules attached to this schedule.

Can you imagine the entry errors and extension errors possible with 64 unit values in dollar fractions extended 64 times into whole dollar amounts? Incidentally, the 64 stock issues in our "true case" grand totaled $1,154,688. Obviously, we are not showing the 64 stocks as we did in Figure 5.2. If you think of Figure 5.2 as being repeated three times, you'll get the complexity idea.

Descriptive Details Required

Up to this point, we haven't told you what the IRS expects of you — your executor, that is — when describing each stock or bond on Schedule B. What we show in Figure 5.2 is a vast simplification. The IRS would like to have each stock and each bond identified in seven ways! The prelude to this requirement is the "Description" columnar heading, which reads—

Form 706	Estate of: ____________ SSN: ________		
	Schedule B - STOCKS AND BONDS		
Item No.	Description	Unit Value	Value at Date of Death
1	80 Airtouch Communications	26 1/2	2,120
2	120 Ameritech Corp.	55 3/8	6,645
3	200 AT&T Corp.	37 3/8	7,475
4	1,500 BankAmerica Corp.	95 1/4	142,875
5	80 Bell Atlantic Corp.	61 1/4	4,900
6	180 Bell South Corp.	39 7/9	7,178
7	134 Image Entmt. Inc.	4 9/16	611
8	64 Lucent Technologies	48 1/2	3,104
9	80 NYNEX Corp.	45 1/8	3,610
10	200 Pacific G & E	23 7/8	4,775
11	80 Pacific Telesis	34 37/64	2,769
12	120 SBC Communications	49 1/8	5,895
13	80 US West Comm Grp	30 7/8	2,470
14	80 US West Media Grp	18 19/32	1,487
15	1,000 Vacu Dry Co.	5	5,000
16	300 UTS Photosource	3/8	113
17	Aggregate accrued dividends 1 1/2 mo. annualized from D/W No.2 ALL STOCKS: COMMON	---	668
	Attachments for backup • Paine Webber statement • Dean Witter statement: No.1 • Dean Witter statement: No.2	From Continuation Schedule(s) If Any	
	(For this schedule) ▶ ▶ ▶ ▶ ▶	Total ▶ ▶	201,695

Fig. 5.2 - True Example of Multiple Stock Entries on Schedule B (706)

Description including face amount of bonds or number of shares and par value where needed for identification. Give 9-digit CUSIP number.

The CUSIP (Committee on Uniform Security Identification Procedure) is a number assigned to all stocks and bonds traded on major exchanges. For short-term trades, it is rarely used.

Supplemental instructions for describing stocks and bonds on Schedule B read—

For stocks, indicate:

- *Number of shares*
- *Whether common or preferred*
- *Issue* [date, series]
- *Price per share*
- *Exact name of corporation*
- *Principal exchange, if listed*
- *9-digit CUSIP number*

For bonds, indicate:

- *Quantity and denomination*
- *Name of obligor*
- *Date of maturity*
- *Interest rate*
- *Interest due date*
- *Principal exchange, if listed*
- *9-digit CUSIP number*

If the stock or bond is unlisted, show the company's principal business office.

Do you know the CUSIP number on any of the stocks or bonds you hold? If not, do you know where to find it? It's on your certificates. Very few ordinary individuals hold stock or bond certificates these days. They hold, instead, a "numbered account" with a brokerage firm, mutual fund, or commodities broker. But, suppose you did have your CUSIP number. If you had 64 items to list on Schedule B (as in our example above), that would be 576 digits (64 x 9) to hassle around with and cross-check. In reality, the IRS doesn't insist on CUSIP numbers, except for officers in large corporations. The CUSIPs are primarily for tracking misconduct by major players in the securities markets. For most decedents, CUSIPs are not vital and can be omitted.

Still, there are six other descriptive details required for each stock, bond, mutual fund, or commodity contract listed on Schedule B. Continuing with our 64 item example above, there could be as many as 384 descriptive details (64 x 6). Are you beginning to get our complexity point? Our suggestion is to prepare a simple description of each item, attach a more detailed description that you request from your broker, and let it go at that. This is the message that we tried to present in Figure 5.2.

The "Accrued Dividend" Problem

Wait! There are still more itemization details required on Schedule B. For each item applicable, the accrued dividends (for stocks) and accrued interest (for bonds) have to be included . . . as a separate entry.

The IRS instruction for listing the accruals reads—

> *List dividends and interest on each stock or bond separately. Indicate* ***as a separate item*** *dividends that have not been collected at death, but which are payable to the decedent or the estate because the decedent was a stockholder of record on date of death. However, if the stock is being traded on an exchange and is selling ex-dividend on the date of the decedent's death, do not include the amount of the dividend as a separate item. Instead, add it to the ex-dividend quotation in determining the fair market value of the stock on the date of the decedent's death. Dividends declared on shares of stock before the death of the decedent but payable to stockholders of record on a date after the decedent's death are not includible in the gross estate.*

Stock dividends are usually declared quarterly, semi-annually, or annually. Interest, by contrast, accrues monthly. Whereas dividends vary, interest is uniform. Consequently, it is when computing the dividend accruals that most of the problems arise. Fortunately, perfect accuracy in your dividend accruals is not so much a virtue as the fact of entering some amount "as a separate item" on Schedule B. Accuracy is not a fetish because the accrual amounts tend to be rather small (order of 1 or 2% or less) of the total value of each stock issue listed. Any "being off a few dollars" is tax treated as *de mimimis*: being immaterial.

The shorter the period of time between the nearest pre-death dividend date and the date of death, the less the influence of accrued dividends on the gross estate. For periods of less than three months, the accrued dividends can be approximated on an annualized basis for all stock, and shown as one aggregate entry. This is what was done in Figure 5.2.

Other Schedule B Instructions

There are several other matters that we should tell you about regarding the preparation of Schedule B. They are informative in the sense that they suggest ways to simplify your estate on items that you probably never thought about before.

A common misconception persists concerning *tax exempt municipal bonds*. These are short, intermediate, and long-term bonds issued by state and local government agencies. **Income** wise, they are federally tax exempt. That is, if they so qualify under Section 103: ***Interest on State and Local Bonds***. These bonds, however, are NOT exempt from inclusion on Form 706. While they may be income tax exempt, they are not transfer tax exempt. A bold-printed warning to this effect in the instructions says—

> ***Bonds that are exempt from Federal income taxes are not exempt from estate taxes.*** *Therefore, you should list these bonds on Schedule B.*

Other government bonds that are listed on this schedule include Treasury bonds, higher education bonds, public housing bonds, FNMA bonds, U.S. savings bonds, U.S. territory bonds, and foreign bonds. Corporate bonds of all kinds have to be included.

As an estate simplifying suggestion, why not convert your entire bond portfolio into **one** tax-exempt muni bond mutual fund? Do it before your demise. Since you have to list any tax-exempt bond fund on Form 706 anyhow, making one entry is certainly simpler than making 5, 10, or more entries for different bonds. We'll have more to say about the virtues of tax exempt bond funds in Chapter 10: Building Needed Liquidity.

The required listings on Schedule B also apply to foreign stocks and bonds. Any foreign securities that you may hold at time of death are subject to a foreign transfer tax as well as to the U.S. transfer tax. To alert you to this reality, the Schedule B instructions say—

> *If you paid any estate, inheritance, legacy, or succession tax to a foreign country on any stocks or bonds included in this schedule, group those stocks and bonds together and label them: "Subject to Foreign Death Taxes."*

Although this instruction does not expressly mention it, we are informing you that there is a Schedule P (Form 706): ***Credit for Foreign Death Taxes***. It is a proportionalized credit against the U.S. transfer tax for the foreign transfer tax paid on foreign assets. To simplify matters in this regard, why not redeem all foreign portfolio assets and reinvest the proceeds into one U.S. mutual fund with a global reach? This way, the foreign transfer tax is reported to you in U.S. dollars. This avoids exchange rate errors when Schedule P is prepared.

The instructions to Schedule B further say—

> *Securities reported as of no value, nominal value, or obsolete should be listed last. Include the address of the company and the state and date of incorporation. Attach copies of correspondence or statements used to determine the "no value."*

Our position is that you should never have in your estate any portfolio assets which have "no value." Not only do the extra explanations and statements complicate your Schedule B, they imply that you have been inattentive to your financial affairs during life. Such implication encourages the IRS to dig for more inattentiveness on Form 706. Therefore, get rid of all no-value portfolio assets before you die. Doing so is a relatively easy decision to make. And, you might even get a capital loss income tax advantage in the process.

In the domain of relatively easy decisions you can make for simplifying your estate while alive, we present Figure 5.3. We urge that you look upon Figure 5.3 as a check-off list for actively simplifying your portfolio estate during life. Whatever you accomplish during life does not appear on Schedule B after death.

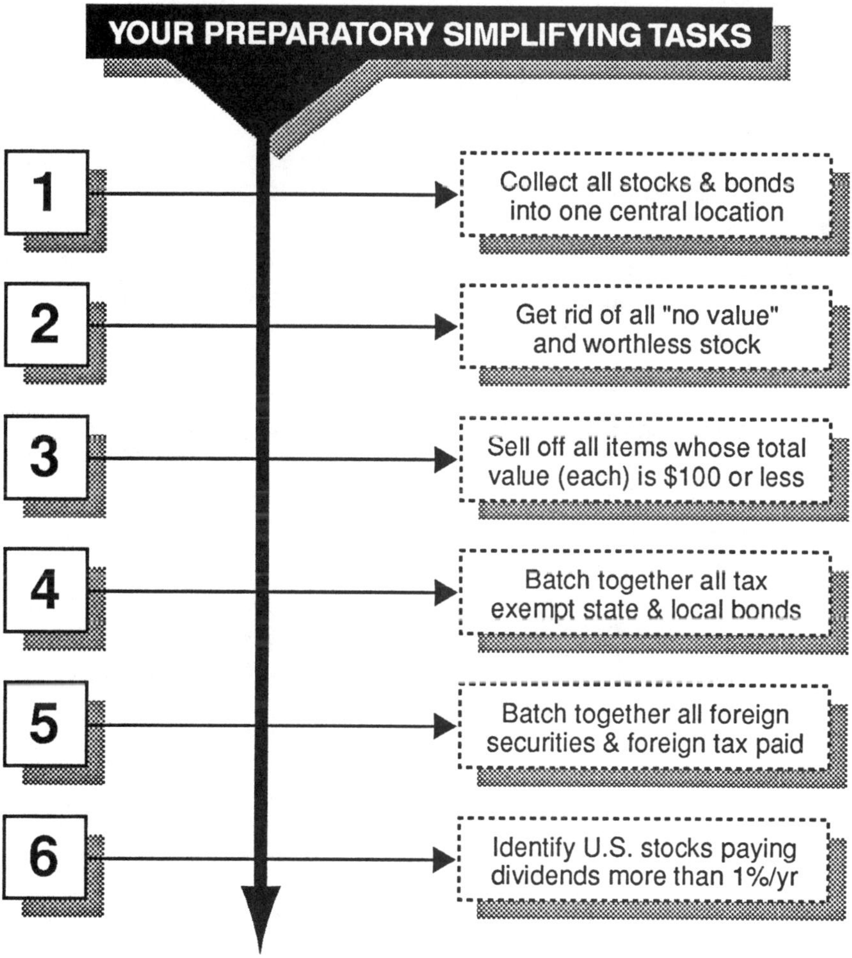

Fig. 5.3 - The 6 "Easy Decisions" Before Making the Hard Ones

Dispositions Before Alternate Date

Except for stock and debt instruments in close corporations, the items on Schedule B are quite liquid. This is certainly true relative to the liquidity of real estate on Schedule A. Schedule B items, though, are less liquid than monetary accounts on Schedule C. Nevertheless, publicly traded items on Schedule B lend themselves to taking advantage of the alternate valuation date (within six months of death) and its dispositional rules. Once one item on Schedule B is selected for alternate date valuation, **all** items on that schedule (and on all asset schedules A through I), must be valued on the alternate date.

There are three particular alternate date rules that you should know about. These are—

Rule 1 — Items distributed, sold, exchanged, or otherwise disposed of *within six months* after decedent's death.

Rule 2 — Items not distributed, etc. under Rule 1.

Rule 3 — Items whose values are affected by the mere lapse of time.

In essence, Rule 1 says—

> *Any property distributed, sold, exchanged, or otherwise disposed of or separated or* ***passed from the gross estate by any method*** *within 6 months after the decedent's death is valued on the date of distribution, sale, exchange, or other disposition,* ***whichever occurs first****. . . . In the "Description" column of each schedule, briefly explain the status or disposition, such as: "Distributed," "Sold," "Bond paid on maturity," etc.* [Emphasis added.]

Rule 2 simply says that if Rule 1 does not apply, enter in the description column: "Not disposed of within 6 months following death." Rule 3 says that if value is affected by the mere lapse of time after decedent's death, "appropriate adjustments" can be made to the alternate date value.

All that we are trying to bring to your attention at this point is that alternate date valuations — especially for portfolio assets — add complications to your after-death estate affairs. If at all possible, you'd like to simplify matters by "slimming down" said assets. One way to do this is to anticipate what is likely to happen within six months after your demise. If you can anticipate what your executor will do (he/she will have full legal discretion to do whatever is necessary), why not take care of such matters yourself?

Anticipate Via Form 1040

The charge can be made that, to suggest that one anticipate his death, is cruel and inhumane. Yet, we all know that the possibility of death passes through one's mind now and then The passing-throughs become more frequent as the years decline in number after age 50. In these anticipatory wonderings, the best predictor of what lies ahead in portfolio matters is your own Form 1040: ***U.S. Individual Income Tax Return***.

Two particular schedules that attach to Form 1040 are vital Schedule B, Form 706 forecasters. The two Form 1040 schedules are:

Schedule B (1040) — Interest and Dividend Income
Schedule D (1040) — Capital Gains and Losses

It is interesting what these two schedules reveal about the complexity of your portfolio assets before death. They are the forerunner to the transfer of those assets to Form 706 (Schedule B) after death. Let us explain. But first, we caution you: **not to confuse** Schedule B (1040) with Schedule B (706), nor Schedule D (1040) with Schedule D (706). There is no tax relationship whatsoever between these same-lettered schedules on Form 1040 and Form 706. Yet, there IS an anticipatory relationship.

Schedule B (1040) is arranged in three parts. In Part I (Interest Income), you list the interest and OID (original interest discount) that you receive from bonds and other monetary accounts that you hold. In Part II (Dividend Income), you list the dividends and other distributions (capital gains, etc.) that you receive on your stock holdings, domestic and foreign. In Part III (Foreign Accounts), you are asked about your foreign securities and trusts, if any. All of these listings, if not disposed of before death, are the very same items that appear on Schedule B of Form 706. The most likely omissions from Schedule B (1040) are tax exempt bonds, close corporation stock, and commodity contracts. As mentioned earlier, these 1040 omissions ARE includible on Schedule B (706). Slimming down the number of items on Schedule B (1040) before death, translates directly into a slimmer number of items on Schedule B (706) after death.

Schedule D (1040) presents a different anticipatory role from that of Schedule B (1040). An entry is made on Schedule D (1040): ***Capital Gains and Losses***, principally when portfolio assets are sold, exchanged, or otherwise disposed of. If you have no or nil items on Schedule D (1040), it could mean that you have few items to enter on Schedule B (706). Or, it could mean that you have refrained from taking any action to sell or exchange your assets before death. If the latter, you are missing an opportunity to simplify your estate.

If you have numerous entries on Schedule D (1040), it could mean that you are aggressively slimming down your portfolio. Any entry on Schedule D (1040) before death is proof of its sale or exchange for "full and adequate consideration." Any item appearing on Schedule D (1040) before death does **not** appear on Schedule B (706) after death. Using Schedule D (1040) intentionally before death constitutes prudent slimming.

We present in Figure 5.4 a summary representation of the anticipatory roles of Schedules B and D, Form 1040. You may not have thought about these schedules in terms of Form 706 before. They are indeed estate-planning useful, if you put your mind to it.

By "putting your mind to it," we mean reducing your total entries on Schedule B (706) to around five or so (excluding accruals). Towards this end, the role of **mutual funds** is one of the great simplifying achievements of our time. Each fund shareholder participates in *thousands* of portfolio assets with just **one** account.

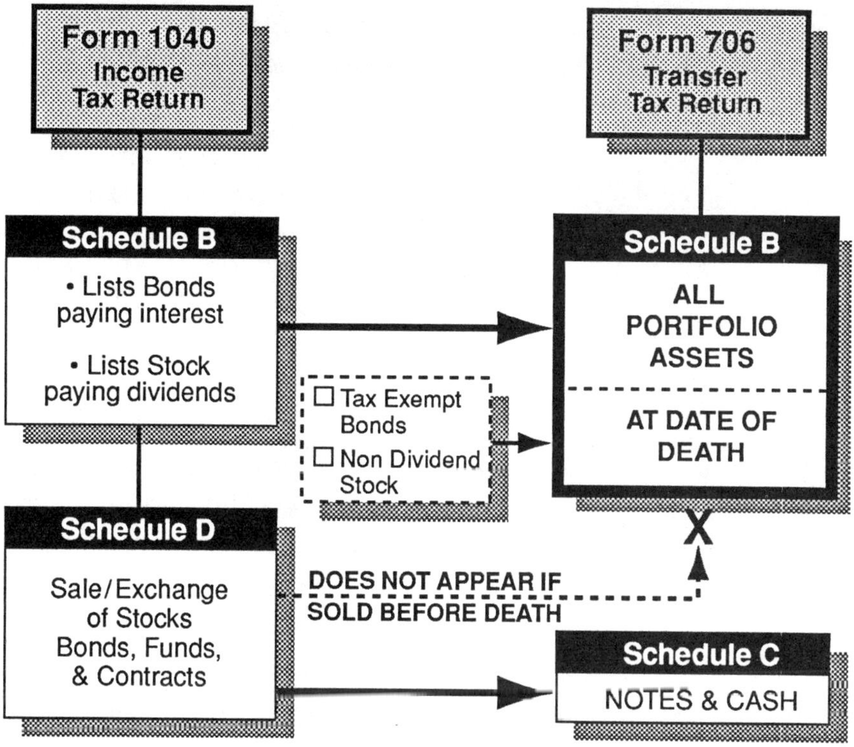

Fig. 5.4 - Anticipatory Role of Form 1040 Schedules for Entries on Form 706

With five such accounts, each with a different investment objective, you can amass all the millions of dollars that you'll ever need.

Tax Now (20%), or Tax Later (37%)

Schedule D (1040) serves a distinctive role of its own relative to Form 706. Each entry on Schedule D (1040) could mean that you sold one or more portfolio assets. When such a sale is made, there is a capital gains (or capital loss) income tax to pay. Many prospective decedents refrain from slimming down their portfolios because of said tax. The universal position is: "Why should I pay the capital gains tax; let my heirs worry about that." Is this the wiser choice? Let us examine the matter.

Suppose you held 1,000 shares in the XYZ Corporation which is publicly traded. You bought the shares for $10,000. After several years, the shares have risen to $15,000 in value. Do you sell the XYZ and pay the capital gains tax on it? Or, do you let the $15,000 be included on Schedule B (706) for transfer tax purposes? Assume that your gross estate (*without* the $15,000) is over $600,000.

If you sell the XYZ stock on Schedule D (1040), you'll have a long-term capital gain of $5,000 [15,000 sales price – 10,000 tax basis]. The capital gains tax rate is 20%. Therefore, you pay $1,000 in income tax (5,000 x 20%). This leaves you with $14,000 in cash proceeds [15,000 – 1,000].

Suppose you did nothing with the $14,000. It would wind up in your gross estate on Schedule C (706): Mortgages, Notes, and Cash. Your transfer tax on this amount would be $5,180 [14,000 x 37%]. The transfer tax rate *starts* at 37% for estates over $600,000, and increases to 55% for estates over $3,000,000. Together, your capital gains tax ($1,000) and transfer tax ($5,180) would total $6,180.

Suppose you did nothing before death. That is, you let the $15,000 of XYZ stock go into your estate and be transfer taxed at 37%. Your transfer tax would be $5,550 [15,000 x 37%]. This amount of tax is $630 less than the combination above: capital gains plus transfer [6,180 – 5,550]. In this case, you're probably right to do nothing before death.

On the other hand, instead of "doing nothing" while alive, suppose you consumed or gave to one of your children $10,000 of the $14,000 after-sale proceeds. You then die, at which time $4,000 goes into your estate. Your transfer tax becomes $1,480 [4,000 x 37%]. This amount plus your $1,000 capital gains tax totals $2,480. Compared to the $5,550 transfer tax above, you have tax saved $3,070 [5,550 – 2,480] on just one during-life portfolio transaction. This is a clear case where "doing something" while alive is better than doing nothing before death.

6

CLARIFYING CO-OWNERSHIPS

A Married Decedent Includes 100% Of "Qualified Joint Interest Property" (QJIP) In His Gross Estate, Then SUBTRACTS The 50% Belonging To His Spouse. A Special Rule To This Effect Applies: IRC Sec. 2040(b). For Nonspousal Joint Tenancy Interests, The Decedent Includes 100% Of All Co-Owned Property . . . UNLESS It Can Be "Shown With Certainty" That A Lesser Percentage Applies. In Tenancy In Common Arrangements, Each Co-Tenant's Specific Ownership Fraction Is Usually Stated Up Front. Otherwise, Tracing The Contributory Interests Of Each Co-Owner — In Money And Money's Worth — Can Be Aggravating And Punitive.

Co-ownership of property is a way of life. It enables two or more persons to join together with a common goal for the property acquired. In the process, there is an implied consent for sharing its acquisition cost, sharing of expenses, sharing of income, sharing of maintenance, sharing of control, sharing of enjoyment, and sharing of profit (or loss) when the property is sold. As long as the co-owners are cooperative and can agree among themselves, there is no particular tax or legal need for their separate ownership interests to be spelled out. As long as all co-owners are alive, and there is no major disharmony between them, the co-ownership arrangement — whatever it might be — can go on year after year without concern.

Problems inevitably arise, however, the moment one co-owner dies. The problems center on what percentage or amount of the property's total value is includible in the decedent's gross estate. This is an area where post-death controversy can raise its ugly head.

The general presumption is that, if the decedent held "any interest" in co-owned property at the time of his death, it is 100% includible in his gross estate. This presumption is overcome where it can be shown with certainty that the decedent owned less than 100%. The "showing with certainty" requires the tracing of each co-owner's separate contributory interest in money and money's worth. The tracing is required throughout the entire holding period of the property: from its acquisition to the death of a co-owner.

Co-ownership cuts across all forms of property holdings. This includes real estate; stocks and bonds; mortgages, notes, and cash; productive machinery and equipment; farming activities; joint ventures; mining activities; operating businesses, and the like. Obviously, the more diverse the types of properties co-owned, and the greater the number of co-owners involved, the more unmanageable the inclusion-in-gross-estate concerns become.

What we want to do in this chapter is to give you pertinent statutory background on the co-ownership problem. Then we want to follow through with as much example specificity that we can. We particularly want to point out how the asset Schedules A (Real Estate), B (Stocks and Bonds), C (Mortgages, Notes and Cash), E (Jointly Owned Property), and F (Other Miscellaneous Property) are co-owner listed. Many of the inclusion accounting details should self-suggest what you could do on your own, for clarifying matters. Obviously, clarification becomes simpler if the number of co-owners can be reduced. The ultimate clarification effort is to sell, exchange, or gift your nonspousal co-owned property while alive.

Basic Law: Section 2033

The mandatory inclusion of co-owned property into one's gross estate stems directly from IRC Section 2033. ***Property in Which Decedent Had an Interest.*** This one sentence tax law reads—

> *The value of the gross estate* ***shall include*** *the value of all property* ***to the extent of the interest therein*** *of the decedent at the time of his death.* [Emphasis added.]

This law became effective with respect to decedents dying after October 16, 1962. It has not changed one iota since!

Nowhere in law is the "extent of the interest therein" defined. This leaves interpretation up to local property law. All that the IRS has done is to broaden the inclusion to include—

> *The value of all property, whether real or personal, tangible or intangible, and wherever situated, beneficially owned by the decedent at the time of his death.* [IRS Reg. 20.2033-1(a)].

The key definitive element in Section 2033 is: *extent of ownership at time of death.* If co-ownership of the property came into existence before death, and remained in existence after death, it clearly is includible in the decedent's gross estate. If death defeated the co-ownership interest in some manner, the property would not be includible. Non-inclusion would occur, for example, if the decedent had only a life interest in property, which terminated at his death. A pension with no survivor benefits is another example.

Once the concept of includibility is established, the next item of concern is the extent of the decedent's percentage or amount of ownership. Determining the precise extent of ownership is not casy to do. The IRS and the courts take the consistent position that—

> *Property which appears to belong to the decedent will be included in his estate in the absence of proof that it did not, in fact, belong to the decedent.*

The above basics are the reason why it is so very important that you, as a prospective decedent, do all that you possibly can ahead of time to clarify each of your co-ownership interests.

Husband & Wife Property

The most common form of co-ownership of property is that between husband and wife during the full term of their marriage. The co-ownership aspects are referred to as "marital property" even though it is unclear which of the spouses acquired the property, when, and how. Such property is generally understood to exclude property acquired from persons outside of the marriage, such as by gift, by will, or by inheritance.

There are two forms of marital property recognized for federal tax purposes. They are *community property* (C/P) and *qualified joint interest property* (QJIP). Both forms are considered 50/50 owned by husband and wife. Today, only eight states (Arizona, California, Idaho, Louisiana, Nevada, New Mexico, Texas, and Washington) have enacted community property laws. The other 42 states have various versions of separate property laws, dower and curtesy laws, tenants by the entirety, and joint tenancy. It is the inconsistency of husband and wife property laws in the 42 states that prompted Congress (in 1981) to enact the QJIP law: IRC Section 2040(b): ***Certain Joint Interests of Husband and Wife.***

By means of Section 2040(b), Congress has decreed a straight 50% surviving spouse exclusion from the deceased spouse's gross estate. The 50% exclusion applies across the board to all property acquired during marriage by either spouse . . . *other than* by "gift, bequest, devise, or inheritance." This exclusion has no bearing whatsoever on the co-ownership of property between nonspouses.

Paragraph (1) of Section 2040(b): ***Interests of spouse excluded from gross estate***, reads (in pertinent part)—

> *In the case of any qualified joint interest, the value included in the gross estate with respect to such interest . . . is* ***one-half of the value*** *of such qualified joint interest.*

The subsequent paragraph (2): ***Qualified joint interest defined***, says—

> *The term "qualified joint interest" means* ***any interest*** *in property held by the decedent and the decedent's spouse as—*
>
> > *(A) tenants by the entirety, or*
> >
> > *(B) joint tenants with right of survivorship, but only if the decedent and the spouse of the decedent are the only joint tenants.*

The term "tenants by the entirety" is the absolute right of survivorship between spouses. The term "joint tenants" includes the right of survivorship, but such right is not absolute. It can be denied by either spouse, in whole or part, by contrary testamentary intent taking effect at death. Tenancy by the entirety applies only to husband and wife, whereas joint tenancy may apply to any two or more co-owners.

Joint Tenancy vs. Tenancy in Common

Where other than spousal property rights are involved, there are two common forms of co-ownership. These forms are joint tenancy and tenancy in common. In either case, the property is physically *undivided.* As such, each co-owner has the right to possess and the privilege to use the whole thing. Cooperative co-owners are allowed to agree among themselves as to who will have possession in fact, since all have possession in law. If they cannot agree, one or more can petition the court to have the property partitioned among them. It then becomes "divided" property. If actual physical division is impracticable, the court will order the property sold and the proceeds divided among the co-owners.

In cooperative co-ownership cases, the owners have generally agreed among themselves as to their divisional interests. In joint tenancies, the presumption is that all co-owners are co-equal. That is, if there are two joint tenants, each owns 50% of the property. If there are three joint tenants, each owns $33^1/3$%; if four joint tenants, each owns 25% . . . and so on. If one of the joint tenants dies, the property interests are re-equalized among the surviving co-owners. Because of this re-equalization, joint tenancy tends to be a *family affair.* When the initial owner dies, his siblings, children, grandchildren, etc. seek to divide up the property interests so that each retains his or her "fair share."

In contrast, tenancy in common is more of a *business affair.* At the very outset, each co-owner is expected to contribute a specified amount of money, property, or services to establish his or her ownership interest in the arrangement. Although all co-owners could contribute equally, seldom is this done. When the agreed amount of initial capitalization is acquired, each co-owner's separate fraction (or percentage) can be determined with mathematical precision. The arrangements could be such that, if there were two co-owners, for example, their ownership interests might be 35/65 (35% + 65% = 100%); if three co-owners, their respective interests might be 25/35/40 (25% + 35% + 40% = 100%); if four co-owners, their respective interests might be 15/20/30/35 (15% + 20% + 30% + 35% = 100%) . . . and so on. The co-ownership fractions (or percentages) can change at any time during the business operation.

Unlike that of joint tenancy, there is no automatic right of survivorship when property is held in tenancy in common. If a co-owner dies, his specific ownership fraction (or percentage) is includible in his gross estate. After inclusion and taxation thereon, the decedent's ownership fraction passes to his heirs or others, as directed by his testamentary dispositions.

The ownership distinction between joint tenancy and tenancy in common is very important. Misconceptions tend to arise after one co-owner's death. Our attempt to clarify the distinction is presented in Figure 6.1. Of the two forms of co-ownership, it is joint tenancy that puts a decedent most at risk, for Form 706 purposes.

Overview of Schedule E

Schedule E is one of the nine asset schedules: A through I. Its official title is: ***Jointly Owned Property***. Schedule E is intended for joint tenancy property only. It is not intended for tenancy in common property. An instruction to this effect on the back of Schedule E says—

> *Do not list on this schedule property that the decedent held as a tenant in common.* [Instead] *report the value of the interest on Schedule A if real estate, or on the appropriate schedule if* [other] *property.*

As the result of this Schedule E instruction, there is no special schedule for tenancy in common property. Specific fractional ownerships less than 100% are commonly entered on Schedules A (Real Estate), B (Stocks and Bonds), C (Mortgages, Notes, and Cash), and F (Other Miscellaneous Property). Asset Schedules D

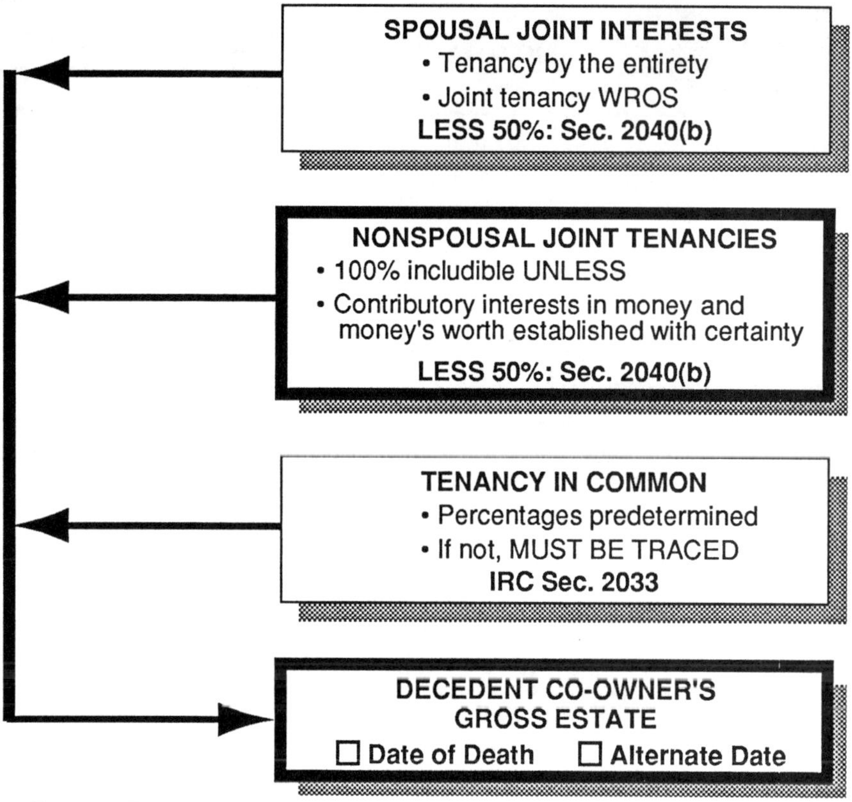

Fig. 6.1 - Types of Co-Ownerships Includible in Decedent's Gross Estate

(Insurance on Decedent's Life), G (Transfers During Decedent's Life), H (Powers of Appointment), and I (Pensions and Annuities) do not lend themselves to co-ownership form.

Schedule E is arranged in two separate parts. These are—

Part 1 — ***Qualified Joint Interests***: *Interests Held by the Decedent and His or Her Spouse as the Only Joint Tenants.*

Part 2 — ***All Other Joint Interests***

In edited form, we show these two parts in Figure 6.2. Part 1, as indicated by its title alone, is clearly intended only for husband

Sch. E (Form 706)	Estate of:		
	JOINTLY OWNED PROPERTY		
Part I	Qualified Joint Interests (Spouses Only)		
Item	Description	Alternate Value	Death Value
	100% Totals		
	"One-Half" or 50% Totals		

Part II	All Other Joint Interests			
Item	Description	PERCENTAGE INCLUDIBLE	Alternate Includible	Death Includible
	Total Other Joint Interests			

Fig. 6.2 - Abbreviated Format of Schedule E Joint Interests

and wife joint tenancy properties. The instructions thereto are essentially a restatement of Section 2040(b) that we cited earlier. The instructions also say—

Community property held by the decedent and spouse should be reported on the appropriate schedules A through I.

As Figure 6.2 indicates, there is a special line in Part 1 which reads—

Amounts included in gross estate (one-half of totals).

The instructons to Part 1 of Schedule E raise a peculiar question. Why are the decedents in the eight community property states allowed to use Schedules A, B, C, and F for spousal property, while married decedents in the other 42 states are directed to use Schedule E only?

Answer: It is one of those shortfalls in common sense that often pervades tax forms design and tax law interpretation.

Our recommendation is that Part 1 of Schedule E be ignored for marital property. Instead, use Schedules A (Real Estate), B (Stocks and Bonds), C (Mortgages, Notes, and Cash), and F (Other Miscellaneous Property). For each appropriate schedule, list 100% of the marital items in one block. Subtotal the 100% amounts. Then show directly below each subtotal, the **subtraction**—

LESS 50% C/P......................................<   >
or
LESS 50% QJIP....................................<   >

Then continue with other appropriate listings for each respective schedule (A, B, C, or F).

The net consequence of our recommendation is that you use Schedule E for its Part 2 function only. The title to Part 2, recall, is: ***All Other Joint Interests***. Or, as we would put it: ALL NONSPOUSAL Joint Tenancy Interests.

Part 2 Inclusions Are Daunting

Please glance again at Figure 6.2 and note its Part 2 format. Its upper portion consists of horizontal lines for entering the name and address of each co-tenant separately. The preprinted instructions above these lines read—

State the name and address of each surviving co-tenant. If there are more than three surviving co-tenants, list the additional co-tenants on an attached sheet.

Thereafter, each co-tenant is assigned a separate capitalized letter for reference identification.

Also note in Figure 6.2 the right-hand portion of Part 2. There are three columns there. Each column (from left to right) is labeled, respectively:

Percentage includible ....[%]
Includible alternate value..........................[$]
Includible value at date of death ....[$]

"Percentage includible." What is that all about?

It refers to the **decedent's** includible portion: NOT that of each co-tenant/co-owner. It also refers to the 300 words of IRC Section 2040(a): ***Joint Interests; General Rule.*** The essence of Section 2040(a) is that 100% of every joint interest is includible . . .

> ***except*** *such part thereof as may be shown to have originally belonged to such other person and never to have been received or acquired by the latter from the decedent for less than full consideration in money or money's worth.*

To carry out this statutory mandate, the IRS instructions for entries in each of the above three columns say—

> *In the "Percentage includible" column, enter the percentage of the total value of the property that you* ***intend to include*** *in the gross estate. . . . In the "Includible alternate value" and "Includible value at date of death" columns, enter only the values that you* ***believe are includible*** *in the gross estate.* [Emphasis added.]

Our interpretation of Section 2040(a) and the IRS instruction to Schedule E, Part 2 is that you have three options. The options are—

(1) Include all nonspousal joint tenancy property at its full 100% value.

(2) Using documentation that establishes each co-tenant's contributory interests in money or money's worth, show specific computations for inclusion amounts less than 100%.

(3) Enter what you "believe to be" the includible amount . . . then let the IRS accept or contest your belief.

In support of these options, the Part 2 instructions on the back of Schedule E say—

> *Generally, you must include the full value of the jointly owned property . . . unless you can show that any part of the property was acquired with consideration originally belonging to the surviving joint tenant or tenants.*

Joint Tenancy Examples

Nonspousal co-ownership of property in joint tenancy form is very common. It is a convenient way of spreading the risks of management and enjoyment of property. It requires no formal procedures for creating the arrangement. Thc co-owners simply agree to include their names on the account, certificate, registration, or title of the affected property. This arrangement is greatly advantageous should one of the co-owners die. For the decedent, the property passes to the surviving co-tenants without the necessity for probate. This one feature alone makes (nonspousal) joint tenancy a popular arrangement among family members.

A common strategy for avoiding probate is this. A mother with two adult children decides to add her two children's names to her various bank accounts, money market accounts, and other investment accounts. She does so "for convenience only." She wants the children to have access to her funds in the event of her sickness, injury, senility, or death. Each child has withdrawal authority only with consent of the mother while she is alive. When the mother deceases, there is no question that 100% of the joint tenancy property is includible in her gross estate. Neither child made any contributory interests in money or money's worth.

Here's another common case. A father with three adult children acquired from his parents an 8-unit apartment complex which was rented. Although his spouse was alive, the rental complex was not marital property: it was inherited. For convenience only, the father added the three children's names to the property deed. He had the title re-recorded as joint tenants with right of survivorship. All three children worked on the property and helped to manage and maintain it. Each year, the father gave each child a computer-generated "Gift

Certificate" signifying a $10,000 per year contributory ownership interest in the 8-unit rental building. When the father dies, it becomes a matter of reconstructing each child's ownership interest in cumulative money and money's worth. In the end, however, no matter which each child's reconstructed interests might be, the IRS would insist that at least 25% of the property's value (1 ÷ 4) be included in the father's gross estate. Conceivably, it might insist on more than 25% being includible.

In another case, an unmarried man and an unmarried woman lived together. They lived in her house which was worth about $500,000. He had a commercial fishing boat and license worth about $285,000. They each kept their own separate bank accounts. However, they pooled together all of their investment money (totaling $365,000) into one growth stock mutual fund. Both names were shown on the account as joint tenants and co-owners. On one of his regular fishing trips, the male co-owner was swept overboard in a violent storm and drowned. His two crew members recovered the body and returned the boat to port. What portion of the $365,000 co-owned investment account is includible in the decedent's estate?

Answer: $365,000 . . . plus growth in the account ($50,000 say) to date of death. A lower amount would be included if the monetary contribution of the decedent could be established with certainty. After exhaustively tracing the various pre-pooled accounts of the decedent, his initial contributory share was determined to be $160,000. With this information, the decedent's percentage includible in Part 2 of Schedule E becomes—

$$160{,}000 \div 365{,}000 = 43.83\% \text{ or } 0.4383$$

The includible value at date of death would be—

$$[365{,}000 + 50{,}000] \times 0.4383 = \$181{,}895$$

Tenants in Common Example

Tenants in common is a different ownership clarification matter from that of joint tenancy. There is more of a business relationship where the percent or fraction of ownership by each co-owner is spelled out ahead of time. This is especially true of an income-producing partnership where each partner's share is reported to the IRS annually.

Partnership reports are done on Form 1065: ***U.S. Partnership Return of Income.*** Each partner's share in the partnership is reported on Schedule K-1 (1065): ***Partner's Share of Income, Credits, Deductions, Etc.*** The Form 1065 states the number of partners. The Schedule K-1 requires the statement of—

Each partner's percentage of:

- *Profit sharing* ...._______%
- *Loss sharing* ...._______%
- *Ownership of capital* ...._______%

The ownership-of-capital percentage is carried to four decimal places, such as 7.2194%, for example. The IRS seldom questions the accuracy of the percentages computed by the partnership entity. What the IRS does question is the valuation of the partnership property, in those cases where the total value is significant.

A recent case on point is that of a decedent who held a 7.2194% ownership interest in a real estate partnership consisting of vacant land, a shopping center, and a mobile home park. The issue was the valuation of the real property at date of death, and the amount of "discounting" applicable to the minority interest of the decedent.

Normal valuation procedures for Form 706 purposes are to professionally value all real estate at date of death. The only exceptions are valuations made within six months before death, or within six months after death. In this true example case, the property was valued at $5,626,000 some *five* years before death. This was unacceptable to the IRS. Although the nondecedent partners objected to the revaluation because of its cost (about $7,000 estimated), it was pointed out that the revaluation fee is a deductible expense against the decedent's taxable estate. The revaluation turned out to be $6,710,000. This amount was $1,084,000 more than previously.

The next disputive item was the percentage of discounting applicable to a minority interest which is inseparable from the partnership. Court-approved discount factors range from 20% to 40%, depending on facts and circumstances. Unless a decedent's executor wants to challenge the IRS in court, a mid-point discount — in this case 30% — is often used.

Thus, the inclusion amount of the decedent's 7.2194% ownership of the partnership was computed as follows:

Total value of property at death	$6,710,000
Decedent partner's interest	7.2194%
Decedent partner's proportionate value	484,420
LESS 30% discount factor	<145,326>
Decedent's includible amount	339,094

This information would go on Schedule A (Real Estate) with an attachment showing the pertinent computations.

Close Corporation Example

A "close corporation" is the operation of small business where five or fewer principals own 50% or more of the stock in said corporation. The stock is not tradable on regular securities markets and, therefore, its computed value must be established.

The ownership percentage of a principal who dies is relatively easy to establish from the corporation's *shareholder registry*. This lists the names, addresses, social security numbers, number of shares owned, and total shares outstanding for the corporation. In the case we have in mind, the decedent principal held 5,280 shares of 18,500 shares outstanding. Thus, his percentage of ownership was 5,280 ÷ 18,500 = 28.54%. He was one of three principals owning together 62% of the corporate stock.

The corporation's gross receipts for the year nearest to the decedent's death were about $16,800,000. A corporation of this gross receipts size must keep such records and ledgers that will enable it to prepare a balance sheet, at least quarterly. A "balance sheet" consists of assets, liabilities, and stockholders equity posted to whatever ending date is designated. The most common assets shown are: (1) Cash on hand, (2) Accounts receivable, (3) Inventory of merchandise, (4) Loans **to** stockholders, (5) Depreciable assets (buildings, structures, improvements, machinery, equipment, vehicles), (6) Land, if any, and (7) Other miscellaneous assets. The most common liabilities shown are: (a) Accounts payable, (b) Notes and loans payable less than one year, (c) Loans **from** stockholders, (d) Mortgages and notes payable one year or more, (e) Retained earnings, (f) Other miscellaneous liabilities, and (g) Stockholders' equity.

The stockholders' equity, as posted on the balance sheet, provides the *first cut* at computing the unit value of the stock shares. In our example case, the posted equity was $1,963,775. Dividing this amount by the 18,500 total shares gives a unit share value of

$1,963,775 ÷ 18,500 sh = $106.15/sh

This value is usually referenced as the: *Unadjusted Book Value.* It is not a reliable measure, but it is a start. One seeks the ADJUSTED book value as the more credible computation.

Land, buildings, and fixtures to land tend to appreciate in value. Yet, they are carried on the books at their acquisition cost, less statutory allowance for depreciation. In our example case, these assets were fair market valued at $2,650,000 *higher* than their carried-on-the-books value. This increases the shareholders' equity from $1,963,775 to $4,613,775 (1,963,775 + 2,650,000).

The next conspicuous balance sheet item for adjustment is the retained earnings: in our case $685,000. Retaining earnings as a liability is permitted only for reasonable business needs: debt payoffs, plant improvements, business expansion, etc. In our example case, the retained earnings were used as a cash kitty for extending "loans" to the three principals. The corporation never paid dividends; it made loans to the stockholders with no set maturity dates or rates of interest. As a consequence of this charade, the retained earnings were removed from the liability side of the balance sheet to the asset side. This increased the stockholders' equity from $4,613,775 to $5,298,775 (4,613,775 + 685,000).

At this point, the adjusted book value per share becomes

$5,298,775 ÷ 18,500 sh = $286.42/sh

Because the decedent was one of the three principals of the corporation, no discounting for lack of marketability was allowed. The decedent's inclusion value at date of death was

5,280 sh x $286.42/sh = $1,512,298

The Ultimate Clarification: Sale, Etc.

We have intentionally gone into some detail in explaining the co-ownership "inclusion problem" at time of death. Unless addressed with specificity ahead of time, the problem can become both aggravating and punitive post-mortem. Particularly so if the co-owned property (the decedent's portion) represents a significant share of the decedent's gross estate. Fortunately, spousal co-ownership inclusions are not the problem they once were. It is in the domain of *nonspousal* co-ownerships where the Form 706 inclusion problems arise. We summarize all of the above plus subsequent matters in Figure 6.3.

Common sense suggests that if you can anticipate your post-mortem co-ownership problems while alive, you should do so. You have any of three valid choices, or a combination thereof. These choices are: (1) *Sale*, (2) *Exchange*, or (3) *Gift*. If done properly before death, and good records maintained, all nonspousal co-ownerships could be eliminated or certainly reduced.

The most straightforward elimination of co-ownership is the outright sale of your portion of the co-owned property. Offer to sell it to your co-owners for "full and adequate consideration" at its fair market value. Exercise great care when selling to close family members. Or, offer to sell your ownership interest to others whom the existing co-owners would approve. If you do sell it, report the disposition on your while-alive Form 1040 for the year of sale.

If a bona fide sale is unlikely, try to *exchange* your ownership interest with another co-owner or two, for some other item or items not co-owned with others. For example, a co-owner may have a car, boat, trailer, camper, golf set, painting, artifact, or some other item you might have wanted but didn't get around to acquiring.

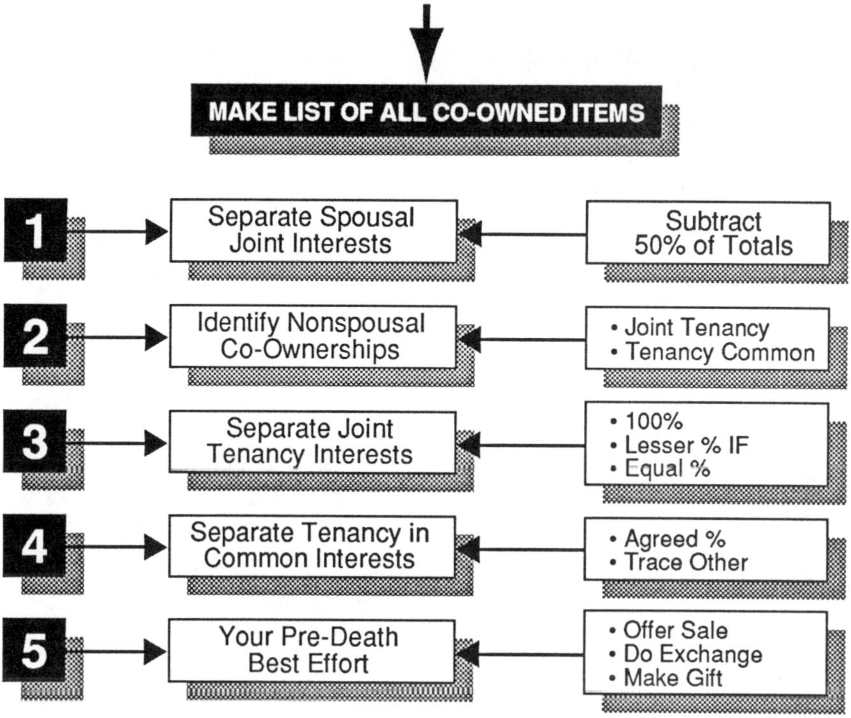

Fig. 6.3 - Summary of Clarification Effort With Co-Owned Property

Because it would not be a "like-kind" exchange, treat it as a sale and report it on Form 1040.

If a sale or exchange is impractical, consider *gifting* your co-ownership interest away. Gift it to anyone you want to, if the donee will accept. You could gift part of your interest to one donee, part to another donee, part to a third donee . . . and so on. Family members would be the ideal donees; they're probably going to inherit it anyhow. Why not set the stage now, and avoid the hassle for your executor?

Whatever you do, we urge that you prepare Form 709: ***U.S. Gift Tax Return***. Technically, this form is required only if the transfer value *per donee* is more than $10,000. Nevertheless, we suggest you prepare it as an "information return" even if no transfer tax results. It puts you on record for stating:

- Donee's name and address
- Relationship to donor
- Description of gift
- Donor's adjusted basis of gift
- Date of gift
- Value at date of gift

One of the constructive features of Form 709 is that it forces you to record thereon: ***Gifts from Prior Periods***. This makes you resurrect any prior tax accountable transfers, and requires that you locate your prior Forms 709 (if any). This information is very helpful to your executor. Our contention is that most prospective decedents do not use Form 709 with the idea in mind of simplifying their estate. This transfer form during life can definitely save headaches, taxes, and post-mortem confusion. We'll address the use of Form 709 more specifically in Chapter 9: Filing Gift Tax Returns. Meanwhile, we urge using the form for clarifying at least some of your nonspousal co-ownership interests.

7

PURGING COLLECTIBLES, ETC.

Every Decedent Or Prospective Decedent Collects Over The Years A CLUTTER ESTATE. Such Consists Of Articles And Effects Which Have Low Or Nil Value For Form 706 Purposes. "Low Or Nil" Is Construed To Mean Less Than 5% Of The Gross Estate. This Is The "Worn And Torn" Domain Of Household Goods, Wearing Apparel, Memorabilia, Depreciable Business Assets, And Obsolete Vehicles, Equipment, Etc. Other Items Are Purgeable If They Can Be Sold Or Gifted Before Death, And Each Disposition Recorded. Your First-Hand Experience Helping Parents And Relatives Purge Their Estates Is Invaluable.

To the IRS, the term "collectibles" means collections of gold coins, rare stamps, antique guns, oriental rugs, works of art, and other items of rarity which are marketable for high value. These items, of course, if on hand at time of death, are transfer taxed. We offer comments and suggestions on these matters, but the IRS meaning is not the primary thrust of this chapter.

By "collectibles," we mean everything in your estate which can be undiplomatically classed as *clutter and junk.* It may not be classified as such by you, but once you are gone, will someone really pay earnest money for it?

Our term includes all of those things collected over the years that were never discarded when they should have been. Our term includes that 30-year-old bicycle still in your garage; your first golf set (or tennis racket); clothes that no longer fit; old books which have no "original manuscript" status; stock certificates of companies no longer in existence; costume and low value jewelry; out-of-date computers, tapes, videos, and accessories; and other paraphernalia which is "worn and torn."

These and similar items need to be cleared out of your estate. Except for individual items whose potential value is $3,000 or more, collectibles clutter up your estate for listing and valuing on Schedule F: Miscellaneous Property. In some cases, dealing with collectibles can take up to 30% to 50% of your executor's time and conscience. The mandated inclusion in your estate of "all property of value" can be troubling to a conscientious executor who feels duty bound to list every paper clip, pot and pan, hand tool, or photo album. Some practical common sense must be used.

Accordingly, in this chapter we offer numerous purging steps for clearing up the clutter in order to simplify your estate. For example, having a safe deposit box *implies* that you may have something to tax hide. By closing your safe deposit box and refiling your papers (or relocating your jewelry), you can remove such adverse implications. Wherever there is a tax to be levied, the IRS is persistent at ferreting out the value in all types of collectibles. The fewer collectibles you have, the simpler it is for everyone.

Schedule F: The Focus

Lest you get the wrong impression of what we mean by the term "purging," we want to clarify it for you. Helpful in this regard is its standard dictionary definition. The word "purge" means—

> *To cleanse or rid of impurities, foreign matter, or undesirable elements; to clear away, off, or out; to free from a charge or imputation of guilt.*

Thus, for our purposes, the term is used as a "cleaning out" process. It is not a process of property concealment nor of tax avoidance.

The first step in any purging operation is to identify those items which are **not** purgeable. For ascertaining such items, we direct your attention to Schedule F of Form 706. The official title of this schedule is: ***Other Miscellaneous Property Not Reportable Under***

Any Other Schedule. If an item is reportable on Schedule A (Real Estate), Schedule B (Stocks and Bonds), Schedule C (Notes and Cash), Schedule D (Insurance on Decedent's Life), Schedule E (Jointly Owned Property), Schedule G (Transfers During Decedent's Life), Schedule H (Powers of Appointment), or Schedule I (Pensions and Annuities), it is not a true candidate for purging. Whether on these schedules or not, if an item truly has nil value or de minimis value, it just shouldn't appear anywhere on Form 706.

For Schedule F overview purposes, we reproduce Figure 1.3 and redesignate it as Figure 7.1. This figure gives you a pretty concise overview. Note that there are three specific "Yes/No" items in the head portion. We'll address these three items later. Meanwhile, note that there are 21 other items in Figure 7.1 which are highly abbreviated.

Sched. F | **Other Miscellaneous Property** | **Form 706**

1. **Articles of artistic or collectible value** ☐ Yes ☐ No
2. **Bonus or award to spouse or other** ☐ Yes ☐ No
3. **Access to a safe deposit box** ☐ Yes ☐ No

Marital deduction property from pre-deceased spouse

☐ Debts due decedent ☐ Proprietorship business(es) ☐ Insurance on life of another

- Partnership interests
- Closely-held corporations

• Claims	• Judgments	• Farm machinery
• Refunds	• Trust funds	• Farm products
• Rights	• Automobiles	• Recreational vehicles
• Royalties	• Household goods	• Reversionary interests
• Leaseholds	• Personal effects	• Remainder interests

Fig. 7.1 - Range of Items Includible on Schedule F (Form 706)

Official instructions to Schedule F appear on its reverse side. There are four particular items listed in the instructions which are clearly not purgeable. These four items are:

1. Debts due decedent (if not listed on Schedule C)

2. Ownership in a business (if not reported on Schedule E or elsewhere)
3. Insurance on the life of another (if decedent or his estate is the beneficiary)
4. Qualified terminable interest property (if decedent is a surviving spouse)

To purge any of these four items intentionally is — or can be — tantamount to tax avoidance. For example, suppose you loaned $5,000 to a friend based purely on a handshake. On date of death, the $5,000 had not been paid back. Your executor, who was not privy to the handshake, omits the $5,000 "debt due decedent" from your gross estate. This is not purging; it is inattention to duty. Suppose that some two years later the $5,000 was paid back. Any omitted payback requires amending Form 706 and attaching thereto a "corrected" Schedule F. If, instead of $5,000, the loan was for $50, its intentional omission would be purging. It's all a matter of "facts and circumstances" and due diligence to reality.

We urge that you review for yourself the official instructions to Schedule F. Your review may trigger thought processes of your own, for distinguishing between what is purgeable and what is not. For example, you have a small claims court judgment for $365. You've tried several times by phone, fax, and certified mail to collect it. Some five years have gone by. The judgment, even with sheriff's service, has not been collected. Purge this item from your estate and go on to other matters.

Articles Having Intrinsic Value

When reviewing an official Schedule F and its instructions, be sure to read and digest every word of Line 1 thereof. That line (on the face of Schedule F) is a question which asks—

> *Did the decedent at the time of death own any articles of artistic or collectible value in excess of $3,000* ***or*** *any collections whose artistic or collectible value combined at date of death exceeded $10,000?* ☐ *Yes* ☐ *No. If "Yes," submit full details on this schedule and attach appraisals.*

You must answer this question either "Yes" or "No." If you leave the checkboxes blank, the IRS will interpret your answer as a "Yes."

What is this question really asking?

It is asking three things, actually. It is asking **at time of death**—

1. Do you have *any articles* (regardless of value) with artistic or intrinsic value? The instructions define such articles as "e.g., jewelry, furs, silverware, books, statuary, vases, oriental rugs, coin or stamp collections." If you have any such articles, the instructions say: "Check the 'Yes' box and provide full details." The first sentence of the instructions to line 1 say nothing about the individual or collective value of such articles.

2. Is *any one article* valued at more than $3,000? If so, the instructions say: "Attach an appraisal by an expert under oath and the required statement regarding the appraiser's qualifications."

3. Is any *collection of similar articles* valued at more than $10,000? If so, attach an appraisal and the required statement. A "collection of similar articles" would be a 12-place setting of fine chinaware or of sterling silver, three original paintings by the same artist, or seven antique hand guns from different manufacturers.

We summarize the above for you in Figure 7.2. The guidelines presented are fundamental to understanding where you can purge and where you may not.

Articles of intrinsic value in your estate at time of death are like a homing beacon to the IRS. If you answer "Yes" and describe a $100 item, the IRS will assume that you have $1,000,000 worth of such item. It will probe and probe . . . and drive your executor wild.

Knowing in advance the "homing beacon" mindset of the IRS, we strongly urge that you make an exhaustive inventory before death of all such articles. Assign your "gut feel" good faith value to

PURGEABLE	NONPURGEABLE
1 Ordinary articles of low or nil value	1 Articles of artistic or intrinsic value
2 If any single item is $3,000 or less, no appraisal is required	2 If any single item is $3,000 or more, full appraisal is required
3 If set of like items is $10,000 or less, no appraisal is required	3 If set of like items is $10,000 or more, full appraisal is required
WORN & TORN Unused, Unuseable, & Unwanted by Family & Nonheirs	***USEFUL & VALUABLE*** Sought by Nonheirs Who Are Willing to Pay For & Improve

Fig. 7.2 - General Guidelines for Purging and Nonpurging

each item or set. Then categorize your items into the following groupings:

- ☐ $3,000 or less, each
- ☐ more than $3,000 each
- ☐ $10,000 or less, each set
- ☐ more than $10,000 each set

This is the kind of preliminary effort you must do, before any bona fide and responsible purging can be undertaken. This inventorying effort applies to all miscellaneous property items, whether having artistic/intrinsic value or not.

The "Safe Deposit" Question

Line 2 on the face of Schedule F addresses *any bonus or award* payable to decedent as a consequence of his employment or death. This is not a purgeable item. Any such amount received, or to be received, will be reported to the IRS by the payer(s) thereof. If applicable, answer the question "Yes" and provide details.

Line 3 on Schedule F is the "safe deposit box" question. The full text of this question reads:

> *Did the decedent at the time of death have, or have access to, a safe deposit box?* ☐ *Yes* ☐ *No. If "Yes," state location, and if held in joint names of decedent and another, state name and relationship of joint depositor. If any of the contents of the safe deposit box are omitted from the schedules in this return, explain fully why omitted.*

Unlike that of Line 2, Line 3 **is** a purgeable item. It is something you can do, and should do, *well before* death. Opening, removing all contents, and surrendering your access key from your death bed is too suspicious.

The term "have access to" a safe deposit box is a tax trap. It means that if you engage a spouse, adult child, relative, or friend to contract for a box in his or her name, you have to answer "Yes" to the question. Otherwise, you could secrete assets in said box and be out of the reach of Form 706. This is not a safe strategy unless you answer "Yes" to the question. Putting some of your assets in someone else's safe deposit box can be a practical convenience, if tax avoidance is not your primary motive.

Answering "Yes" to the question and supplying information such as "Nothing of value" will not be accepted. Nor will a statement such a "Private papers only — birth certificate, marriage certificate, military discharge, divorce decree, last will and testament, etc." It is true that these important papers have no market value. However, they imply that you have also commingled various financial instruments, such as life insurance policies, Treasury Note accounts, certificates of deposit, pass books, stock certificates, expensive jewelry, foreign currency, and/or a horde of green paper cash. Dealing with adverse tax implications is always a problem.

Your best course of action is to get rid of your safe deposit box altogether. Then your executor can answer "No" to the question with a clear conscience. If you do have items of value that would fit into such a box, earmark said items for listing on Schedules A through I, as appropriate. The official question applies clearly to commercially available safe deposit boxes within the confines of a regulated financial institution. An employee there has to log each of your entries to said box. If items are removed after death, an officer of the institution has to witness inventorying the contents, and any removal therefrom. If you have some kind of portable safe box at home for important papers and records, you can still answer the question "No."

Household Furniture & Things

The instructions to Schedule F say—

> *Include . . . household goods and personal effects, including wearing apparel.*

That's all! We need more instructions than this.

IRS Regulation 20.2031-6(a): ***Valuation of household and personal effects***, adds the following—

> *A room by room itemization of household goods and personal effects is desirable. All the articles should be named specifically, except that a number of articles contained in the same room, none of which has a value in excess of $100, may be grouped. A separate value should be given for each article named. In lieu of an itemized list, the executor may furnish a written statement containing a declaration that it is made under penalties of perjury, setting forth the aggregate value as appraised by a competent appraiser or appraisers, or by a dealer or dealers in the class of personality involved.*

This regulation was adopted in 1958. Since then, monetary inflation has taken its toll. In mid-1958, the CPI (Consumer Price Index) was set at 28.5; in mid-1998 the same index was 162.5. Hence, the $100 value figure above can be read as $570 [100 x (162.5 ÷ 28.5)]. Our experience has been that you can group items together if the value of each article or set of articles is less than $1,000. Keep in mind that, usually, the term "household goods and effects" applies to used, worn, and partially damaged furniture, fixtures, furnishings, appliances, and utensils.

How do you value a 30-year-old damaged sofa, a scratched up chair, a cabinet full of pots and pans, a broken down bed mattress, or a dishwasher that clanks when turned on?

The answer is: You don't! You purge immediately all junk-type items from any listing on Schedule F. Omit altogether any description of them. The IRS is more tax interested in items of furniture that truly have some useful value. Our term "useful value" means worthy of being sold through bulletin board notices, newspaper ads, or Internet postings.

For example, your Schedule F might show—

- Living room furniture — 8 ft sofa, travertine table, 4 stuffed chairs, curio cabinet, 3 end tables, decorative flower stand $5,000
- Mahogany dining set — 10 ft table, 8 chairs, buffet......3,000
- Master bedroom set — king size bed, 2 dressers, 1 vanity, large mirror..2,500
- Other miscellaneous household articles.........................1,000

These are your estimated values. Ordinary household furniture and furnishings do not appreciate in value. If you know approximately what you paid for the articles, estimate their current value at about 20% of their original cost. This is what we call: "estimated purging." You mention only those things that are potentially useful to persons other than your immediate family.

Of course, if you have a grand piano, an elaborate cut glass display cabinet, an elegant chandelier, or a big-screen high definition TV, list such items separately. If appropriate, have such items professionally appraised. While this is not purging in and of itself, it is laying the groundwork for doing so. There may be some appraised items that you may prefer to sell or gift, if you have no foreseeable need for them.

Selling or gifting an item before death legitimately removes it from one's estate. If sold, and the proceeds not consumed, there would be some inclusion on Schedule C (Notes and Cash).

Personal Clothing & Memorabilia

Except for hardly worn outer clothing (e.g., business suits, evening gowns, fur coats, dress shoes, etc.), wearing apparel tends to be self-purging. Many persons periodically get rid of their out-of-style clothing, items that are too small because of weight gain, and other accessories which are worn, torn, or damaged. Other than donations to family members and charitable organizations, most such apparel is not readily marketable.

Even if there is truly no apparel of value in your estate at time of death, we urge that you make some entry on Schedule F. An example would be—

Personal clothing and effects..$100

Even if your used clothing value was less than $100, enter as a minimum figure $100 anyhow. This is for Schedule F purposes. It tells the IRS that you are aware that your personal clothing and effects are reportable assets on Form 706, but they really are of nil value. Our experience has been that rarely does the IRS question the personal clothing estimates of "ordinary" decedents. Show a listing for at least $100 and then purge aggressively on your own.

As always, there are exceptions to any general purging recommendations we make. We had one case, not long ago, where the decedent — a 55-year-old mid-level corporate executive — had 39 business suits, 112 dress shirts, 3 tuxedos, about 50 silk ties, and 15 pairs of shoes. (All total, about 219 articles of outer clothing.) The suits and tuxedos cost new between $350 and $800 each. The shirts and ties cost about $50 each; the shoes cost between $150 and $300 each pair. There is no way that one's executor can bulk estimate this type of clothing, and have the estimate acceptable to the IRS (on Form 706).

Here's a case where a men's clothing dealer has to be called in to inventory and appraise each item of value. The above items were all in good condition (most "like new"); they were cleaned and laundered regularly. Here's a case also where "fair market value" is construed as the *wholesale* value of each item: not the retail value. One's executor is not expected to open a retail shop to sell separately

219 articles of clothing to the general public. The wholesale value of men's clothing rarely exceeds 25% of the original purchase cost. The clothing dealer appraised all of the above at $8,000.

The above decedent was not married. The usual practice with married decedents is to list jointly owned husband and wife items at 100% on Schedule F, then subtract 50%. This practice, of course, does **not** apply to the personal clothing and effects of a decedent, whether male or female. Consequently, wearing apparel is always listed on Form 706 at 100% of its estimated or appraised value.

The term "effects" in the phrase: *personal clothing and effects*, is construed to mean various forms of personal memorabilia. This includes photo albums, family letters, sketch books, diaries, genealogy lists, tourist souvenirs, military uniforms, hygienic supplies, and other knickknacks which truly have no market value whatsoever. For ordinary decedents, don't even list such items on Schedule F. Include their nil value within the term "effects": as personal effects. Give them away as opportunity permits, or tag them for your children, relatives, and friends to pick up later. Except for articles of artistic or intrinsic value, and for photos and papers of famous persons, omitting memorabilia from Schedule F would not likely be noticed by the IRS.

Vehicles, Machinery, & Equipment

Unlike personal clothes and memorabilia, there is a ready market for used vehicles, machinery, and equipment. This is especially true if, even though broken or damaged, the items can be repaired. The panorama of such hardware items includes autos, boats, trailers, aircraft, hot-air balloons, farm machinery, nonfarm machinery, welding equipment, power tools, bicycles, exercise equipment, sport equipment, copy machines, computers, monitors, etc. etc. At minimum, these items have salvage value for stripping off hard-to-get parts for servicing old equipment (called: "cannibalizing").

Highway vehicles (autos, trucks, vans, trailers, campers) are always in demand: whether in good, fair, or poor condition. The average of high/low "Blue Book" values gives you a good handle on what value you might get for your vehicles at retail.

No lump sum estimates will be accepted by the IRS for highway vehicles, off-road vehicles, machinery of all kinds, office and shop equipment, power tools, and the like. Our position is that unless you use each of these items more than once a year, you should purge them. Advertise them and sell them any way that you can. If, after a few months, there are no buyers, offer them to a charitable organization. If a charitable organization doesn't want them (because they are not in working order), put them in a dumpster . . . or pay to have them hauled away. Get them out of your estate before it is too late.

Depreciable Business Assets

Many persons who are employees, self-employeds, or partners engaged in a trade or business, acquire tangible assets for carrying on said business. If an article has a useful business life of more than one year, it has to be capitalized and depreciated over its useful life. Statutory class lives (or recovery periods) are prescribed over 3, 5, 7, 10, 15, 20, 25, 27.5, 39, and 50 years [IRC Sec. 168(c)]. Adopting and applying these cost recovery periods requires the setting up of a *depreciation schedule* for each separate article or group of articles of the same class. The IRS form for this purpose is Form 4562W: ***Depreciation Worksheet***. With this form, an allowable depreciation deduction is computed for each item, each year. All prior years' depreciation is cumulatively shown.

Items scheduled on Form 4562W include vehicles, machinery, and equipment of *all kinds* used in the trade or business. Also included are nonresidential structures of all kinds: shops, barns, sheds, signs, docks, roadways, fencing, towers, derricks, irrigation systems, and the like. Also included are breedstock (such as horses, dogs, cattle, alpacas, snakes, exotic animals, etc.), vinestock (berries and grapes), and treestock (fruit and nuts, mostly). Anything and everything that is productive in a business must be entered onto a depreciation schedule.

The tendency is that once an item is entered on Form 4562W, it stays there forever. In one sense, it is easier to add another depreciation schedule than to pursue the effort to remove an item. In another sense, items simply "disappear" from Form 4562W when they are no longer business useful or have been superseded by more efficient items. What most owners of business property fail to realize is that all assets remaining on one's premises or under his control at time of death ARE INCLUDIBLE in his gross estate. They have to be inventoried and appraised.

There are four legitimate ways of removing (purging) unused or unusable business assets from Form 4562W. The four ways are: sale, gift, junk, or abandon. Any of these ways constitutes purging for "full and adequate" consideration. If done before death, the IRS cannot drag the items back into your estate after death. Our depiction of the effort required is presented in Figure 7.3.

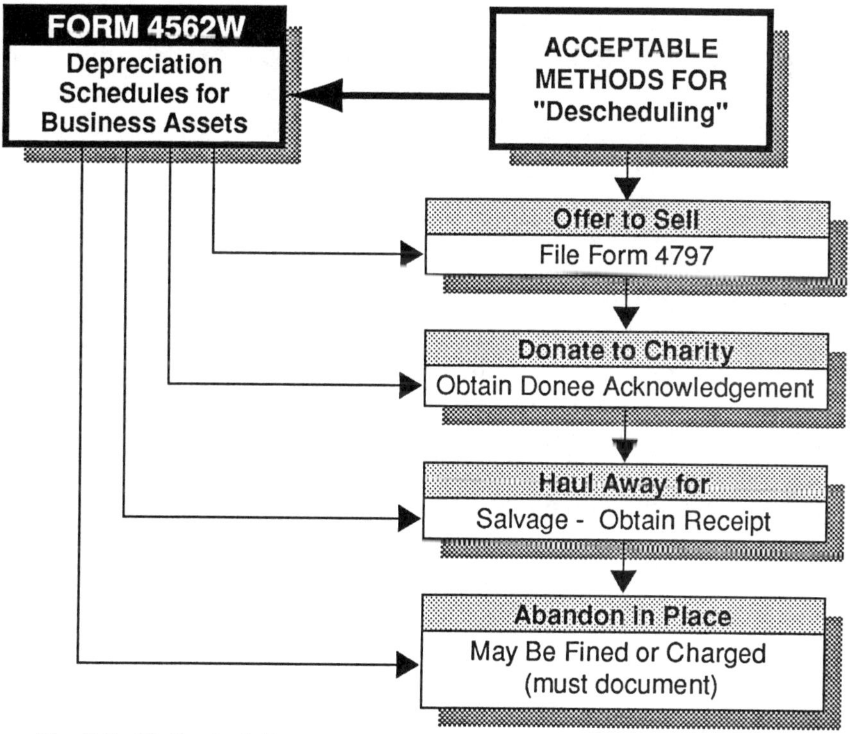

Fig. 7.3 - Methods & Documentation for Purging Depreciable Assets

The cleanest way to rid business assets from your estate is to sell them. Sell them at any price that you can get. When you do so, prepare and file Form 4797: ***Sales of Business Property.*** The proceeds generated may or may not be taxable, depending on your "adjusted basis" (cost minus depreciation allowed) at time of sale. If truly sold, the only thing includible in your gross estate is the unconsumed proceeds from the sale.

If you cannot sell your unused or unusable business assets, your next best effort is to try to donate them to a charitable organization, or have them hauled away as junk. Either method requires documenting your effort(s) through receipts, descriptions, and date(s) of disposition. Most charitable organizations will refuse nonworking items, unless they have competent volunteers who will repair them. If the nonworking items consist of metal, plastic, wiring, glass, and parts that can be recycled, you may be able to get them hauled for free. Otherwise, you will have to pay a hauling fee and a dump fee. Receipts for these fees, however, constitute your assurance that such items are not includible in your gross estate.

Abandonment, as a means of purging your business assets, is tricky. Much depends on where the abandonment takes place. If it takes place on public roadways (vehicles and trailers) or on public waterways (boats and barges), there may be a fine imposed. The fine will include the cost of hauling, junking, or destroying the abandoned property. If the abandoned items are located on leasehold property (whether public or private), the completion of abandonment depends on the terms of the lease. If the lease has expired or is mutually terminated, the abandoned items automatically become the property of the lessor. Purging documentation on the abandonment of business assets is more difficult to acquire than that from selling, gifting, or junking.

Assist Parents & Relatives

It is always difficult to make a decision to get rid of an item that you have used over the years but no longer have use for. It's a tough decision. You have to think, decide, and act. Rather than doing so, you put it off . . . and put it off. Meanwhile, your "collection" of lifetime unused, unusables, unwanteds, and unvalueds mounts and mounts. Whether at home, at office, or at business, your shelves get full. Your closets get full. Your garages and storage sheds get full. Your yards, parking spaces, and vacant lots get full. You rent public storage spaces, and they get full. All because you just won't get rid of anything. Unwittingly, perhaps, you have created a massive *clutter estate.*

There is an antidote to the clutter estate syndrome. It is: offer to assist your parents, grandparents, uncles, and aunts who are going through the purging process. They are older than you, and have probably reconciled themselves to the purging decisions that have to be made. Your assisting them will provide you experience first-hand on how and why purging should be done.

Suppose, for example, you have an 83-year-old mother who is failing fast. Your father predeceased her. He made no purging decisions on his own, as he left those decisions up to your mother. She is bewildered, confused, in pain, and probably experiencing some dementia. She still has property and accounts in her name with your father. In addition, she has three cars, none of which she can drive. There is a lot of estate clutter which your mother has forgotten about. Her eyesight and hearing are bad; she has difficulty walking, going up or down stairs, and stooping and bending. She wants to clear out things, but physically can't do it. There's that old exercise contraption that your father had, which she has been wanting to get rid of for years.

Do you see what we mean? Everyone over 55 years of age (some persons younger) has a clutter estate. It makes no difference whether one's gross estate is small (less than $600,000), medium (less than $3,000,000), large (less than $10,000,000), or extra large (over $10,000,000). The larger the estate, the larger the clutter and the greater the drag and dead weight it imposes.

Executor Experience Preferred

Suppose that you were the designated executor (or co-executor) for a parent or relative who is failing fast. At least two medical doctors have informed you that your parent or relative may not live more than six months. You know from other information communicated to you that the prospective decedent's gross estate will be more than $1,000,000. This tells you right off that Form 706 **will be** required. In six months' time, there is no way to legitimately avoid filing Form 706. But you can make things simpler for yourself, as executor, if you promptly and properly take matters into your own hands. The experience that you gain in doing so will help you decide your own purging priorities.

For the sake of illustration, let us assume that your failing parent or relative has his or her own residence which is full of furniture, furnishings, fixtures, files, appliances, and "things." As the executor-to-be of the estate, with six months to go, here's what you could do:

I — Canvass all designated heirs and close family members as to their preference for assets less than $3,000 each item, or less than $10,000 each grouping of items. Convey the items to them and record.

II — Contact at least one (preferably two or three) *public auction house(s)*, and invite estimating agents to the prospective decedent's residence. Request estimates and listings of what household items are auctionable, and those which are not.

III — Contact a hauling service to haul away the nonauctionable/nonmarketable clutter and stuff.

Public auction houses advertise regularly in telephone directories and on the Internet. They offer monthly auction services either on-site or at their outlets, and provide pre-auction estimates.

Public auction dealers are in the business of getting the best price possible, when liquidating an estate. They invite the public to visit their premises before each auction. If you've never been to an estate auction, we urge that you attend one. Or, at least, visit an auction house and look around. You'll get a good idea of what sells . . . and what won't sell. Once an auction is over, items which did not sell are usually junked. How nice it would be to have the foreknowledge — and fortitude — to purge an estate of nonsalable items well ahead of Form 706 time.

8

COMPILING PRIOR TRANSFERS

Tax Rates For Estates Over $3,000,000 Flatten Out At 55%. This Induces Prospective Decedents To Engage In "Silent Transfers" Of Property Interests Years Ahead of Time. The Transfers Include Life Insurance, Retained Life Estates, Reversionary Interests, Revocable Transfers, Appointed Powers, Estate Freezes, Lapsing Rights, Annuities, And Other Ingenious Strategies. To The Extent That These Strategies Give The Appearance Of Escaping Taxation, They ARE INCLUDIBLE In Your Gross Estate. Your Reconciling These Matters Now Will Greatly Simplify Tasks For Your Executor.

For Form 706 purposes, the term "transfer" means the gratuitous conveyance of property, interest in property, enjoyment of property, or rights to property for less than full and adequate consideration. Most such transfers occur between family members, closely-held businesses, and private trust arrangements. Most such transfers are motivated by the desire to escape tax — or, certainly, to minimize tax — on the property transferred. The motivation is most pronounced for prospective decedents whose gross estates are expected to exceed $3,000,000. From this amount up, the transfer tax is a flat 55%.

All gratuitous transfers are tax characterized as those for *insufficient consideration*. It is the extent of insufficiency that escapes — or can escape — tax. Let us explain "insufficiency" with a numerical example.

Suppose you have a parcel of property whose fair market value is $300,000. You sell it to an unrelated party for $300,000. This is a bona fide sale, inasmuch as you received "valuable consideration" for it. All applicable taxes apply. But suppose you "sold" it to your son, to your daughter, to your business associate, or to your trust for only $100,000. This constitutes a transfer for **insufficient** consideration. There is $200,000 of insufficiency. If the alleged sale took place 10 years before death, say, the $200,000 might readily escape taxation altogether.

An attempt to recapture escaped taxes is what Schedule G (***Transfers During Decedent's Life***), Schedule H (***Powers of Appointment***), and Schedule I (***Annuities***) are all about.

In this chapter, therefore, we want to familiarize you with the inclusionary aspects of Schedule G, particularly. We'll include comments on Schedules H and I, as well. More importantly, though, we want to explain why you should research and compile all of the information that you can on those prior transfers. You want to do so now, so as to avoid the pyramiding of penalties on your executor later. The ***Penalties*** section of the Instructions to Form 706 say—

> *The law provides for penalties for willful attempts to evade payment of tax.*

Umbrella Law: Section 2043

Section 2043 of the Internal Revenue Code is titled: ***Transfers for Insufficient Consideration***. This is the "umbrella law" for all transfers during life where tax reduction or tax avoidance constitute the primary motivation. Legitimate motivations include estate planning arrangements, property settlement arrangements between spouses, or educational trust arrangements for children and grandchildren. Legitimate motivations imply that any applicable tax at the time of transfer has been addressed. If not, Section 2043 becomes operative. It is one of those laws that loiters in the background, and is cocked and set to snare you, unexpectedly.

Section 2043(a): ***In General***, reads in full as—

If any one of the transfers, trusts, interests, rights, or powers enumerated and described in sections 2035 to 2038, inclusive, and section 2041 is made, created, exercised, or relinquished for a consideration in money or money's worth, but is not a bona fide sale for an adequate and full consideration in money or money's worth, there shall be included in the gross estate only the excess of the fair market value at the time of death of the property otherwise to be included on account of such transaction, over the value of the consideration received therefor by the decedent.

In the introductory example above, it is the $200,000 of insufficiency that is includible in one's gross estate. But where on Form 706 would you include such an amount?

Answer: You have to know, or be informed, that the inclusion is reported on Schedule G. Its title: ***Transfers During Decedent's Life***, is suggestive of where all Section 2043 inclusions are to appear. We say "suggestive" because the instructions to Schedule G make no specific reference to Section 2043.

A section in the Schedule G instructions is headed: ***How to Complete Schedule G***. This instruction starts off by saying—

*All transfers (other than outright transfers not in trust and bona fide sales) made by the decedent at any time during life must be reported on the Schedule regardless of whether you believe the transfers are subject to tax. If the decedent made any transfers **not described in the instructions above**, the transfers should **not** be shown on Schedule G. Instead, attach a statement describing these transfers: list the date of the transfer, the amount or value, and the type of transfer.* [Emphasis added.]

This is an odd instruction: if "not described in the instructions above," do not show the insufficient consideration transfers on Schedule G. Instead, "attach a statement," etc. The "instructions above" refer to Sections 2035, 2036, 2037, and 2038 **only**. In other words, Section 2043 inclusions are *attached* to Schedule G; they are not directly reported on it. The reportings are indirectly included on Schedule G via a line which reads:

Total from continuation schedules (or additional sheets) attached to this schedule. . . . ____________

Addressments on Schedule G

In the General Information portion of Form 706, there is a Schedule G target question. It reads—

Did the decedent make any transfer described in section 2035, 2036, 2037, or 2038? ☐ Yes, ☐ No. If "Yes," you must complete and attach Schedule G.

Although there are other inclusionary questions in the General Information portion of Form 706, none specifically addresses Section 2043: ***Transfers for Insufficient Consideration.*** Therefore, for Schedule G purposes, one concentrates primarily on Sections 2035, 2036, 2037, and 2038.

The official titles to each of these four sections are:

Sec. 2035 — ***Adjustments for Certain Gifts Made Within 3 Years of Decedent's Death.***

Sec. 2036 — ***Transfers With Retained Life Estate.***

Sec. 2037 — ***Transfers Taking Effect at Death.***

Sec. 2038 — ***Revocable Transfers.***

Section 2035 is referred to as the "3-year mandate." Its subsection (a): ***Inclusion of Certain Property in Gross Estate***, reads in full as—

If—

(1) the decedent ***made a transfer*** *(by trust or otherwise) of an interest in any property, or* ***relinquished a power*** *with respect to any property, during the* ***3-year period*** *ending on the date of the decedent's death,* ***and***

(2) *the value of such property (or an interest therein)* ***would have been included*** *in the decedent's gross estate under section 2036, 2037, 2038, or 2042 if such transferred interest or relinquished power had been retained by the decedent on the date of his death, the value of the gross estate* ***shall include*** *the value of any property (or interest therein) which would have been so included.* [Emphasis added.]

We've listed above the titles to Sections 2036, 2037, and 2038. Section 2042 is titled: ***Proceeds of Life Insurance***. This section requires includibility of all insurance proceeds on the life of the decedent. It also requires includibility of proceeds on the life of persons other than the decedent **if** — *the decedent possessed at his death any of the incidents of ownership, exercisable alone or in conjunction with any other person.* The term "incidents of ownership" has its own interpretive twists. Generally, said term includes reversionary interests exceeding 5% of the cash value of the policy immediately before the death of the decedent. Instructions to Schedule G require that insurance on the life of the decedent be reported on Schedule D, and that insurance on the life of another be reported on Schedule F.

Section 2035(a) is the reformation of a prior Section 2035 rule: *Transfers in Contemplation of Death.* This prior rule was changed in 1976 for decedents dying after December 31, 1976. Under the prior rule, inclusion was required for "any transfers" made "at any time," if "contemplation of death" appeared to be a significant motive. Under current Section 2035(a), the time-band for inclusion is within three years of death. Three years is a more practical contemplation period for transfer tax enforcement purposes.

Inclusions & Exceptions

Now that we have called your attention to the inclusionary "3-year mandate," specifically what is so included? The answer to this is where Section 2035 has to be read closely. The answer is found in subsections (a), (b), and (c). Subsection (a) identifies four sections of the tax code which are includible; namely: Sections

2036, 2037, 2038, and 2042 (above). Subsection (b) requires that any gift tax paid be includible; and subsection (c) requires that any interest in property used to pay death taxes be includible.

The creation and transfer of life insurance policies is a very common death bed practice. Said practice is nurtured aggressively by the insurance industry, which asserts that Section 2042 does not apply to *irrevocable* insurance trusts. That may be, if the irrevocable trust is created well before three years before death. However, any insurance trust transfers within the 3-year period are includible!

Any *gift tax* paid on bona fide transfers during the 3-year period also is includible. The premise here (Subsec. 2035(b)) is that a premature depletion of the gross estate has taken place by the amount of gift tax dollars paid. The whole idea of the 3-year rule is to discourage those death bed transfers and other schemes that seem to pop up out of nowhere. When a prospective decedent is failing fast, family members often intervene to expedite the predeath transfer processes.

Subsection 2035(c) further extends the premature depletion premise. Arrangements made to pay death taxes, remove tax liens, and pay for special appraisals of family farms, businesses, and real estate are includible amounts. The rationale is that such amounts need not be expended until after death.

In Figure 8.1, we try to summarize the types of property interests that are includible under Section 2035.

There are only two exceptions to the 3-year mandate. The first exception applies to bona fide sales. On this point, subsection (d) expressly reads:

> *Subsection (a) shall not apply to any bona fide sale for an adequate and full consideration in money or money's worth.*

The second exception applies to marital gifts and small transfers that are not tax accountable. Subsection (c)(3) states that inclusion shall not apply to any transfer *not required by Section 6019* to file a gift tax return. As per Section 6019 (Gift Tax Returns), no filing is required for:

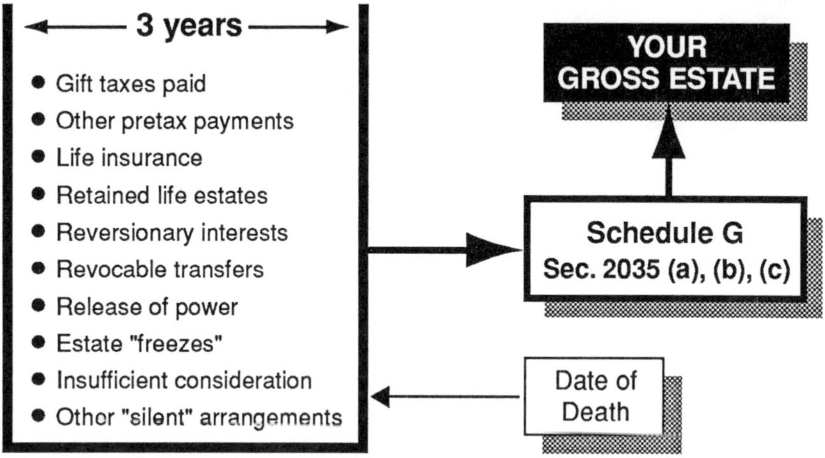

Fig. 8.1 - Mandated Focus on Transfers Within 3 Years of Death

(i) gifts of $10,000 or less per year per donor per donee [Sec. 2503(b)]
(ii) qualified transfers for educational or medical expenses [Sec. 2503(e)]
(iii) qualified gifts to spouse [Sec. 2523]
(iv) qualified charitable and similar gifts [Sec. 2522]

Whenever a tax law provides for specific exceptions, no other exceptions, exclusions, or exemptions can be read into such law

Certain More Than 3 Years

The prior "contemplation rule" read as—

*The value of the gross estate shall include the value of all property **to the extent of any interest therein** of which the decedent has **at any time** made a transfer, by trust or otherwise, in contemplation of his death.* [Emphasis added.]

As in current law, bona fide sales of property for full and adequate consideration are excluded. Though a sale removes property from the gross estate, such removal is replaced by the proceeds received from the sale.

The "at any time" concept of the prior contemplation rule is retained in Sections 2036, 2037, and 2038. The titles of these sections, again, are:

Sec. 2036 — Transfers with Retained Life Estate
Sec. 2037 — Transfers Taking Effect at Death
Sec. 2038 — Revocable Transfers

For these transfers, not only does the 3-year rule apply, but **also** does the "at any time" rule. Life estate, transfers at death, and revocable transfers are includible because they are often made long before three years before death. Such arrangements are recognized as legitimate "estate planning" measures.

All three of the above sections contain the includibility phrase: *to the extent of any interest therein* . . . at time of death or immediately before death. In other words, if one's interest (possession, enjoyment, income) in the property transferred is less than 100%, the lesser amount is includible. For at-death transfers of interests, includibility applies only if the decedent's reversionary interest in the property was more than 5% of its transferred value.

A "retained life estate" (Sec. 2036) is the partial transfer of property by which the transferor retains the right to its possession, enjoyment, or income until the very moment of his demise. A transfer "taking effect at death" (Sec. 2037) is the passing of the right to the possession, enjoyment, or income of property only after surviving the decedent, and only when the property reverts to the decedent or to his estate for disposition other than to the survivor. A "revocable transfer" is where property has been legally conveyed to a trust or other entity, whereby the transferor reserves the right to alter, amend, revoke, or terminate the arrangement at any time before his death. The functional distinctions between these three types of transfers are portrayed in Figure 8.2. At the time of each transfer, appropriate tax accountings and reportings are made. Transitional convenience is the primary motivation for said transfers: not tax avoidance.

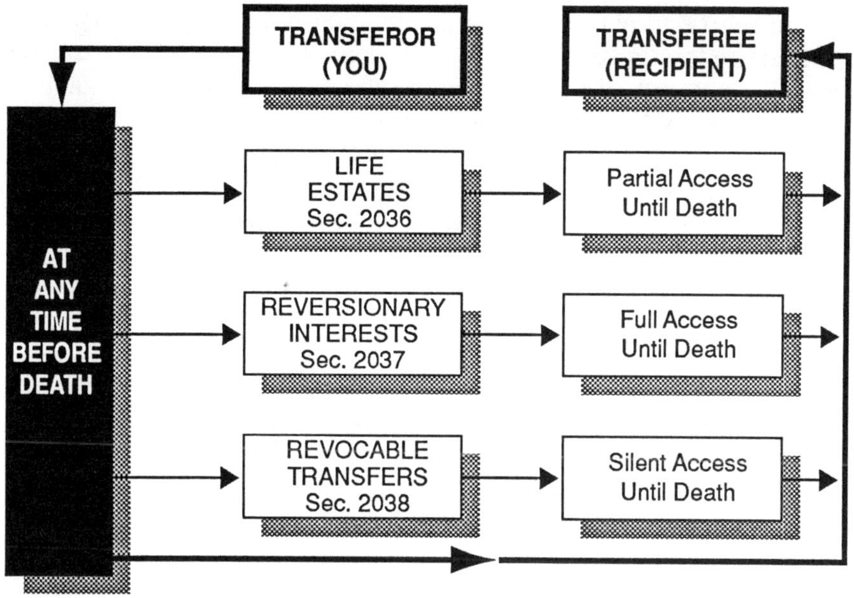

Fig. 8.2 - Includibility of Certain Transfers Before 3 Years Before Death

Include "Lapsing Rights"

In contrast to the Figure 8.2-type transfers before death, there are "lapsing right" transfers. These are tax avoidance schemes predicated upon old law Section 2036(c): ***Inclusions Related to Valuation Freezes***. A "valuation freeze" is a strategy whereby marketable property interests are transferred at a contrived low value predicated upon specific retained interests, which are artificially inflated in value. A year or two (or three later), the retained interests lapse, collapse, or expire. The transferee is left with the possession of property at its true market value. Valuation freeze transfers are practiced by family-owned active businesses in corporate, partnership, or trust form.

Ingenious rationales are used to support the high retained values in the form of distribution rights, buy-sell agreement rights, guaranteed payment rights, liquidation rights, put or call rights, conversion rights, option rights, voting rights, and other rights which must be exercised at a specific time, at a specific amount. The high value of the retained rights at the time of a transfer causes the property transferred to a junior member of the family to be artificially low in value. To seal the deal, a gift tax or other transfer tax is computed and paid. Under "old law" (1976), any such tax payment froze the valuation at that time.

For transfers occurring **after** October 8, 1990, the old law on valuation freeze was repealed. In its place, Sections 2701 through 2704 have been added. These four new sections are:

Sec. 2701 — Special Valuation Rules in Case of Transfers of Certain Interests in Corporations or Partnerships [2,300 words];

Sec. 2702 — Special valuation Rules in Case of Transfers of Interests in Trusts [560 words];

Sec. 2703 — Certain Rights and Restrictions Disregarded [130 words]; and

Sec. 2704 — Treatment of Certain Lapsing Rights and Restrictions [480 words].

These "new law" rules seek to retroactively prevent any contrivance (after October 8, 1990) that distorts the retained interests in family wealth transfers. The yardstick for reference is the **marketability** of the retained interests to nonfamily members. Thus, if an intrafamily created right has no marketability to a third party, said right is statutorily assigned a zero value. This maximizes the value of the transferred property interests . . . and maximizes the corresponding gift or transfer tax. Exceptions apply when market quotations are readily available for a right conferred by the retained interest or for the transferred interest.

Three Compilation Periods

For instructional purposes, we have intentionally quoted specific wording of selected inclusionary laws. As you can sense, not every situation is all black or all white. Unless you, as a potential decedent, go to the effort of resurrecting and compiling your transfers of the past, your designated executor will have to do so. As he probes your past, he will find himself at "crossed swords" with your transferees. They will resist your executor and will engage an attorney to fight him. The adversarialness that follows will run up your estate administrative expenses unconscionably. Though recalling and documenting your transfers of property interests (for less than full and adequate consideration) may be unpleasant for you, it is better that *you* do it than your executor.

Most helpful in your resurrection and compilation efforts is to divide your intensity of recall into three distinct time periods. These periods are:

I — Within 3 years before death
II — Back to 1990
III — Back to 1976

The focus of your recall for these periods is summarized in Figure 8.3. All three time periods would go on Schedule G: ***Transfers During Decedent's Life***. The official instructions to Schedule G (Form 706) should be read with care.

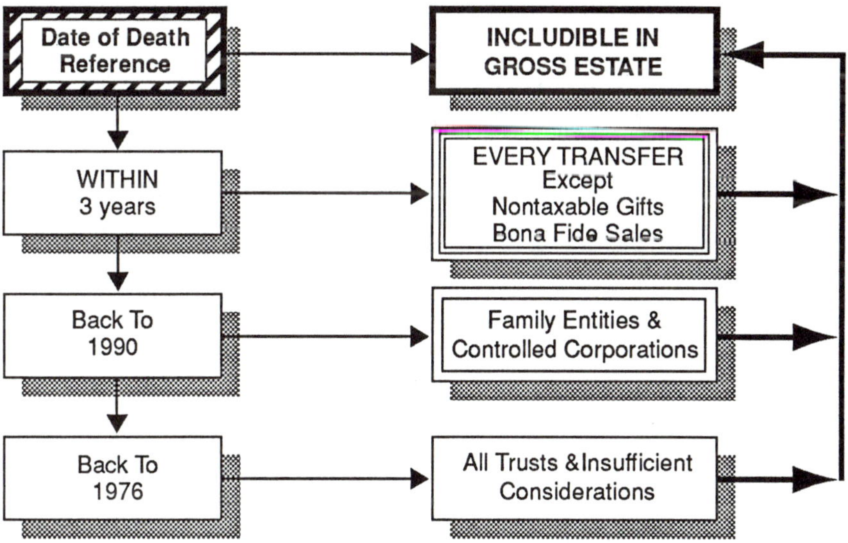

Fig. 8.3 - Intensity of Recall for Prior-to-Death Transfers

Period I is an absolute MUST. This is that "contemplation of death" time span where gratuitous transfers are accelerated. Congress, for practical reasons, has softened its stance on prior transfers going back to day one. Still, it is unforgiving for specifically designated transfers within three years of death. Although obviously you will not know the exact date of your demise, you will know when you reach that frame of mind when you want to get things in order. That's the time to start recording everything you do for easing the transfer of your property to your family, heirs, and friends. Document and record your effort, whether or not each transfer is includible in your gross estate. Your executor will sort things out, when the right time comes.

If you do an outstanding job in Period I, your faulty memory may be forgiven in Periods II and III. If you'd had a family business which you've transferred progressively to your siblings and children (and grandchildren), you are expected to keep accurate business records of those transfers. Dig up those records back to 1990, photocopy them, and place them in a Period II file for your executor.

Period III (back to 1976) applies only to your early transfers for insufficient consideration. It is quite possible that the original transferee may have sold or exchanged the transferred item for full and adequate consideration. Such a transaction would be difficult to trace, by you or anyone else. The only items that you would likely have records of back to 1976 are those for which gift tax returns were prepared and file. If so, dig them up and place them in a Period III file for your executor. Your executor will have to respond to a line on page 1 of Form 706 which reads—

Adjusted taxable gifts . . . made by the decedent after December 31, 1976 $________

Powers of Appointment

A power of appointment is the grant of enjoyment rights to property belonging to someone else or to some entity, which is not the creation of the decedent. A decedent does not need to grant himself power over his own property; he already has it. But someone else — by will, by trust, or by other testamentary appointment — can grant the decedent (while alive) power over that person's property. The term "power" is the right of the grantee (recipient of the power) to exercise his own discretion in the appointment and consumption of income or principal from the grantor's property. A designated grantee may be assigned appointment powers by several grantor family members. Such appointments are well established estate planning arrangements. IRC Section 2041: ***Powers of Appointment***, recognizes these arrangements.

There are three functional types of appointed powers. These are: (1) general power, (2) limited power, and (3) administrative power. For instructive overview purposes, we present in Figure 8.4 a simplified distinction between these powers.

As per subsection 2041(b)(1)—

> *The term "general power of appointment" means a power which is exercisable in favor of the decedent* [grantee], *his estate, his creditors, or creditors of his estate.*

Under a general power, the grantee has almost as much authority over the property as he would have if it were entirely his own. Consequently, in the absence of Section 2041(a) — includibility in gross estate of the grantee decedent — granting a general power could afford the grantor an easy way to avoid the estate transfer tax. General powers of appointment are like a Damocles sword over the heads of both the grantor and grantee. The appointed property could be taxed in both gross estates! Because of this possibility, professional estate planners go to great lengths to avoid any appointment being inadvertently classed as a general power.

If a power to invade, consume, or appoint income or principal is limited by an *ascertainable standard* relating to the health, education, support, or maintenance of the decedent, it is deemed **not** a general power [Sec. 2041(b)(1)(A)]. Being so deemed, a limited power of appointment is not includible in the decedent's gross estate. An "ascertainable standard" means that the power is exercisable for the holder's "support and comfort," "support in his customary manner of living," "education and health," "medical and dental

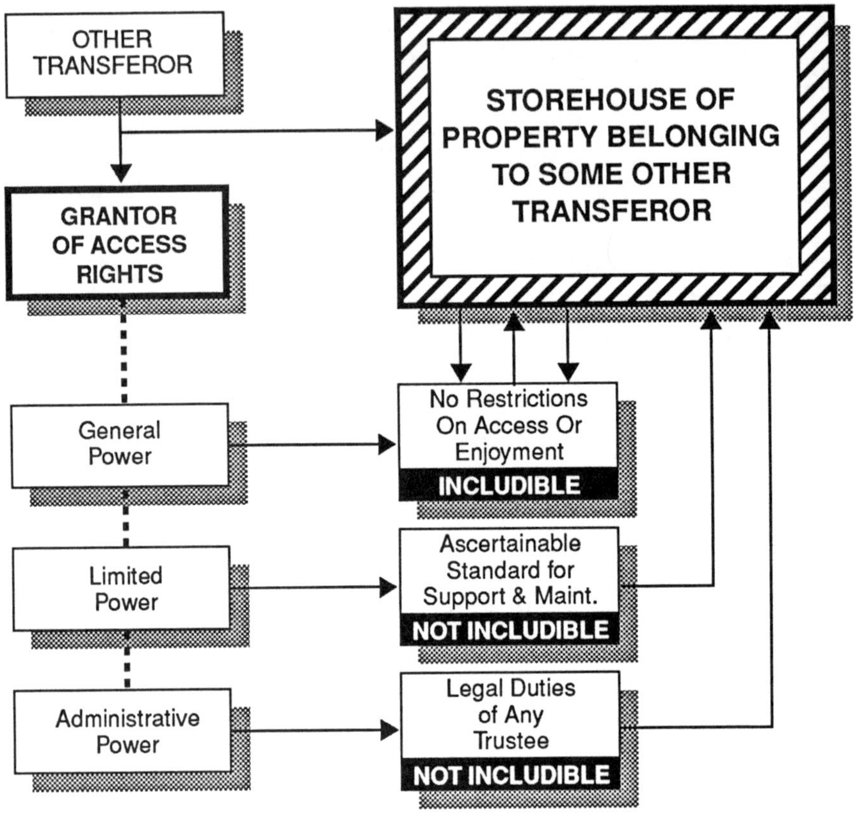

Fig. 8.4 - Prior "Powers" That May Have Been Granted to Decedent

expenses," "expenses for nursing and invalidism," and similar support and maintenance requirements beyond the bare necessities of daily living.

A power to amend only the administrative provisions of a trust instrument, which cannot substantially affect the beneficial enjoyment of trust property or income, is **not** a general power of appointment. The mere power of management, investment, custody of assets, or the power to allocate receipts and disbursements between income and principal, is one's ordinary responsibility when acting in a fiduciary capacity over appointed property.

The IRS takes the powers of appointment matters very seriously. It goes by a "5 by 5 rule" to establish the includibility or nonincludibility of appointed powers in a decedent's estate. This rule is the greater of—

(A) *$5,000 or*

(B) *5 percent of the aggregate value . . . of the assets* [appointed].

If the value of the appointed property is **less** than the greater of (A) or (B), it is deemed a *lapsed power*. A lapsed power is non-includible. Other powers which are excludable are those general powers which terminated or from which the appointee was released before three years before death.

Preferably, for simplifying your own gross estate and reducing the tax thereon, you should have no appointed powers which, in the remotest way, could be IRS construed as general powers. This means reviewing carefully the express wording in all pertinent documents (family wills, trusts, and insurance arrangements) where you have been granted appointment rights. Unless you need access to the appointed property for your own support and maintenance, contact the grantor (if living) or his fiduciary agent to rectify things. Otherwise, you — your executor, actually — will be burdened with completing Schedule H: ***Powers of Appointment*** on Form 706.

Inclusion of Annuities

While it is possible to avoid having to complete Schedule H, it is much less likely that you can avoid Schedule I: ***Annuities***. This is because annuities play a major role in most pension, profit-sharing, stock bonus, individual retirement, and self-employment retirement plans. Fundamentally, an "annuity" is a contractual arrangement for the payment of a fixed amount of money at regular intervals of time, for the life of the annuitant, his surviving spouse, or for a term of years certain. An annuity contract is purchased from an annuity insurer for an agreed face amount. Once all terms of the contract are fulfilled, any proceeds thereafter revert to the guarantor of the contract (for the risk he has taken). Schedule I is the last of the nine asset schedules (A through I) that comprise your gross estate.

Section 2039(a) sets forth the general rule on the includibility of annuities. In pertinent part, this estate tax law reads—

> *The gross estate shall include the value of an annuity or other payment receivable by a beneficiary by reason of surviving the decedent under any form of contract or agreement . . . if . . . the decedent* [received or] *possessed the right to receive an annuity or other payment . . . for any period which does not end before his death.*

The amount specifically included in your gross estate can be less than 100% of the annuity market value at time of death. The amount includible is that portion of the face amount which you (or your employer on your behalf) paid out of pocket for purchasing the contract. For example, suppose the face amount of your annuity contract was $100,000. And, further, suppose that you and your employer, if any, paid $60,000 out of pocket for the contract. At date of death, the contract value was $38,600. What is your includible portion?

It is—

60,000/100,000 x $38,600 = $23,160

The rationale for not including the $15,444 [38,600 – 23,160] is that it is the guarantor's money: **not** yours. Any part of the annuity proceeds that contractually revert to the guarantor are clearly not part of your estate.

What we have tried to do in this chapter is to point out that, perhaps unknowingly on your part, you may be the "deemed beneficiary" of some other person's property transfers. Some of these transfers may be unwanted by you. Unless you intentionally resurrect them, reconcile them, compile them, or disclaim them, they will add to your gross estate. The additional tax burden will deprive your heirs of some of the property enjoyment that you had otherwise intended for them.

9

FILING GIFT TAX RETURNS

Gifting While Alive Not Only Helps Simplify Your Estate Later, It Provides Opportunity To "See For Yourself" Threefold Tax Benefits. These Include (1) The $10,000 PER DONEE Annual Exclusion, (2) Partial Or Full Use Of The $600,000-Plus Unified Exemption (Which Increases Annually To $1,000,000 By Year 2006), (3) The Generation Of Donee Income On Which You Pay No Tax. Each Form 709 Is A PER DONOR Return Prepared On A Calendar Year Basis. It Requires The Listing Of Each Donee's Name On Schedule A, And The Documentation On Schedule B Of Prior Taxable Gifts And Cumulative Exemptions.

One of the least understood and most undcrused documentation of gratuitous transfers is the gift tax return: **Form 709**. The gift tax — like the death tax — is an excise tax for the transfer of property for less than full and adequate consideration. The type of property covered is real or personal, whether tangible or intangible, made directly or indirectly, in trust, or by any other means. The gift tax is a transfer tax in exactly the same sense that the death tax is a transfer tax. It is NOT an income tax nor a property tax.

Back in 1976, Congress *unified* what was previously two separate tax rate schedules, and two separate exemption amounts, into one package. As a result, the gift tax rates and the death tax rates are identical. The lifetime exemption amounts ($600,000 to $1,000,000: recall Figure 1.1) are also identical. The applicable gift or death exemption amount is *per individual*, whether living or deceased. In other words, one can use his or her transfer tax exemption amount during life, or at time of death. The portion unused during life is credited to his or her estate at time of death.

The gift taxing rules have one unique feature which the death taxing rules do not have. The first $10,000 of a gift is not taxed; it is an *exclusion*. Furthermore, it is an *annual* exclusion. Still further, a gift of $10,000 can be made to any number of donees (recipients) by a single donor, in a given year, and no gift tax applies. For example, if you had five children, siblings, or relatives, you could gift away $50,000 . . . without tax. If you made the gifts five years in a row, you could gift transfer $250,000 without tax.

If married at the time of each of the five separate gifts, in five sequential years, your spouse, too, could transfer $250,000 without tax. Between the two of you as separate donors, you could transfer legitimately $500,000 out of your combined gross estate. Still, each of your separate lifetime exemption amounts ($600,000 to $1,000,000) would remain intact!

Failing to use the role of gift tax returns in estate planning endeavors stems from the term: "tax return." People just don't like filing tax returns. Believe it or not, this one type of return can be used advantageously to both *simplify* and *reduce* your gross estate when your final day comes. This is because the gift tax return has a **cumulative accounting feature** which no other IRS return has.

Consequently, in this chapter we want to acquaint you with Form 709: ***U.S. Gift Tax Return***, and explain how it can be used for recording and compiling all of your estate plans and strategies. The key in this regard is the use of Schedule B on Form 709: ***Gifts from Prior Periods***. Our contention is that a file of Forms 709 provides a documentation trail that is authentic and convincing. Such a file removes the suspicion of tax avoidance, should any of your prior transfers be silent, insufficient, or inadequately documented.

Death Bed Usage

It is standard procedure when the IRS examines a death tax return (Form 706) to request a listing of all gifts made within three years of death. (We covered the 3-year rule in Chapter 8). The IRS requests the names of all persons to whom gifts were made, whether more than $10,000 or less than $10,000. For the less than $10,000 gifts, the IRS requests some documentation of each such gift. It wants to see a letter of gift intent, an affidavit of acceptance, a canceled check, a bank statement of deposit, an electronic transfer confirmation, or whatever else is appropriate to dispel IRS suspicion. Without convincing documentation on the nontaxability of gifts for $10,000 or less, the IRS has no choice but to presume that, potentially, hordes of cash and/or property may have disappeared, underhandedly, from the decedent's gross estate.

There is also a "standard procedure" in human nature. When death is imminent, or likely to be so, there is a mad dash — the death bed syndrome — to gift away money and property. Most such gifting is not properly documented. The attention and focus are on reducing the prospective decedent's gross estate as rapidly as possible. Heirs and relatives encourage this procedure. Rarely does any heir or relative think of documenting each gift via a gift tax return. Let us illustrate the typical scenario with a true case.

A widower had two daughters and five grandchildren: totaling seven donees. He gifted each of them $10,000 in each of the three years before his death. These gifts reduced his gross estate by $210,000 (7 x $10,000/yr x 3 yrs). Though his estate was reduced, the gifts were not made properly.

Each year he wrote two checks. One check went to Daughter A for $30,000 ($10,000 for herself and $10,000 for each of her two children). The second check went to Daughter B for $40,000 (herself and three children). Instead of there being seven nontaxable gifts each year, there were two *taxable* gifts: one for $20,000 [30,000 – 10,000] and the other for $30,000 [40,000 – 10,000]. Despite professional advice to the contrary, each daughter wanted the checks written as stated. Each wanted to control the money gifts to their own children. Thus, in IRS eyes, there were NOT seven gifts each year; there were only two such gifts. Both were taxable. And since no gift tax returns were filed, the amount of $150,000 ([20,000 + 30,000]/yr x 3 yrs) was added back into the widower's gross estate when he died.

In a situation like the above, preparing a gift tax return becomes the ideal document. Each year, the donor prepares one Form 709 and lists on it the name, address, and relationship of each of the seven donees. For the amount of gift to each, he enters $10,000. The 21 gifts of $10,000 each would have been properly reported to the IRS on its very own forms.

Overview of Form 709

Now that we have exemplified the benefits of Form 709 as a prima facie document of your gift transfers, let us overview the form with you. Officially its full title is: ***U.S. Gift (and Generation-Skipping Transfer) Tax Return***. Note the parenthetical inclusion of "generation-skipping transfer," or GST for short. In other words, Form 709 is applicable for gifts to your parents, to your siblings (of your same generation), to your children (one generation below you), to your grandchildren (two generations below you), to your great-grandchildren (three generations below you), and to others yet unborn down your generational line. Our contention is that Form 709 can address all of your wealth transfer intentions while you are alive, even though some of those intentions may not be carried out until after your demise.

Form 709 is filed on a calendar year basis. It consists of four pages of statements, columns, and lines. This number compares with 44 pages for Form 706: the death tax return. Form 709 is accompanied by eight pages of official instructions, compared with 22 pages for Form 706. For prior transfer accounting purposes, Form 709 covers everything that Form 706 covers. Indeed, a very prominent question on Form 706 asks:

> *Have Federal gift tax returns ever been filed? ☐ Yes, ☐ No. If "Yes," attach copies of the returns and furnish: (a) Period(s) covered, and (b) Internal Revenue office(s) where filed.*

In highly abbreviated and outline form, the contents of Form 709 are listed in Figure 9.1. The appearance of complexity stems predominantly from generation-skipping transfers (GSTs). If one postpones his GST intentions until later in life, Form 709 boils down to page 1, plus Schedule A (Part 1) and Schedule B, only.

Form 709 | **U.S. GIFT TAX RETURN** | **Year**

Name, Address, & Tax ID of Individual Donor

Page 1

- **Part 1 - General Information . . . [18 lines]**
- **Part 2 - Tax Computation . . . [20 lines]**

Page 2 — **SCHEDULE A**

☐ **Computation of Taxable Gifts . . . [22 lines, 5 columns]**

- **Part 1 - Gifts Subject Only to Gift Tax**
- **Part 2 - Gifts Subject to BOTH Gift Tax & GST Tax**
- **Part 3 - Taxable Gift Reconciliation**

Page 3

Continuation of Schedule A . . . [18 lines]

SCHEDULE B

☐ **Gifts from Prior Periods . . . [5 lines, 5 columns]**

Page 4 — **SCHEDULE C**

☐ **Computation of Generation-Skipping Transfer (GST) Tax . . . [22 lines, 5 columns]**

- **Part 1 - Generation-Skipping Transfers**
- **Part 2 - GST Exemption Reconciliation**
- **Part 3 - Tax Computation**

Fig. 9.1 - General Contents of Form 709 for Each Individual Donor

This is the situation for most ordinary transfers of money and/or property.

Of particular note, which is not evident in Figure 9.1, is that Form 709 is a **per individual** return. It is not a husband and wife return, even if married at the time of each gift transfer. This is so, even though provisions on the form allow for *gift splitting* between husband and wife. An instruction to this effect says—

> *A married couple may not file a joint gift tax return. However, if after reading the instructions below, you and your spouse agree to split your gifts, you should file* **both** *of your individual gift tax*

returns together (in the same envelope) to avoid correspondence from the IRS.

The gift splitting rules between spouses are hairy for combined gifts in excess of $20,000. Consent and cross-consent portions of the form have to be addressed and signed. We suggest, therefore, that you disregard the gift splitting lines on Form 709. Each of you prepare your own return, independent of the other. Each spousal gift return becomes an attachment to Form 706 when each spouse deceases. There is no joint death tax return, even if both spouses die simultaneously in the same event.

Transfers Subject to Form 709

In the broadest general sense, Form 709 accommodates all conceivable forms of gratuitous transfers. It covers all transfers by gift whether present interests are given, or future interests are given. A gift is a *present interest* if the donee has all immediate rights to the use, possession, and enjoyment of property and its income. A gift is a *future interest* if the donee's rights to the use, possession, and enjoyment of property and its income will not begin until some future date.

The present vs. future distinction is important with regard to the annual exclusion of $10,000 per donee. Gifts of present interest are allowed the exclusion, whereas gifts of future interest are not allowed the $10,000 exclusion. Also, future interests require revaluation of the gifted amount when said interests "trigger in." The gift of a present interest to more than one donee as joint tenants in property, or as joint beneficiaries in a trust, qualifies for the annual exclusion for *each donee.*

As to the actual types of transfers subject to being reported on Form 709, selected excerpts from the official instructions say—

The gift tax applies not only to the gratuitous transfer of any kind of property, but also to sales or exchanges not made in the ordinary course of business, where money or money's worth is exchanged but the value of the money or money's worth received is less than the value of what is sold or exchanged. . . . The exercise or release of a general power of appointment may be a gift by the individual possessing the power. . . . The gift tax may also apply to the forgiveness of debt, to interest-free loans, to the assignments of the benefits of an insurance policy, and to the giving up of some amount of an annuity in exchange for the creation of a survivor annuity. . . . Transfers to family members of interests in corporations, partnerships, and trusts are gifts. The lapse of any voting or liquidation right is a gift.

And so on. It is hard to find any gratuitous transfer of property or money which is not subject to gift tax accounting, where the gross amount to any one donee exceeds $10,000. For example, municipal bonds that are exempt from federal income tax are *not* exempt from federal gift tax. Nonresident aliens gifting tangible property located in the U.S., whether to a U.S. citizen or to a foreign citizen, are subject to filing Form 709.

There are three types of transfers that are not subject to Form 709. These are payments to: (1) political organizations, (2) educational institutions for tuition, and (3) health care providers for medical expenses. To the extent that a payment is for other than political, educational, or medical use, it is a gift to the individual on whose behalf the payment is made.

Schedule A, Part 1 Listings

In the head portion of Form 709 there is a statement that reads—

Enter the total number of separate donees listed on Schedule A — count each person only once. ▸ _______

The message behind this statement is that you have to start at Schedule A before any gift tax can be computed. If, for example, you entered 3 in the space above, the processing assumption by the IRS would be that no tax would apply to the first $30,000 of your gratuitous transfers. Keep in mind that Form 709 is prepared for each full calendar year: one year at a time. Each year for which you file a Form 709, the $10,000 annual exclusion per donee applies (if "present interests" are conveyed).

As Figure 9.1 indicates, Schedule A is titled: ***Computation of Taxable Gifts***. Below this title is Part 1 which is subtitled: ***Gifts Subject Only to Gift Tax***. Between this title and subtitle (not indicated in Figure 9.1), there is a preprinted question which asks—

> *Does the value of any item listed on Schedule A reflect any valuation discount? Yes* ☐, *No* ☐. *If the answer is "Yes," see instructions.*

This is your tip-off that the IRS is apprehensive, rightfully, about your intentionally undervaluing nonmarketable property interests. Unpleasant tax penalties can be imposed. So, beware!

Undervaluation improperly leads to conservation of the unified (exemption) credit. Consequently, the essence of the instructions regarding valuation discounts is—

> *If the value of any gift you report in Schedule A reflects a discount for lack of marketability, a minority interest, a fractional interest in real estate, blockage, market absorption,* ***or for any other reason****, answer "Yes" to the question* [above]. *Also, attach an explanation giving the factual basis for the claimed discounts and the amount of discounts taken.* [Emphasis added.]

Once you get past the above question, Schedule A consists of five columns. These columns are lettered and headed:

- A — Item number
- B — Donee's name, address, relationship to donor, and description of gift
- C — Donor's adjusted basis of gift
- D — Date of gift
- E — Value at date of gift

Columns B, C, and E are where all of the *disclosure action* lies.

Before describing your disclosure actions more fully, the format of Schedule A is instructive. Said format is presented in Figure 9.2. Note that Column B takes up most of the horizontal white space.

Schedule A	COMPUTATION OF TAXABLE GIFTS			Form 709
A	B	C	D	E
Item No.	• Name, address: Each Donee • Description of Gift	Donor's Adjusted Basis	Date of Gift	VALUE at Date of Gift
			Total Gifts	
			Per Donee Exclusions	< >
			TAXABLE GIFTS	

Fig. 9.2 - General Format of Schedule A, Form 709

This implies that the information you enter in Column B must be full and complete. Instructions say that—

> *If you need more space than that provided, attach a separate sheet, using the same format as Schedule A.*

Columns B, E, & C Explained

Column B requires that each donee be separately listed by name, address, and Tax ID (social security number for individuals and EIN for trusts). Corporations and partnerships do not qualify as donees of gratuitous transfers. The Column B instruction for trusts says—

> *If the gift was made by means of a trust, enter the trust's identifying number* [EIN] *and attach a copy of the trust instrument.*

Professionally prepared trust instruments can be quite voluminous: 35 to 50 pages on average. Therefore, use good judgment and attach only the vital pages that describe each beneficiary and his or her relationship to the donor. If, as the donor, you make transfers to more than one trust, your transfer accounting life will be complex.

Actually, the instructions to Column B say nothing about entering the Tax IDs of individuals. From your own experiences, you surely must know that whenever there is any transfer of property, the IRS wants to know the *identifying numbers* of all parties involved. This is so that its computer can cross-match that which a transferor reports, with that which a transferee reports. Accordingly, list all names and IDs of individuals in a chronological order by age: oldest first, youngest last. If there is more than one transfer to the same donee, list the present interests first, then the future interests.

Column B also requires a description of each transfer to each donee. The instructions for the descriptions say (in part)—

> *Describe each gift in enough detail so that the property can be easily identified. . . . For interests in property based on the length of a person's life, give the date of birth of the person. . . . For life insurance policies, give the name of the insurer and the policy number.*

Other instructional descriptions parallel those on Form 706 for its nine asset schedules: A through I. Recall Figure 1.2 (on page 1-7) and the asset descriptions in Chapter 1 and Chapters 4 through 8. A point to keep in mind is that whatever you distribute after death can be pre-distributed during life.

As indicated in Figure 9.2, Column E is headed: *Value at date of gift.* The valuation instructions at this date are identical to those instructions on Form 706 for "Value at date of death." All valuations entered on Form 709 or 706 must be supported with full information on how each value was determined. Whether one transfers an interest in property during life or after death, it has to be fair market valued on the date of the transfer.

Column C in Figure 9.2 is headed: *Donor's adjusted basis of gift.* One's "adjusted basis" in property is his acquisition cost (or other basis) plus additions, less allowances for depreciation, amortization, and depletion (if any). Only the donor has these records; the donee does not. In the case of a gift, the donor's basis is transferred to the donee . . . along with the property. This basis information is needed, should the donee subsequently dispose of the property in a taxable transaction.

In contrast to Form 709, there is no basis information required on Form 706. This is because, upon death of a decedent, the distributee of property gets a "stepped up" basis to its market value at death.

At this point, we think it is instructive to present a general comparison of the features of Form 709 (gift) with Form 706 (death). We do so in Figure 9.3. Note that we show Schedule B of Form 709; we'll explain this schedule more fully later. In the meantime, our intention in Figure 9.3 is to have you recognize the direct interrelationship between Forms 709 and 706. Our message is that you have a choice in the timing of your transfers. You can transfer during life, at death, or some combination of the two. Either way, the exemption allowances and tax consequences are much the same.

How Gift Tax Computed

The gift tax computational process is vastly different from your experiences with income taxation. The gift tax is purely a transfer tax. That is, it is a tax on the privilege of transferring money or property gratuitously to some member of your family, who receives the money or property tax free. Gift taxing has nothing whatever to do with the income (if any) from the transferred money or property. When making gifts, there is an exemption threshold which increases from $600,000 to $1,000,000, depending on the year of the gift (recall Figure 1.1 on page 1-5).

If you look at an official Form 709, you will find that there are 15 steps for establishing the amount of taxable gifts (for the gift year). Plus, there are 20 more steps for arriving at the tax (if any) on a single gift, or on a combined series of gifts. That's a total of 35 steps. When you are gifting money or property in excess of $10,000 per donee, you are expected to tax account for your transfers, each and every year. But rather than going through the 35 steps, we have a simpler way of presenting the true substance of how the gift tax is computed.

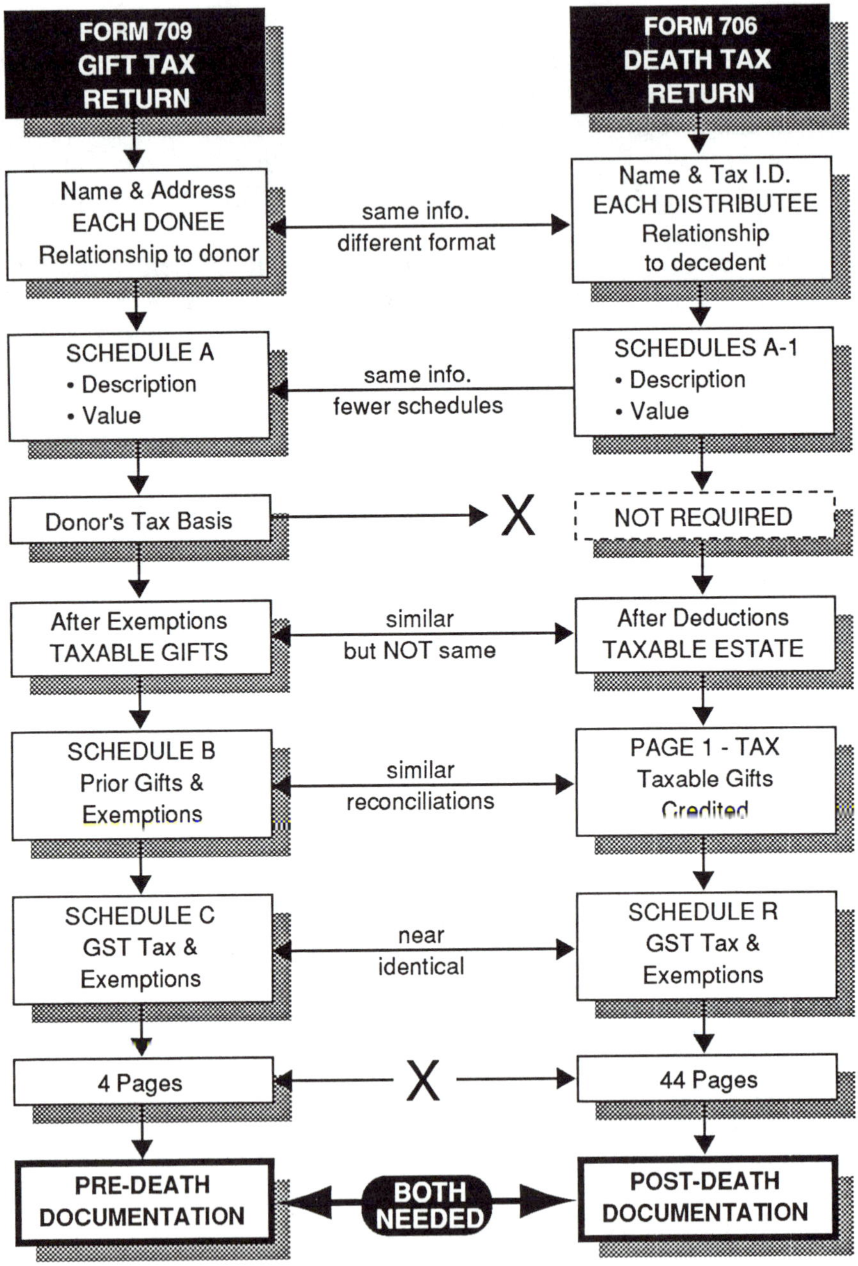

Fig. 9.3 - Highlights of Key Differences Between Forms 709 and 706

Let us assume for the moment that this is the first time you have ever needed to prepare a gift tax return. You have three adult children; you are planning to give each of them $100,000 in money or property (at their choice). Assume again, for the moment, that your maximum exemption amount is $600,000. How much gift tax would you pay?

Our simplified computational process goes like this:

Step 1 —	Total value of gifts by donor	$300,000
Step 2 —	Total annual exclusions: 3 donees	<30,000>
Step 3 —	Amount of taxable gifts	270,000
Step 4 —	Maximum exemption amount	<600,000>
Step 5 —	Taxable amount. Subtract step 4 from step 3 (do not enter less than zero)	-0-
Step 6 —	Unused exemption amount. If step 5 is zero, subtract step 3 from step 4	330,000

As the above example illustrates, you processed $300,000 in gifts. Because of the $10,000 annual exclusion per donee, your taxable gifts are reduced to $270,000. And, because of the exemption allowance, no actual gift tax applies. Therefore, the common question asked is: "If there is no gift tax to pay, why do I have to file a gift tax return?

There are *two* reasons why you have to file. One reason is that, in the example above, you have already consumed $270,000 of your gift-death "unified" exemption allowance. There **has to be** a record of this, somewhere. If you made no other gifts, then died several years later, your estate can not claim the full exemption allowable for your death year. If the maximum exemption amount was $700,000 for your death year, the applicable amount to your estate would be $430,000 [700,000 – 270,000]. On your death tax Form 706, your executor is asked:

Have Federal gift tax returns ever been filed?

If you have made a taxable gift of any amount, you had better check the box ☐ Yes.

Reason Two for filing a gift tax return is that gift taxing is a *cumulative* tax. If you make a series of different-year gifts while alive, you further reduce your applicable exemption at time of death. Indeed, while alive, you might well wipe out all of your unified exemption amount. When you reach such point, the gift tax will apply.

Prior Gifts on Schedule B

Schedule B of Form 709 is titled: ***Gifts from Prior Periods.*** Obviously, if you are preparing Form 709 for the very first time, you will have made no prior gifts. You can skip Schedule B. But if you make a taxable gift any year later Schedule B must be used. You'll see the rationale for this, when we explain its columns.

Like Schedule A, Schedule B has five columns: A, B, C, D, and E. Unlike Schedule A, however, the columns in Schedule B are functionally different. You can sense the difference as we list the headings below:

A — Calendar year (of prior gift)
B — Internal Revenue office where prior return was filed
C — Amount of unified credit against gift tax for periods after December 31, 1976
D — Amount of specific exemption for periods ending before January 1, 1977
E — Amount of taxable gifts

Column A shows the year in which a Form 709 was previously filed. If five prior Forms 709 were filed, for example, there would be five separate calendar year entries. List chronologically, starting with the farthest year back.

Column B asks for the IRS office where you filed each of your prior year Forms 709. This means that you should have kept a copy of each of your prior returns. Each such return gives your name, address, Tax ID, and other information which the IRS keeps in its data base as far back as 1970. As we have previously mentioned, gift taxing is a cumulative process. The result is that each subsequent gift pushes you higher and higher up the gift-death tax rate schedule.

Column C carries the cumulative tracking concept further. Corresponding to each year in Column A, you enter the amount of exemption credit that you claimed for that year. You obtain this amount from page 1 of each prior Form 709 at the line marked: *Unified credit* [applied]. At the bottom of the column, you show the cumulative total of all prior year exemption amounts. At some point, you may exhaust the maximum exemption allowable. When and if you do (exhaust your exemption), such fact will be noted on your Form 706 death tax return.

We will skip over Column D. For our readers it is inapplicable. It applies only to a short specific period of time before 1977 when the gift tax and death rates and exemptions were "unified." We have long since passed that period.

Column E (amount of taxable gifts) is the bottom line of Schedule A for each prior Form 709. The term "taxable gifts," recall, is the total market value of actual gifts, less the $10,000 exclusion for each donee listed in Schedule A. There is no reference in Schedule B to any prior donees. This is because it is the *donor* who has to pay the gift tax: not the donees.

In Figure 9.4, we portray the interrelationship between Schedule B (for prior years) and Schedule A (for current year). We also show how the two are totaled on page 1 (tax computation) of your current Form 709. Particularly note how the cumulative prior exemption credits *subtract* from the maximum allowable exemption amount for the current year. The gift-death exemption credit is a once-only maximum amount. You can use bits and pieces of it over several years of lifetime gifting. But in the end — at death — you cannot exceed the maximum allowable.

Tax Effect of Prior Gifts

Gift taxing invokes a unique concept of its own. Unlike income taxing which is a separate year tax, gift taxing is a *cumulative* tax. As successive year gifts are made, all prior taxable amounts are added to the current year taxable amount. At this point, a cumulative tax is determined. From this cumulative tax, all prior year taxes are subtracted. This gives the current year gift tax. The gift tax rates start at 18% for taxable gifts up to $10,000; the rates go to 55% for cumulative taxable gifts over $3,000,000. There **is** a valid rationale for cumulative gift taxing.

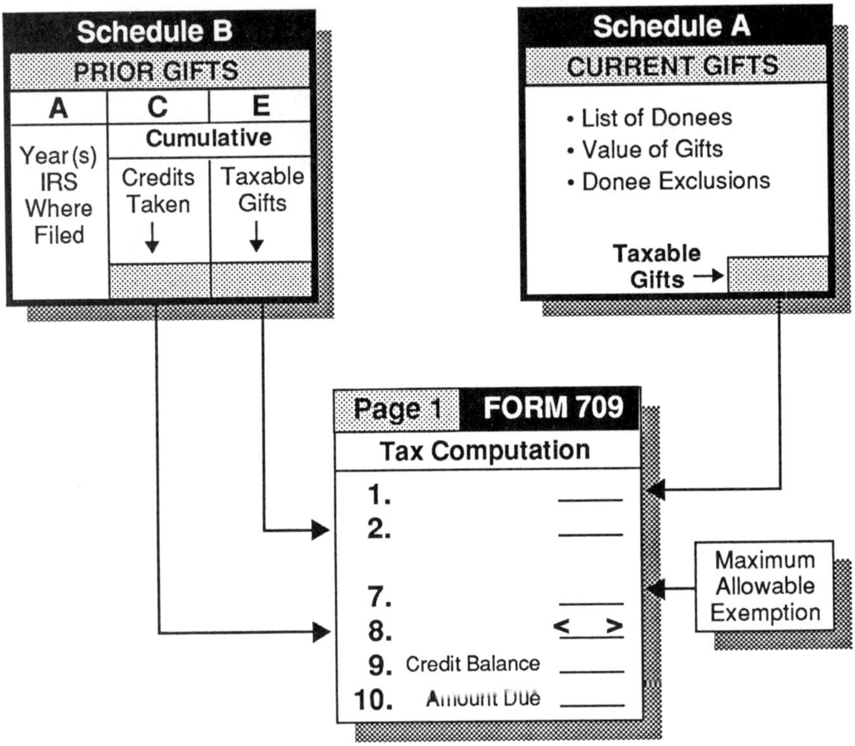

Fig. 9.4 - The "Prior Gifts" Accounting Role of Schedule B on Form 709

The death tax is a transfer tax on your accumulation of wealth throughout all of your years of living. If you made no gifts during life, your death tax would be one gross up figure. If you made a series of gifts (without the effect of cumulative taxing), your death tax would be substantially lower than if no gifts were made. Congress intended that the gift tax and the death tax be unified and equal. The only way to achieve this "unification" was to require that gifting be cumulatively taxed, rather than being separately taxed each year. In this manner, every individual is free to make gifts or not make gifts, as he or she sees fit. The tax rates and exemption credits favor neither gifts nor death.

The cumulative gift taxing process is best explained by abbreviating the 20 computational steps on page 1 of Form 709. About half of these steps require tangential explanations which distract from the focus of our discussion. By omitting these tangential matters, the gist of the page 1 ***Tax Computations*** follows:

Step 1	—	Current year taxable gifts (from Schedule A, after exclusions)	$__________
Step 2	—	Prior year taxable gifts (from Schedule B, Col. E)	__________
Step 3	—	Cumulative total taxable gifts (add steps 1 and 2)	__________
Step 4	—	Tax computed on step 3 (from Form 709 instructions)	__________
Step 5	—	Tax computed on step 2 (from Form 709 instructions)	__________
Step 6	—	Current year gift tax (subtract step 5 from step 4)	__________
Step 7	—	Maximum unified credit* (preprinted on Form 709)	__________
Step 8	—	Cumulative prior credit allowed (from Schedule B, Col. C)	__________
Step 9	—	Unused balance of credit (subtract step 8 from step 7)	__________
Step 10	—	Current tax due (if any) (subtract step 9 from step 6)	__________

*Increases from $600,000 to $1,000,000 by year 2006.

"Basis Spread" Dilemma

The difference between the market value of property and the donor's basis in it is the *basis spread* of a gift. For example, if an item gifted is marketable at $100,000 and the donor's basis in that item is $35,000, the basis spread is $65,000 [100,000 – 35,000].

The $65,000 spread is the potential amount on which the donee would pay capital gains tax, if he sold the item after its being gifted to him. From the donor's position, this creates a dilemma. Does he gift now while alive, or does he wait until death. If the $100,000 item were transferred at death, there would be no basis spread for the donee. For the donor, however, there is an includible $100,000 in his gross estate, which, had it been gifted, would not be there.

Fortunately, there is a way around this dilemma. It is called: *sale-gifting*. The donor **sells** the basis spread asset to the intended donee at full market value. After the sales contract is drawn up, the donor turns around and gifts the contract to the donee. What follows is a true example of how the process can work.

An elderly widow was diagnosed with terminal cancer. She had two children, a married son and a married daughter. The donor wanted the son to have her residence which was worth $235,000. Her basis in that residence was $65,000. She went through the sale-gifting process in 1998. The son acquired the residence at a tax basis of $235,000. She filed a sale of residence Form 2119, on which she reported a realized gain of $170,000 [235,000 – 65,000]. Because it was the sale of her own home, she was entitled to a $250,000 capital gain exclusion [IRC Sec. 121(a), (b)]. Thus, she paid no income tax on that sale. In the sale year, she filed Form 709. In Column C of Schedule A she listed (as donor's adjusted basis of gift) $235,000. In Column E (value at date of gift), she also listed $235,000. Her taxable gift thus became $225,000 (235,000 – 10,000 exclusion]. She paid no gift tax, however, because the $225,000 was less than the $625,000 unified credit (at step 7 above) to which she was entitled.

10

BUILDING NEEDED LIQUIDITY

For Even Modest Estates, The Death Tax Can Approach $500,000 Or More. To Meet This Obligation, A Purposeful Liquidity Buildup Plan Is Required. Once You Have Realistically Estimated Your Tax, Natural Instinct Is To Pursue Sensible Efforts To Minimize It. Still, There Comes A Time When Selling Assets (Before Death) Is Unavoidable. Ideally, One's LIQUIDITY POOL At Death Should Approach 35% Of His Gross Estate. "Selling Everything," Except Business Interests And Personal Home, Can Make Sense. Installment Payments May Apply When A Business Is Closely Held.

Liquidity? What is that?

It is having money available to pay your debts when they come due. It is being able to write a check before the deadline without having to scramble to sell off assets to do so. Having sufficient liquidity to pay one's death tax is a special preparatory concern of its own.

What is so special about the death tax? "I'm able to pay my income taxes on time each year," you say to yourself. "As for my death tax, it'll be business as usual for me."

What's so special? It is the *magnitude* of the amount of tax money required. Let us explain.

For a "high-end" income taxpayer, one's *taxable* income (after deductions and exemptions) would be around $150,000. For a single person, the income tax on this amount is around $42,000.

In contrast, for a high-end decedent taxpayer, one's taxable estate (after deductions and exemptions) would be around $3,000,000. The death tax on this amount is around $1,000,000. Furthermore, the $1,000,000 would have to be paid within nine months of the decedent's death [IRC Sec. 6075(a)]. If this were your estate, how would you raise the $1,000,000 if you had not planned on it ahead of time?

You get the idea, don't you? The death tax is a much higher amount relative to income tax, property tax, and the like. Ordinarily, one doesn't keep on hand the liquidity needed to pay his death tax promptly. Yet, as part of one's estate planning and simplifying measures, thinking ahead about paying the death tax makes sense.

This is what this chapter is all about. We want to help you estimate what your death taxes might be. We also want to suggest some measures that you can take to have the money available when needed. Oh, yes, you can get up to 12 months' extension of time to pay your death tax. In the 12-month interim, however, you have to pay interest at about an 8% to 10% rate. On a $1,000,000 death tax, for example, a 12-month extension would cost you an additional $90,000 (or so). Accordingly, it is best that you **not** rely on extensions of time to pay. They do not reduce your liquidity needs.

Estimating the Tax

To know how much liquidity to provide for, you need some estimate of what your death tax might be. An "estimate" is just that: an estimate. We can give you a reasonably good approach by simplifying the 28 computational steps on Form 706 (U.S. Estate Tax Return). We can shorten this number to 12 steps as follows:

Step 1	—	Total gross estate	$________
Step 2		Total allowable deductions	<________>
Step 3	—	Taxable estate (subtract step 2 from step 1)	________
Step 4	—	Total prior taxable gifts	________
Step 5	—	Adjusted taxable estate (add steps 3 and 4)	________

Step 6	—	Tentative tax (Table A: unified rate schedule)	________
Step 7	—	Total gift tax previously paid	< ________ >
Step 8	—	Estate tax before credits (subtract step 7 from step 6)	________
Step 9	—	Maximum exemption credit	< ________ >
Step 10	—	Residual estate tax (subtract step 9 from step 8)	________
Step 11	—	Other applicable credits	< ________ >
Step 12	—	Net estate tax (subtract step 11 from step 10)	========

A few comments on the above are instructive. Step 1 is the summary of all of your assets Schedules A through I on Form 706, at time of death. If you made any taxable gifts before death, and filed Forms 709, said gifts will be pulled back into your "accountable estate" at Step 4. This accounting pullback is a safeguard against your inadvertently claiming two maximum exemption credits: the one preprinted on Form 709 AND the one preprinted on Form 706 (at Step 9). Because the same exemption amount is gift-death *unified*, only one maximum amount is allowable. If you paid any gift tax prior to death, that amount is treated as a *prepayment* towards your death tax (at Step 7). Making prepayments before death via gift tax returns is encouraged as one form of liquidity preparation.

Except for marital and charitable deductions, most other deductions (at Step 2) rarely exceed 3 to 5% of your gross estate. For rough estimating purposes, such de minimis amounts can be ignored. So, too, can other credits (at Step 11), such as state death taxes, and transfer taxes paid by a predeceased spouse (if any). The Step 9 maximum exemption credit ranges from $192,800 (the year 1997 equivalent of $600,000 in asset value) to $345,800 (the year 2006 equivalent of $1,000,000 in asset value). For compromise purposes, we'll use the year 2002. The scheduled maximum credit for that year is $229,800. [Recall Figure 1.1 on page 1.5.] If any GST (generation-skipping transfer) tax is applicable, it simply *adds on* to the amount at Step 12 above. The GST tax is a separate computational process of its own.

With the above comments in mind, we present in Figure 10.1 approximately what your death tax would likely be. Note that we show estimates for gross estates at $500,000 intervals, between $1,000,000 and $5,000,000. For amounts between these intervals, use the estimating rates in the right-hand column. For gross estates less than $1,000,000, use 10% for estimating purposes. For gross estates more than $5,000,000, use 50%; for gross estates more than $10,000,000, use 55%.

Gross Estate	Tentative Tax	After Unified Credit	Estimating Rate
1,000,000	345,800	116,000	12%
1,500,000	555,800	326,000	22%
2,000,000	780,800	551,000	28%
2,500,000	1,025,800	796,000	32%
3,000,000	1,290,800	1,061,000	**36%**
3,500,000	1,565,800	1,336,000	38%
4,000,000	1,840,800	1,611,000	40%
4,500,000	2,115,800	1,886,000	42%
5,000,000	2,390,800	2,161,000	44%

- ☐ The tentative tax figures are based on de minimis (3% to 5%) administrative deductions.
- ☐ The unified credit is based on Year 2002; the exclusion amount is $700,000 which is equivalent to $229,800 in credit dollars.

Fig. 10.1 - Rates for Estimating Death Taxes for Selected Gross Estates

Filing Thresholds & Credits

If your gross estate is less than the filing threshold for Form 706, there is no death tax. Consequently, estimating your potential tax is only necessary when your gross estate exceeds the exclusion amounts prescribed in Section 2010: ***Unified Credit Against Estate Tax***. This IR Code section does not explain the difference between an "exclusion" and a "credit." All that you are told is that the two are "unified" for gift-death tax computational purposes.

An *exclusion* is the dollar amount of one's gross estate (including prior taxable gifts) that is exempted from death tax. A *credit* is a dollar-for-dollar offset against one's tentative death tax. Using the regular (unified) gift-death tax rate schedule (where the rates range from 18% to 55%), there is an equivalence between exclusion and credit. We posted the equivalences for you in Figure 1.1 (on page 1-5), and called them: applicable *exemption* amounts. The average taxpayer understands the word "exemption" better than "exclusion" or "credit."

On the other hand, the term "exclusion amount" is more fitting when considering the threshold beyond which the filing of Form 706 is required. For threshold filing purposes, subsection 2010(c): *Applicable Credit Amount*, lists the following exclusion amounts:

Year of Death (or Gift)	Exclusion
1998	$ 625,000
1999	650,000
2000–2001	675,000
2002–2003	700,000
2004	850,000
2005	950,000
2006 or thereafter	1,000,000

Now you see why we used a gross estate of $1,000,000 as our starting point in Figure 10.1. Eventually, no death tax returns will be required for gross estates (including the "pull back" of taxable gifts) of $1,000,000 or less.

For threshold filing purposes, the terms "gross estate" and "exclusion amount" MUST INCLUDE any prior-to-death taxable gifts. Otherwise, one could alter his Form 706 filing requirements by giving away most of his estate before death. For example, if one gave $800,000 in taxable gifts, which reduced his net estate to $700,000, he might get the impression that no Form 706 is required. This is not so. His gross estate for filing purposes is $1,500,000 (700,000 + 800,000).

Once one exceeds his Form 706 filing threshold, he has to think in terms of an *exemption credit amount.* This is a switching of hats, so to speak. The credit amount is the exclusion amount converted to tax rate dollars. For example, consider an exclusion amount of $700,000 (our assumption in Figure 10.1). The unified tax rate schedule for amounts between $500,000 and $750,000 states that the amount of tax is—

$155,800 + 37% of excess over $500,000
= 155,800 + 0.37 (700,000 – 500,000)
= 155,800 + 74,000 = 229,800

In other words, you go through the eight steps enumerated earlier, to arrive at a tentative tax. For the year of death designated in subsection 2010(c), you apply the maximum exemption credit allowable. Once you consume the maximum *unified* credit, the death tax world is irreversible.

Overcoming Sticker Shock

You need to have some idea of what your death tax is likely to be. This is what Figure 10.1 is for. It gives you a ballpark estimate. Such an estimate is good enough for its "sticker shock" effect. You need this shocking effect to face reality. Death tax is not cheap. We haven't even touched on the GST tax. Said tax adds to those amounts in Figure 10.1.

Strictly for illustration purposes, consider the mid-point of Figure 10.1: a $3,000,000 gross estate. The death tax would be approximately $1,000,000. Rarely would anyone keep such amount in ready liquid form. Nor should one. Yet, the $1,000,000 death tax figure serves as a shocker. It shocks one into disbelieving the figure, and into scrambling around for getting verification of it.

There is no better way of overcoming the death tax shock than by getting second, third, and fourth opinions on what your death tax is likely to be. First, you have to estimate what your gross estate would be. Then phone, visit, or internet various tax professionals in your area. Pay a consulting fee and get each one to state his estimate of the amount of said tax. If you really want to go into orbit, ask your consultants to estimate your GST tax by using Schedule R on Form 706. Don't veer off into sensational ways of reducing the death plus GST tax. If you do, you'll be skimmed and creamed by professional sharks out there. Your objective is simply to get a consensus of the magnitude of the tax payment that your executor will face.

Consensus verification is shock therapy of its own. If you get three or four estimates all within 10% to 20% of each other, your sticker shock should gradually disappear. In its place, unfortunately, anger may appear. Anger may cause you to do foolish things. It may lead to your underreporting and undervaluing your assets, or to wild schemes of secretive transfers, or to offshore tax havens where there is high risk of embezzlement and bankrupting your estate.

We want you to continue your lifestyle and plan of wealth building, the way you have been doing for years. We just want you to face reality. Once you do so, your mind will gravitate toward ways and means for building up liquidity *within* your gross estate. Yes, you can build up liquidity by mortgaging your primary assets to the hilt, or by purchasing multi-million-dollar life insurance policies. These measures can exacerbate your estate and pump your death tax shock level up, several notches more.

Look at it this way. You'll do whatever you can to sensibly reduce the death tax bite. In the end, though, you'll either pay a large amount of money to the IRS, or almost as large an amount to an entourage of attorneys, agents, brokers, and other professionals.

Assign Liquidity Ratings

Your objective is to build up liquidity within your own estate. Doing so requires that you prepare a comprehensive listing of all assets that you possess. Follow the information that we presented in prior chapters, or obtain from the IRS its Form 706 and instructions. Schedules A through I of Form 706 comprise the totality of your assets. List your assets in any order that is convenient. Then assign to each asset a reasonable market value. You don't need to get professional appraisals at this point. A little inquiry and research on your own is sufficient. All you want is a rough idea of what your estate is worth.

Once you have listed all of your assets and their approximate values, go through the list and assign to each asset a liquidity rating. A "liquidity rating" is indicative of the relative ease with which you can convert an asset into cash or "money in the bank." We suggest that your most liquid assets be assigned a rating of 1; your least liquid be assigned a rating of 5.

For example, if you have "X" number of dollars in a checking-only account, you know that by writing a check that money is promptly available. We'd assign that asset an LR1 (the "LR" for liquidity rating). Similarly for savings accounts, credit union accounts, money market accounts, certificates of deposit, and other interest-bearing monetary accounts with established financial institutions. Any account that you can liquidate and write a check on the proceeds within 10 days, we'd assign an LR1.

We'd assign other ratings based on the number of days it takes to have check-writing access to the proceeds from asset conversions. The number of access days that we would use are as follows:

LR2 — within 30 days
LR3 — within 60 days
LR4 — within 90 days
LR5 — 120 days or longer

Examples of the types of assets that would fall in these categories are presented in Figure 10.2.

As you probably already are aware, business ownership interests and commercial/industrial/agricultural real estate are difficult to liquidate in a short period of time. That's why we assign them an LR5. For business entity property, special valuation rules apply [Sec. 2032A: Valuation of Certain Farm, Etc., Real Property] and special exclusion rules apply [Sec. 2033A: Family-Owned Business Exclusion]. Because of the rigidity of these rules against asset dispositions, a special 10-year installment payment rule applies. This installment rule is Section 6166: *Extension of Time for Payment of Estate Tax Where Estate Consists Largely of Interest in Closely Held Business*. Here, the term "largely" applies only to business interests that exceed 35% of one's gross estate. In

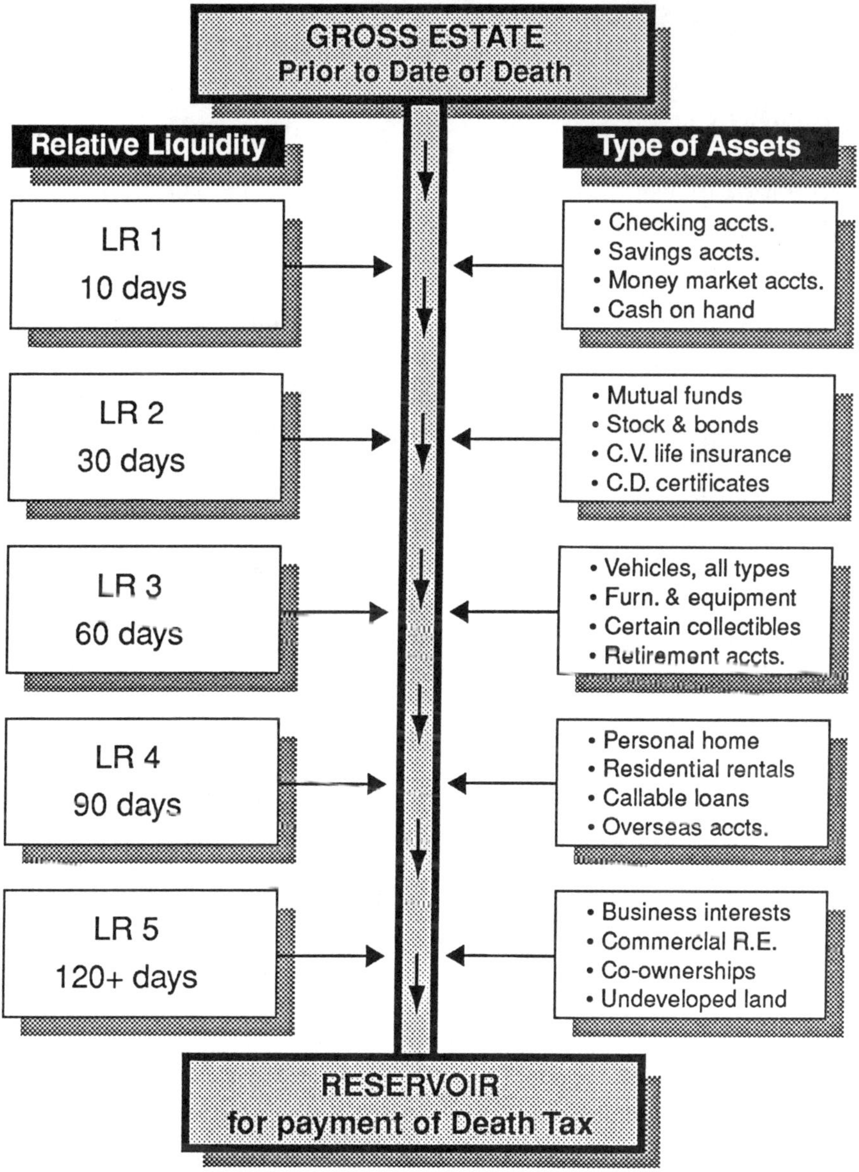

Fig. 10.2 - Suggested Liquidity Ratings for Assets Includible in Gross Estate

short, if your gross estate consists of 50% or more of LR5 assets, you will have not only liquidity problems, but also valuation and filing problems. Consequently, our comments on building liquidity within your estate relate only to the LR categories 1 through 4.

Prepare to Sell Assets

For the payment of death taxes, the IRS will not accept property, securities, collectibles, or other marketable assets. It wants cash. It wants cash in the form of your personal or business check, a cashier's check, an approved electronic transfer, or other instant cash arrangement. Instructions to Form 706 for paying the tax say—

> *Make the check payable to the Internal Revenue Service. Please write the decedent's name, social security number, and "Form 706" on the check to assist us in posting it to the proper account.*

For death tax payments, the cash needs range from about $100,000 to over $1,000,000. This magnitude of cash is not an item that you can "max out" with your credit cards. You need access to a large reservoir of ready liquidity. One way would be to establish a $1,000,000 line of credit with your bank. But you would have to pledge most of your assets as collateral. Another way would be to buy a $1,000,000 single premium life insurance policy. The single premium could cost you as much as $500,000 in upfront cash. This could cause you to sell assets to pay the premium. Or, if you want to be stubborn about it, you could deliberately default on your payment to the IRS. That agency would have no choice but to seize all of your assets and public auction them at bargain basement prices. If the auction proceeds, after IRS expenses are taken out, are insufficient to pay the tax, the IRS can go after the assets of your heirs (called: *transferee taxation*).

One way or the other, the IRS is going to get cash from you. It is, therefore, to your advantage to start planning on selling some of your assets while alive. We'd have you start the "planning to sell" process at least 10 years or more before your anticipated death. This gives you time to build your liquidity slowly and purposely.

What assets do you sell?

Firstly, those assets rated LR1 already are virtually liquid in form. You could raise cash from these assets in 10 days' time. So there is not much decision required in this category. When you need some money, it is standing by for you. When convenient, purposely increase the amount in this category.

Your decisional effort for selling assets should focus on LR categories 2, 3, and 4 (recall Figure 10.2). All assets in these categories are candidates for sale. Follow just one "don't sell" principle. That is, don't sell what you — absolutely and positively — personally need to live out the rest of your life. This includes your home, household essentials, vehicles, and other items of active enjoyment. Then *think about* preparing to sell everything else. This may sound harsh, but it is facing reality. Most heirs want cash rather than property items.

We know of a recent case where a widow was an accomplished (classical) pianist. She had a famous-name grand piano of superb workmanship and tonal quality. With the onset of rheumatoid arthritis in her hands and fingers, she could no longer play. Although she was urged to sell it in order to simplify her estate affairs, she willed it to one of her grandsons who occasionally had played on it. A few months after her death, her grandson sold the piano. He wanted the cash. And so do most heirs.

When selling assets, sell in "waves." Sell items in category 4 first, then in category 3, and lastly in category 2. If this is too painful for you, enlist the aid of your executor. Making or not making sell decisions will provide invaluable experience to your executor. Whatever you do sell in categories 2, 3, and 4, assign the proceeds to your category 1 assets. This way, you are building up liquidity gradually . . . and sensibly.

The Ultimate Liquidity Plan

Generally, we urge that you plan on selling — somewhere along the line — at least 35% of the value of your estimated growth estate. If you glance back at Figure 10.1 for a moment, 35% represents the approximate midpoint of that table. In other words, we are saying that the ideal estate plan is to have sufficient funds on hand to pay your death tax promptly. Ideally, you'd like to achieve such position without there being any "forced sale" after death.

Let us carry the liquidity goal to its extreme. What is so wrong with having a completely liquid estate . . . with only two exceptions? Exception one would be your principal residence or retirement abode. Exception two would be your ownership interests (if any) in a long and closely-held business enterprise. Why not everything else in liquid asset form?

The ideal goal, in our view, is that which we depict in Figure 10.3. That arrangement is what we call one's *ultimate liquidity plan.* We do not recommend Figure 10.3 for persons in their pre-retirement years. Such persons should concentrate more on wealth building than on wealth conserving. But once you are in full retirement or semi-retirement, the arrangement in Figure 10.3 **is** achievable and much desired.

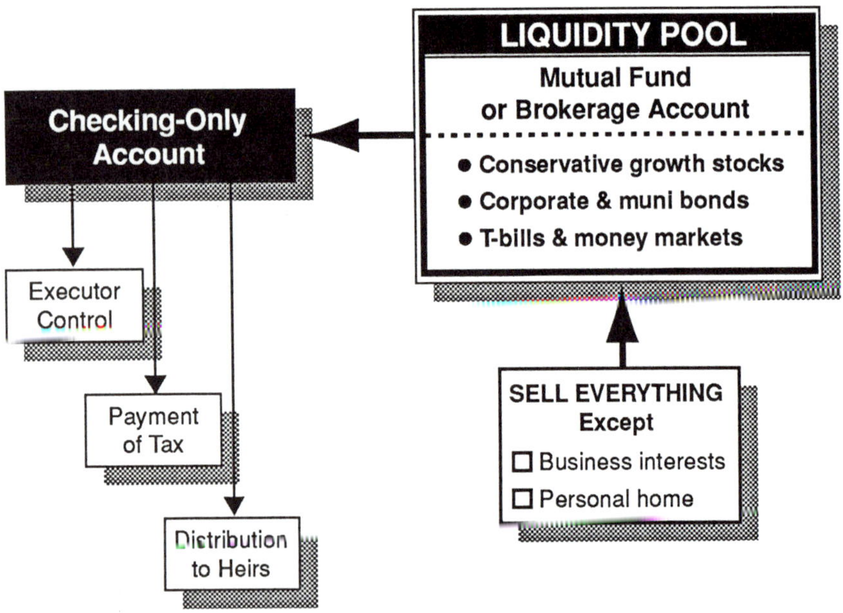

Fig. 10.3 - The Ultimate "Contemplation of" Liquidity Plan

The core feature of Figure 10.3 is your associating with a reputable investment management firm. There are many out there.

A well established mutual fund or brokerage firm is desired. Select among those with which you've had experience in the past. Seek no-load or low-load sales commission arrangements. Low operating expenses, capital preservation, and conservative investments comprise your target interests. If, by this time in your life, you haven't made the many millions of dollars that you once thought you could, now may not be the time to continue trying.

The arrangement in Figure 10.3 is not intended to deny you further growth in wealth. The arrangement is tempered so that the risk of loss becomes less of a factor in your portfolio activities. All investment firms allow switching between stocks, bonds, and money market accounts as you see fit. Just be sure that you have the capability of switching out of your core investments into a checking-only account on short notice. Ideally, also, you would include your executor's name and signature authority on your checking and investment accounts. This is strictly for convenience only. Upon your demise, it permits your executor to take immediate control of your liquid assets.

Tax Reduction Efforts

No matter what your final death tax bill turns out to be, or to what extent your gross estate consists of liquid assets, your heirs will deem the tax to be "too high." Heirs think in terms of total dollars that they are not receiving. They would have wanted you to pursue sensible efforts to reduce said tax. There are indeed *five* such efforts that you can pursue. None is magic and none is sensational. They are as follows:

Effort 1 — Consume as much of your estate as sensible, while alive. Too many prospective decedents feel compelled to save as much as possible for their children and heirs. While this may be an admirable trait, there is no law requiring it. Your only obligation is to provide for minor children, disabled dependents, and surviving spouse, if any. Otherwise, you are free to spend your own money as you see fit. Helpful in this regard is setting for yourself a *spenddown* limit below which you do not want to shrink your estate. For example, you could set your gross estate at $1,000,000 . . . and spend all in excess of that amount.

Effort 2 — Pay off all debts for which you are obligated more than 30 days. This includes mortgages, notes, loans, judgments, pledges, income taxes, property tax, . . . whatever. By paying off your more-than-30-day debts, you reduce your gross estate by the amount of money used to pay off that debt. Not only does this simplify your estate accounting, it eliminates any continuing burden on your heirs.

Effort 3 — Make frequent annual $10,000 gifts to your children, grandchildren, siblings, and other close family members. Make each gift by separate check. Save the canceled checks as documentation for yourself **and** for your donees. Too often, prospective decedents wait until some diagnosis of terminal illness is made, before gifting away any of their assets. Then they struggle furiously to make as many $10,000 gifts as they can. The longer the headstart before any terminal diagnosis is made, the more that can be transferred out of your estate without tax.

Effort 4 — Use the full exclusion amount (tabulated earlier) to make irrevocable gifts to your adult children (or other adult heirs). File gift tax returns (as discussed in Chapter 9), and cumulatively track your taxable gifts until you have consumed all of your applicable unified exclusion amount. Being able to do this, of course, assumes that your gross estate exceeds $1,000,000 by at least the exclusion amount. Preferably, gift those assets which are likely to appreciate in value, such as real estate, growth stock, fine art, etc. Even if you liquidate and use some of your core investments in Figure 10.3 to gift your exclusion amount, any subsequent earnings thereon would remain out of your estate.

Effort 5 — Make deductible bequests to charitable organizations and/or to your spouse (if any). Section 2055: ***Transfers for Public, Charitable, and Religious Uses***, places no limit on the amount of deductible transfers you can make. The same is true of Section 2056: ***Bequests, Etc., to Surviving Spouse***. With either of these two statutory deductions, you could reduce your taxable estate — and therefore your death tax — to virtually nil. With public, charitable, or religious transfers, your heirs derive no gratuitous benefits whatsoever. With marital bequests, that which is removed from your estate is includible in your spouse's gross estate. However, your surviving spouse may use what you transfer to him/her to repeat the tax reduction efforts above.

We summarize the above reduction efforts in Figure 10.4. If you put your mind to it, you **can** soften your final tax bite. We urge that you consider doing so, before falling prey to magic-sounding trusts, expatriation of funds, and stealth transfers.

Acceptance Letter by IRS

Sooner or later, your death tax has to be paid. Statutorily, it is required to be paid in full within nine months after date of death. This is referred to as the *return due date*. This is the official reference date for any extensions of time to pay, or for the approval of extended installment payments.

In those cases where it is impossible or impractical to pay the full amount when due, or if the correct tax cannot be determined because the gross estate is "unascertainable," an extension of payment time may be requested. This requires the filing of Form 4768 (for estate tax) and Form 2758 (for GST tax), and accompanying said form(s) with a substantial payment in cash. As per Section 6161(a), an extension up to 12 months beyond the return due date may be granted. Interest, however, is charged on the late payment at a rate (of 8% to 10% per annum) determined by Section 6621.

When the entire full amount of the death tax has been paid, you will receive an acceptance letter from the IRS. The letter is bold print headed:

ACCEPTANCE OF ESTATE TAX RETURN
(NOT A BILL FOR TAX DUE)

The letter goes on to say—

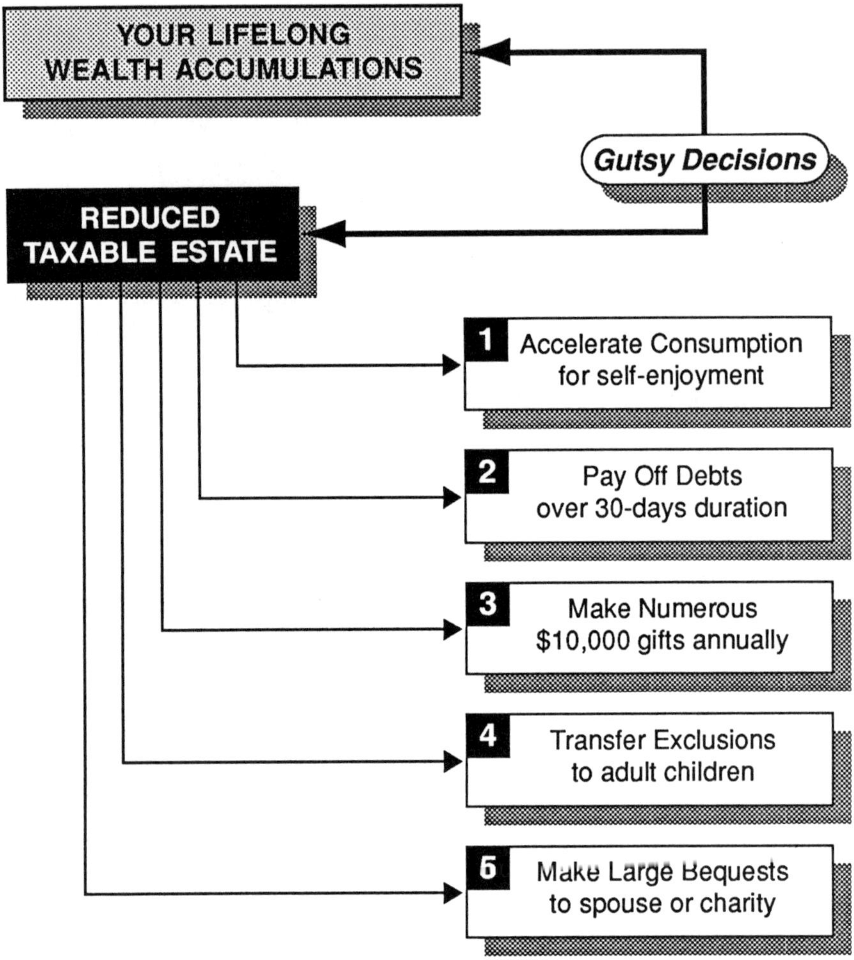

Fig. 10.4 - Sensible Tax Reduction Efforts Without Sensational Risks

> *This letter **and** proof of payment, such as cancelled checks or receipts, will establish that your personal liability for the tax has been settled. . . . This letter is evidence that the Federal tax return for the estate has either been accepted as filed or has been accepted after an adjustment to which you have agreed.* ***You should keep this letter as a permanent record.*** [Emphasis added.]

11

UPDATING YOUR WILL

Your Will Is Your CENTERPIECE PLAN For Defining And Distributing Your Estate. When Updated In Conformity With Ongoing Efforts To Simplify Your Estate, It Becomes A "Directional Compass" For Your Executor. This Directionality Is Most Important When Bequesting A Marital Residence To Your Spouse, A Closely Held Business Or Farm To Your Adult Children, And Rental Real Estate To Your Trust. Thereafter, Empower Your Executor To Convert All Else Into Monetary Form For Prompt Distribution To Those Heirs And Legatees Of Your Choice.

Everyone needs a will; not everyone needs a trust. Still, estate planners hawk the virtues of a trust as taking care of everything, including simplifying your estate. The truth is that a will takes effect immediately upon death, whereas, chronogically, a trust takes effect later. Technically, a will suspends the starting of trust activities until the decedent's estate is settled. Settlement includes preparing and filing Form 706: U.S. Estate Tax Return, and the payment of the death (transfer) tax thereon. Settlement also includes settling probate (legal) issues, if such issues arise.

A will does not avoid probate, though it can greatly simplify the process. On the other hand, a trust *may* avoid probate IF all property intended for the trust is predeath titled in the name of the trust. A trust, however, **does not avoid** Form 706 and its tax. Nor does a will.

A will can more readily simplify the preparation of Form 706 than can a trust. This is because a will focuses on a relatively short span of time after death (nine months or so), whereas a trust focuses on many years after death. Because of its short after-death time focus, a will is the ideal instrument for setting forth in clear, unequivocal terms what your specific intentions are. A will can be modified, updated, and changed with minimum fanfare. This is because a will, typically, is five pages or so in length, whereas a trust is 35 pages or more in length. The best estate planning is to rely on a will first . . . *then* a trust (if truly needed).

Accordingly, in this chapter, we want to address the primary ingredients of a will, and urge that you update your will with our comments in mind. One viewpoint is to think of your will as a set of instructions to your executor. It is also an opportunity to provide your executor with important information for the preparation of Form 706. In this regard, for example, you can recap in your will the taxable gifts that you made prior to death. This recap is not only helpful to your executor, it is also helpful to your heirs. Heirs tend to forget what you have given them during life. Your will is one way of reminding them of the past. Has your will preparer ever mentioned this opportunity to you? We have other pointers to mention which your will preparer may have overlooked.

Have Separate Instruments

Because of the exhilarating popularity of trusts and the mysticism surrounding them, the tendency these days is to combine a will and a trust into one instrument. If you are married, the one instrument serves four purposes: (1) your will, (2) your trust, (3) your spouse's will, and (4) your spouse's trust. The testamentary instrument serving these purposes can easily reach 50 pages or more. All sorts of contingencies have to be addressed.

Even if you and your spouse die simultaneously, and each of your gross estates is 100% liquid monetarily, there are **four** separate tax accounting functions to perform. There is a Form 706 for your gross estate. There is a separate Form 706 for your spouse's gross estate. After each Form 706 is separately accepted by the IRS, there is a separate Form 1041 (U.S. Income Tax Return for Trusts) for your trust, AND a separate Form 1041 for your spouse's trust. There are no joint 706 forms; there are no joint 1041 forms. Each Form 706 is identified with the individual social security number of the decedent. Each Form 1041 is identified with an employer identification number of the trust entity.

No matter how willing and cooperative a husband and wife may be, each is a separate human individual. They are two different minds and two different bodies. Rarely do they think exactly alike as to their testamentary dispositions. Even more rarely do they die simultaneously. The time span between the two deaths can alter the gross estate of the surviving spouse, can accelerate gifts, and cause revisions to prior testamentary dispositions. In Figure 11.1, we try to dramatize the uncertainty and confusion that can arise when there is one testamentary instrument seeking to accomplish four major post-death accountings simultaneously.

Our position is that, for best testamentary planning, there should be separate instruments for each post-death accounting phase. There should be a separate will for the husband and a totally separate will for the wife. If both feel the need for a trust, there should be a separate trust instrument for the husband, and a separate trust for the wife. Professional preparers will gladly prepare four separate instruments, if you insist that they do so. Many such preparers will agree with our position. We fail to see any real saving in time, money, or property distribution efficiency by having one instrument "take care of everything."

Incidentally, Part 1 of Form 706 *requires* that a certified copy of your will be attached. It does **not** require the attachment of your trust instrument (if any). Part 4 requires that a certified copy of your death certificate be attached. If your will provides for transfer of property into a trust, Part 4 requires only that your trust EIN be entered. When Form 1041 is first filed for a trust, a certified copy of the pertinent instrument is required. In anticipating all of these attachments, a will should be no more than five pages in length; a trust no more than 15 pages. Otherwise, the deluge of paper attachments may prompt the IRS to make intensive inquiry into your estate affairs.

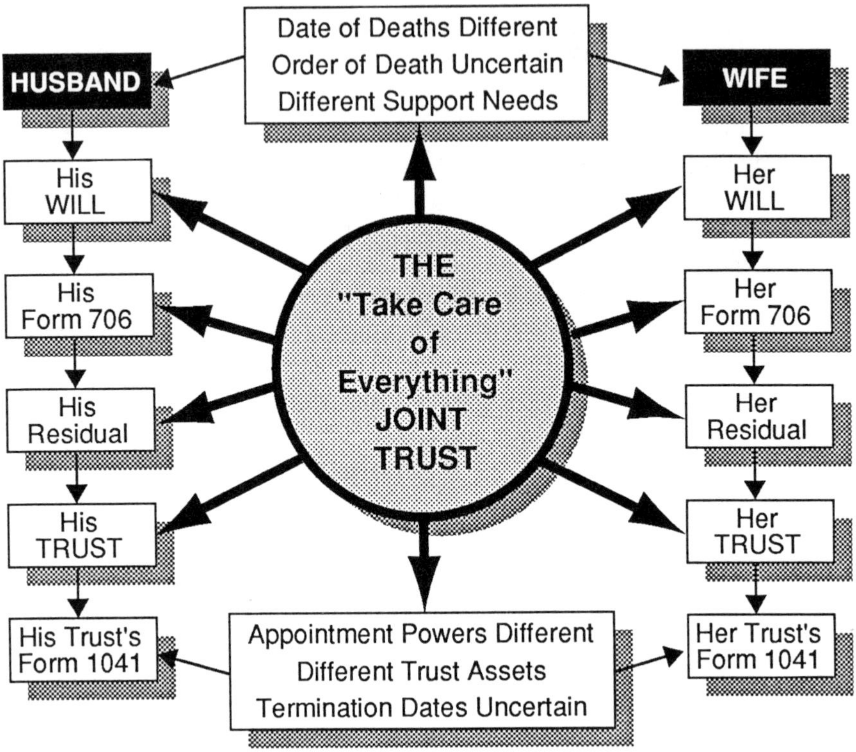

Fig. 11.1 - Chaos & Confusion When "Just One" Testamentary Instrument

Check Preamble Paragraphs

The anatomy of a will requires certain preamble paragraphs that set the stage for who you are and what you intend. You have to testify (to the world, essentially) who you are, where your domicile is, your state of mind, and what prior instruments (if any) that you wish to revoke. You want to "clear the table" and start anew, perhaps. To do so, you need to review your current will, and update the preamble paragraphs as necessary.

Obviously, if you change your county, state, or country of residence, you need to reflect that change in your LAST WILL AND TESTAMENT. You need to conform this information with that which your executor must enter on Form 706. After your full name and social security number, your executor must enter—

Legal residence (domicile) at time of death (county, state, ZIP code, or foreign country). Year domicile established.

After your full name and domicile, a statement is required as to your sound mental condition. The typical statement goes like this—

I, ______________, being of sound and disposing mind and memory, and not acting under duress, menace, fraud, or undue influence of any person whomsoever, do make, publish, and declare this to be my Last Will and Testament. . . .

While alive, your will has no legal effect. After death, your state of mind when the will was prepared — and witnessed — can be challenged. In anticipation of this possibility, make sure that you engage in a series of conversations with your witnesses. They may be called upon to testify in your behalf.

Following your statement of mental competency, there is a revocation paragraph. The idea here is to make sure that your updated will is indeed your latest one. That nothing will pop out of the woodwork to supersede it. Typically, the language goes something like this—

I hereby revoke any and all former Wills, Codicils to Wills, and Testamentary Dispositions by me at any time heretofore made. I specifically revoke my former Will dated _____ and executed at _______; my former Life Insurance Contract dated ________ and executed at ___________; and my Inter Vivos Trust dated _________ and executed at ______________.

The revocation paragraph is your chance to fine tune your latest will, based on the experience and knowledge that you have gained since your prior will. We urge that you **not** amend or correct your old will with hand-entered notations and comments. Doing so invites protracted legal challenges and probate. Most wills should be reviewed and updated at least every five years: more often in some cases. If for no other reason, you at least want to verify the existence and latest address of each of your witnesses.

Verify Heirs & Legatees

An "heir" is a living person within your immediate family bloodline: parents, siblings, spouse, children, and grandchildren. A "legatee" is any other person or entity whom you name in your will as a distributee of some portion of your property. You do not need to name every possible heir, only those you intend to provide for. If you are married and have children, you must name and recognize all of them. This includes any spouse or child who has predeceased you. If you have minor children, or have designated other minors, such as grandchildren, you must show their dates of birth. If any heirs or legatees live outside of the U.S., you should indicate their foreign addresses. All of these items have to be verified: correct spellings, correct dates, and correct addresses.

If you are married, divorced, widowed, remarried, unmarried, or single, you should expressly state so. If you are divorced or widowed, give the name of that spouse and date of divorce or date of widowhood. If you have remarried, cite the date on which the new marriage is legal. If you are unmarried but living with someone, state the other person's name only if you intend to provide for him or her. If you have never been married (meaning: single), state so.

If you have adult children, there may be one or more for whom you may not wish to provide. Or, there may be an ex-spouse whom you wish to omit. Still, you must name such persons in your will and expressly state that you — knowingly and intentionally — are not providing for them. Though you are not required to give a reason, it is advisable to do so. A written reason by you helps your executor to fend off challengers from participating in your estate.

Whatever may be your situation, make sure that you include a "$1 clause." Such a clause might read as:

I have intentionally made no provision for any person other than those named in this Will, whether such person claims to be an heir of mine or not. If any person or persons other than those provided for herein should prove a right to participate in the distribution of my estate, to each and all such person or *persons proving a right to so participate, I give, devise, and bequeath the sum of One Dollar ($1.00) only.*

If you want to make this clause more forceful, you can insert the name(s) of the person or persons whom you expressly want to omit from your will.

Instruct Your Executor

The most important person who will administer your estate affairs after death is your executor (executrix, feminine). As the legal owner of the property and assets in your estate you have the power to nominate and appoint as executor whomever you want. Your choice of such person should not be a figurehead. You don't want someone who, a few days after your death, rushes off to an attorney or other professional and dumps everything in his/her lap. You want an executor who will take charge, and who will engage a professional (attorney, accountant, appraiser, tax preparer) only when necessary. For a limited duration of time, your executor has all of the legal and administrative powers prescribed by state law. You can add to these prescribed powers as you see fit.

Many professional will preparers recite in the will all of the powers and duties prescribed by your state's probate code. This adds unnecessary pages of legalese. Your executor, once confirmed with "Letters Testamentary" can do anything that you could do with your own property while alive. The job of your executor is to get things done, and settle your estate efficiently and promptly. These work matters are summarized for you in Figure 11.2.

When appointing your executor, you should also appoint a successor executor, and, possibly, a successor successor executor. The appointment of co-executors is not advised, though it can work advantageously in some cases. Authorize any appointee to resign or withdraw at any time, providing he or she does so in writing. The next appointed executor down the line takes charge.

After clearly naming your executor(s), you want to follow with a "delegation of powers" paragraph. Such a paragraph might read as—

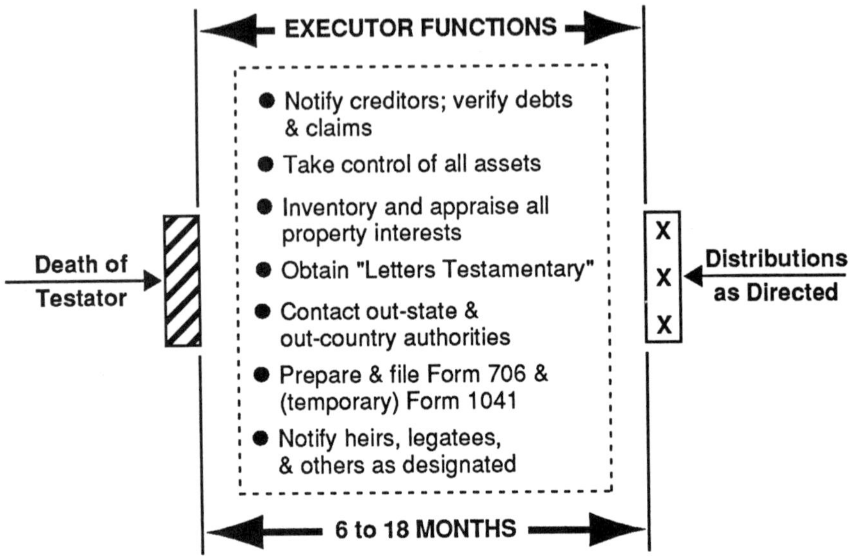

Fig. 11.2 - "Real Work" That Your Executor Has to Accomplish

I direct that my Executor or Executrix, whoever it may be, shall have full power to sell, exchange, rearrange, transfer, or otherwise dispose of as much of the property of my estate as he or she deems advisable and necessary, in order to distribute and settle my estate as directed herein, by ***independent administration*** *without giving notice and without judicial accounting of any kind. I specifically direct that all taxes, debts, and expenses applicable to my estate be paid prior to final distributions, and that all assets be distributed and my estate be settled* ***within nine (9) months*** *of my demise.*

The term "independent administration" means that your executor does not have to seek approval from an attorney, probate judge, or any distributee for conducting day-to-day transactional affairs. Where business interests, real estate, or co-owned assets are involved, it is prudent to seek judicial approval, if any contention is anticipated. The way some heirs and legatees react, after the death of a testator (will writer), is an interesting quirk of human nature.

By directing that taxes be paid before final distribution of assets, your executor can invoke Sections 2205, 2206, and 2207 of the

Internal Revenue Code. The gist of these sections is that **each heir or legatee shall share proportionately in the tax** . . . *unless otherwise directed by the will of the decedent.* Thus, if any beneficiary receives a distribution before the full tax is paid, . . . *the executor shall be entitled to recover from such beneficiary* . . . a proportionate amount of the tax. Distributions before tax are possible through such arrangements as life insurance, pensions, annuities, life estates, trusts, joint tenancies, and so forth.

Clarify Property Interests

The central purpose of a will is to distribute your property after death to persons of your choice. You can only distribute property which you own; you cannot distribute someone else's property. If married, your spouse has separate distributive rights from you. Consequently, every testator must declare what property is his own and clarify his interests therein with certainty.

There are four distinct classes of property which a testator may own. These classes are—

Real property,
Tangible property,
Intangible property, and
Personal effects.

Real property consists of parcels of land with or without structures thereon, and rights thereto. Tangible property consists of objects which can be seen, felt, and moved. Vehicles, machinery, equipment, collectibles, works of art, natural resources, etc. are examples. Intangible property (stock, bonds, mortgages, notes, bank accounts, etc.) has no physical body form, and has no intrinsic value of its own. Intangible property consists of "pieces of paper" rather than actual physical objects. Personal effects are items, both tangible and intangible, which have little market value relative to real, tangible, and intangible property.

If married, you need to make a clear distinction between marital property (50/50 owned) and separate property. Separate property is that which was acquired before marriage, or during marriage if acquired by gift or inheritance from parents and relatives. If separate property, define it by source of acquisition, approximate value, title form, and your intentions regarding keeping such property separate and apart from your marital estate.

If you co-own a trade or business, or rental real estate with persons other than your spouse, you should name your co-owners and indicate the extent of your ownership interests therein. Also, indicate where each co-owner's interests are recorded on books of account and titles. This gets us back to the principles we discussed in Chapter 6: Clarifying Co-ownerships. Your updated will is an excellent way for "setting the record straight" on such matters.

If you have property located out of state or out of country, identify that property with certainty. Identify what it is, where it is, and how acquired. If transferred to accounts overseas from U.S. accounts, indicate when the transfer(s) was(were) made, and that all proper U.S. tax returns have been filed. In fact, attach a copy of the latest such return to your will.

If you are a widower or widow, it is advisable to add the name of one or more of your adult children to property titles and accounts. This is strictly for convenience only. You can do this with your own separate property, but not that which is co-owned with other persons. A will paragraph to this effect might read as follows:

> *I hereby declare that all of my property, real and personal, tangible and intangible, of whatever kind or nature, wherever situated is my separate property, regardless of the form in which it may be held at the time of my demise. For reasons of convenience only, and with no predeath gift intended, I have knowingly and purposefully placed all of my property, both real and personal, in joint tenancy with one or more of my children. This joint-tenancy arrangement shall have no bearing on each child's proportionate share of my estate upon my demise.*

Prior Transfers & Disclaimers

We have already given you a discourse in Chapters 8 and 9 about prior transfers (for insufficient consideration) and taxable gifts. Your will is an excellent way to confirm these matters for the convenience of your executor. It saves time and possible animosity towards your executor by recipients who may have to be interrogated. You confirm these prior matters by a separate declaratory paragraph in your will. You also annex to your will copies of pertinent income or gift tax returns. This confirmational role of annexing returns is rarely ever mentioned by professional will preparers. Do you recall anyone mentioning annexing your gift tax returns to your will?

A declaratory paragraph in your updated will re the above might read as—

> *I hereby declare that I have made a series of gifts, some outright and some with retained interests, to various heirs and legatees of mine, commencing on ________________. In each case a gift tax return has been filed, and will be filed as appropriate after the date hereof. Photocopies of said returns are annexed hereto. I specifically declare that I have made no transfers whatsoever for insufficient consideration, nor have I received any such transfers from other persons.*

So much for prior gifts and transfers; now for disclaimers. A "disclaimer" is an unequivocal statement that you do not want included in your gross estate certain property items that you expect to inherit from your parents, uncles, aunts, siblings, and other relatives. Disclaimers are a valid way of whittling down — and simplifying — your gross estate. The statutory requirements for a valid disclaimer are set forth in IR Code Section 2518(b): ***Qualified Disclaimer Defined.*** The key ingredient required is an unqualified refusal of acceptance, in writing. Isn't your will a written instrument? Of course it is.

Accordingly, your disclaimer paragraph might read as—

> *I hereby irrevocably and unqualifiedly disclaim and refuse forever to accept the following property interests transferable from the persons indicated, namely:*
>
> *(1)*______________________
> *(2)*______________________

*(3)*__________________________

To this date, I have neither accepted nor derived any benefit whatsoever from these properties. If there should be any other property transferable to me from the persons above named, I hereby likewise disclaim and refuse to accept any and all of such property.

The beauty of a qualified disclaimer in one's will is that the disclaimed property completely bypasses the will. By so doing, it is not subject to death tax in the testator/decedent's estate. It goes directly to the decedent's surviving heir(s). It's almost like the disclaimed property being in a separate trust of its own.

Property Intended for Trust

Depending on the magnitude of your gross estate, you may feel the need for a trust. Whereas a will is limited to a one-time distribution of your estate, a trust may distribute your property over many years. Consequently, in testamentary terms, a trust is more flexible than a will. But it is also more complicated. This is why we urge that you weigh the pros and cons of a trust thoroughly. If your gross estate is in the neighborhood of $3,000,000 or more, a trust indeed can be a useful planning adjunct to your will. Because of their revocability during life, living trusts are quite popular.

By its very nature, a trust instrument is lengthy, abstract, and impersonal. It tends to be overly legalistic. Though you pay for the trust preparation effort, the instrument itself is written primarily for "the legal system" that will endure long after your demise.

Typically, the *preliminary* wording in a living trust is written like this:

I hereby give and bequeath to my surviving spouse (or child or children) all personal automobiles, silverware, books, pictures, household furniture, furnishings, jewelry, clothing, wearing apparel, and other similar items of personal effects used in and about the household. As to the rest, residue, and remainder of my estate, whether real, personal, tangible, intangible, or mixed, wheresoever situated, I hereby give, devise, and bequeath it all to my husband (or wife) as ***trustee*** *to be held in trust and administered and distributed in accordance with the following provisions and subject to the following uses, terms, and conditions.*

This is what we call a "dump-in" trust. You bequeath the "pots and pans" and other items of little value, and dump everything else into the trust. Attorneys call the above wording a "pour over" will. Whatever you wish to call the wording, *it is a cop-out.* All preparatory effort and forethought on your part that we have discussed in previous chapters is turned over to a trustee. The trustee turns your estate over to an attorney. The attorney turns the custody of your assets over to a bank or trust company. Then a prolonged — very prolonged — **legal milking** process begins.

Our preference is that you designate in your will only those specific property items that you want in your trust. For example, you might declare as follows:

I hereby declare that that portion of my estate itemized below, ***and no other****, shall pass into the trust known as the ____________ ________________ TRUST. The terms and conditions of said trust are set forth in that instrument titled "Declaration of Trust" dated ______________ at ________________ attached hereto as a supplement. The property so transferred shall be limited to the following, in kind or value, net after prorations for debts, taxes, and expenses, namely:*
Property A____
Property B____
Property C____
or the equivalent thereof.

The phrases "in kind or value" and "or the equivalent thereof" are supportive of the substitutive power of your executor for carrying out your trust property intent. This wording is more applicable to a testamentary (after death) trust than to a living (before death) trust. However, in anticipation of death, you can — and should — use the same kind of specific property wording in a living trust.

Treat Will as "Centerpiece"

There is a deep rooted, fundamental problem with trusts. Having one lulls you into a false sense of security. You have a trust, therefore you don't have to think or do anything, any more. You have no compass; no sense of direction; no need to make decisions; no need to simplify your estate — just push everything off into your trustee's hands. Then lull yourself along in peace and bliss. Unless your personally appointed trustee has the stomach and smarts to persist in your interests, the "pros of the day" will milk your estate for all of its worth. Once you are deceased, you have no control whatsoever.

Instead of relying on a trust in blind faith, treat your will as your **centerpiece plan**. Regard it as your navigational compass. Use it to steer you through the hidden shoals and shark infested waters that target your estate. Because a will is a much simpler instrument than a trust, you can review it, change it, amend it, and update it whenever you like.

As we depict in Figure 11.3, your will constitutes the vital transitional guide from the moment of death to the settlement (distribution) of your estate. Control in this regard is the role of *your executor* — **not** your trustee — when preparing and filing Form 706. And, also, paying the death tax therewith. As to this tax, IRC Section 2002: ***Liability for Payment***, says—

> *The tax imposed by this chapter* [Estate Tax] *shall be paid by the executor.*

Note that there is no mention of a trustee. Therefore, while alive, you should think, act, and make decisions like an executor.

Editing & Witnessing

Your latest updated will should conform closely to the prior efforts you have taken to simplify your estate. It should not be a

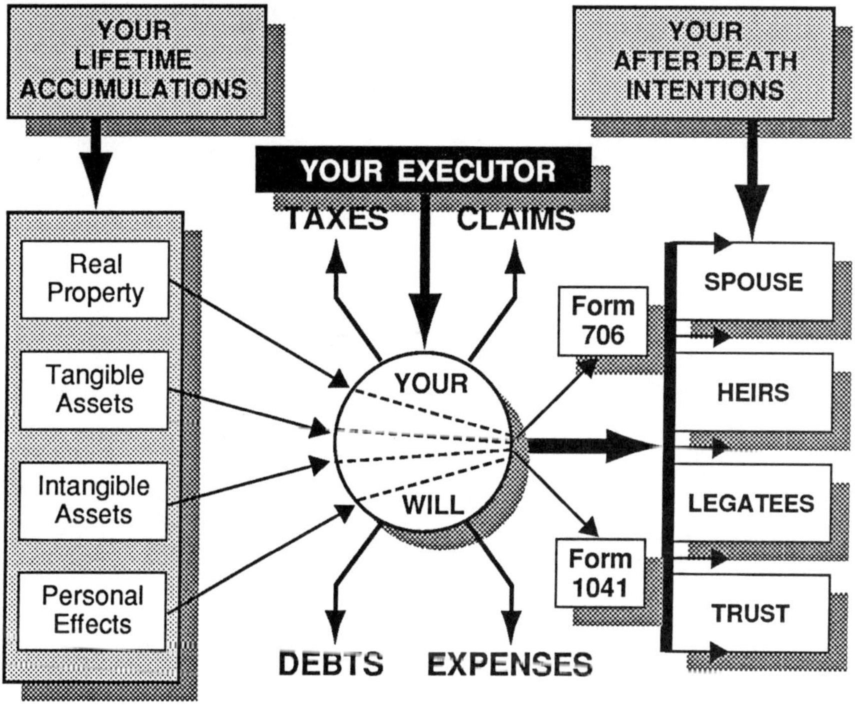

Fig. 11.3 - The "Centerpiece Concept" of Your Will (Before Any Trust)

stereotyped or boilerplate will. It should be meaningful and specific. This requires that you edit your will thoroughly, particularly if some attorney or other professional prepares it for you.

Good editing requires mental insight into how your gross estate will appear on Form 706, and how your residual estate will be distributed. If you are married, make a substantial bequest to your spouse, such as the marital residence and other property. Such bequests are deductible from your gross estate for taxation purposes. If you are not married and have no children or grandchildren, one or more charitable bequests may be in order.

If your residual estate consists of a closely held business, farm, or rental real estate, bequeath it to those adult children who pledge to continue the activity. This permits an extension of time for paying the taxes thereon. If you have no adult children, assign the property to a trust with instructions that it be sold within a specific period of time (such as within five years, for example).

After fully editing your will, you face the concluding task. Said task is the signing of your will in the presence of two witnesses. Typically, the witness paragraph reads as follows—

IN WITNESS WHEREOF, I have hereto set my hand this ____ day of __________.

(your signature)
Your name typed in caps

The foregoing document consisting of ___ pages, including this page, was on the date thereof by ______ (your name) ______, the maker thereof, signed in our presence and in the presence of each of us, and at the time of subscribing said document (he/she) declared that it was (his/her) Last Will and Testament, and at (his/her) request and in (his/her) presence and in the presence of each other, we have subscribed our names as witnesses thereto.

(Signature of witness) *Residing at* ____________________

____

(Signature of witness) *Residing at* ____________________

____

Selecting competent witnesses is not a perfunctory task. We have sound advice in this regard. Never let an attorney and his secretary witness your will. Attorneys want to keep your signed original in *their possession* so as to assert themselves as your "personal representative" upon your demise. Never select persons as witnesses who are named in your will. They have a conflict of interest. Never select two persons who are husband and wife. They could be killed or seriously injured in a common disaster. You always need at least one witness to prove your will. In some jurisdictions, a Notary Public will do.

12

INITIATING YOUR OWN 706

The FORM 706 EXPERIENCE Is A Rarity While Alive. It Unfolds ONLY When Actually Filling Out The Form, Starting On Page 1 At Line 1: Decedent And Executor. Part 3: Elections By Executor, And Part 4: General Information Can Also Be Filled Out. Part 5: RECONCILIATION Can Be Filled Out After Schedules A Through I (ASSETS) And Schedules J Through U (DEDUCTIONS) Are Completed. If "Generation-Skipping Transfers" Are Made, Schedules R And R-1 Are Required. Part 2: TAX COMPUTATION Is The Last To Be Filled Out. Net Distributive Amounts (After Expenses And Taxes) Are Entered In Part 4 To "Top Off" The 706 Experience.

The "706" refers to IRS **Form 706**. Its short title is: ***U.S. Estate Tax Return***. The term "estate" refers to your property holdings and interests that remain unconsumed at the time of your death. The term "tax" is the liability assessed against your estate for the pure privilege of passing/transferring your property to others . . . gratuitously. The preparation and filing of Form 706 applies generally to gross estates over $600,000. This filing threshold increases slightly each year until 2006 when it becomes $1,000,000.

We have cited above only the "short title" of Form 706. Its full title is: ***U.S. Estate (and Generation-Skipping Transfer) Tax Return***. Definitely note the word "**and**" in this long title. This word means that IN ADDITION TO the estate tax, there is a GST tax. The two taxes — estate tax and GST tax — are added together near the bottom of page 1 of Form 706. In previous chapters, we have not said much about the GST tax. However, in this chapter, we want to expand your knowledge a little more about GST matters.

In order to expand your knowledge and enhance your appreciation of Form 706, we offer a novel approach. WE WANT **YOU** TO INITIATE THE PREPARATION OF YOUR OWN FORM 706! To our knowledge, no one else has ever suggested that a prospective decedent do this. This is not a wacky idea at all. It makes good sense. It is the best way in the world to really know what your executor has to endure when you are gone. Why not share in your executor's duties now?

Accordingly, in this chapter we want to whisk you through Form 706 in its entirety. Obviously, we cannot expect that you totally complete the form and sign your own name to it. That's for your executor to do. Nevertheless, you can prepare a *comprehensive draft* of it. Then include the draft with other important papers in your estate file. Doing so will put you many steps closer to reality than your contemporaries.

Fill Out Part 1 on Page 1

The best way to gain familiarization with Form 706 is to start filling it out! We mean it. Fill out Part 1 on page 1. Below the form title, Part 1 comprises about two vertical inches of space. It consists of 14 entry blocks. All but two or three of the entries can be completed by you.

The title of Part 1 is: ***Decedent and Executor***. You are not the decedent — not yet, anyway — and you are not the executor. Still, we want you to start filling out the form as though you were both decedent and executor. This will give you a different perspective of what your afterlife will be.

The first three entry blocks in Part 1 are quite simple. They are:

1a *Decedent's first name and middle initial (and maiden name, if any)*
1b *Decedent's last name*
2 *Decedent's social security number*

The mere fact of thinking like an executor for a decedent puts you in an entirely different frame of mind when addressing a tax form.

The next four entry blocks are:

3a *Legal residence (domicile) at time of death*
3b *Year domicile established*
4 *Date of birth*
5 *Date of death*

Obviously, you can't fill out your own date of death. You have to leave item 5 blank. Whatever that date turns out to be, it has to be corroborated by your death certificate.

The next three entry blocks pertain to your executor. They are:

6a *Name of executor*
6b *Executor's address*
6c *Executor's social security number*

If you have updated your will as we have urged you to do in Chapter 11, you can fill out these blocks now. The instructions for ***Name of Executor*** say—

> *If there is more than one executor, enter the name of the executor to be contacted by the IRS. List the other executors' names, addresses, and SSNs on an attached sheet.*

The next two entry blocks are:

7a *Name and location of court where will was probated or estate administered*
7b *Case number*

If **all** of your assets were in joint tenancy with your spouse, or in joint tenancy with one or more of your adult children, or in a living trust, you could enter N/A (Not Applicable) in these two blocks. We suggest otherwise; leave **7a** and **7b** blank. You really do not know whether your estate will be probated. Much depends on the savvy and self-reliance of your executor.

Three Checkboxes in Part 1

The last three entry blocks in Part 1 read:

8	*If decedent died testate, check here and attach a certified copy of the will.*	▸ ☐
9	*If Form 4688 is attached, check here*	▸ ☐
10	*If Schedule R-1 is attached, check here*	▸ ☐

If you are not already familiar with the term "testate," it means: *having made and left a legally valid will.* We prepared you for this in Chapter 11. So, check the box at item 8.

Form 4688 is an application for an extension of time (beyond the statutory nine months) to file Form 706 and/or to pay the tax. Our thesis throughout this book has been no extensions. Allow yourself and your executor six months to get the return done and the tax paid. So, leave the box at item 9 blank.

The checkbox at item 10 cannot be addressed until you complete Schedule R: ***Generation-Skipping Transfer Tax***, as well as Schedule R-1: ***Direct Skips from a Trust***. The preprinted instructions on the back side of Schedule R-1 say, in part—

> *Schedule R-1 (Form 706) serves as a payment voucher for the GST tax imposed on a direct skip from a trust, which the trustee of a trust must pay. The executor completes the schedule and gives 2 copies to the trustee. Both the executor and trustee sign the R-1s and attach one copy to Form 706 with a check or money order.*

We'll address Schedules R and R-1 later; meanwhile, leave the box at item 10 blank.

Now that you have completed Part 1 as much as you can, skip over Part 2: ***Tax Computation***. You can not complete Part 2 until you have completed Parts 3, 4, and 5, and all schedules on Form 706. There are nine asset schedules to complete (A through I) and seven deduction schedules (J through U). Schedules R and R-1 are not deduction schedules.The next part that you can do is Part 3: ***Elections by the Executor***.

Four Elections by Executor

Part 3 (at the top of page 2) consists of four rather technical questions. You **and** your executor may have to do a little research on these questions. By "research" we mean studying the IRS instructions that relate to the questions, and reviewing the applicable sections of the Internal Revenue Code. The four questions, as they appear on Form 706, consist of approximately 65 words. The IRS instructions thereon comprise about 4,800 words. The applicable IR Code sections (2032, 2032A, 6166, and 6163) consist of about 11,000 words. Obviously, you cannot — should not — answer these questions off the top of your head. Each requires a checkbox answer: ☐ Yes, or ☐ No.

In abbreviated form, the questions read as follows:

1. *Do you elect alternate valuation?*

2. *Do you elect special use valuation?*

3. *Do you elect to pay the taxes in installments?*

4. *Do you elect to postpone part of the taxes?*

As to Question 1: alternate valuation, we suggest a "No" answer. The alternate valuation law (IRC Sec. 2032) says that you can revalue everything up to six months after death. Our premise is that, if you have done the simplifying efforts that we have proposed in previous chapters, you should be able to complete the entire Form 706 in six months' time. Simply instruct your executor to sell everything that he needs to *before* the six months, and treat the proceeds amount as the date of death value.

As to Question 2: special use valuation, we also suggest a "No" answer. If "Yes," the instructions tell you to prepare Schedule A-1: Section 2032A Valuation. This schedule and its instructions take up six pages on Form 706. Glance through these pages and read the 20-step checklist for this election. When you do, we are convinced that "No" will be your answer.

As to Question 3: installment payments, your answer might be "Yes," or it might be "No." It depends on there being any closely held business, farm, or real estate in your estate that exceeds 35% of the value of your gross estate. We see merit in a "Yes" answer if your estate has illiquid assets to the extent described in IRC Section 6166. We discussed this in Chapter 10: Building Needed Liquidity.

As to Question 4: postponement of taxes, we suggest a "No" answer. The postponement rule of Section 6163 applies only to reversionary or remainder interests. These are ownership interests covered by Section 2033 (any interest at time of death) and Section 2037 (transfers taking effect at death). Subsection 2037(b) defines the term "reversionary interest" as—

> *Any possibility that property transferred by the decedent* [before death] *may—*
> *(1) return to him or his estate, or*
> *(2) be subject to a power of disposition by him* [at death].

With all of the preplanning and simplifying efforts that we have urged upon you in Chapter 8: Compiling Prior Transfers, you should feel quite comfortable with a "No" answer to Question 4.

Importance of "Letters Testamentary"

The questions in Part 3 above (and others in Part 4 below) require that your executor make probing inquiries into your estate affairs. His inquiries are going to generate hostility and taunting by prior transferees, asset holders, financial institutions, out-of-state sources, and out-of-country authorities. Beneficiaries and their attorneys are going to be particularly hostile. To these inquirees, presenting them with a copy of your will appointing your executor will not convince them of his authority. They want to see a court-approved legal document called: ***Letters Testamentary***. The dictionary definition of this term is—

> *A written instrument from a court or officer thereof informing an executor of his appointment and of his authority to execute the will of the decedent.*

How does your executor get Letters Testamentary?

Answer: He has to petition the Superior Court, Probate Division, for such letters in the county where you reside. Each state has its own petitioning process and legal forms. The type of initiating legal form is: *Petition for Probate of Will, Letters Testamentary, and Independent Administration* . . . or other title words to this effect. On the petition form, your executor requests that—

a. ☐ Decedent's Will be admitted to probate.
b. ☐ He be appointed Executor with Letters Testamentary.
c. ☐ Authority be granted to administer estate independently.
d. ☐ Bond not be required.

Other matters also appear on the petition form. The principal such "other matter" will be a public *Notice of Death and of Petition to Administer Estate*. The Notice is addressed to all heirs, beneficiaries, creditors, contingent creditors, and other persons who may have a financial interest in the will or the estate of the decedent. A hearing date is set, after which — if there are no objections or challenges — the presiding judge affixes his signature to an ***Order for Probate***. Thereupon, the court clerk issues the Letters Testamentary. This one-page document is typified in Figure 12.1.

We can hear your cries of anguish now. "You mean *my* estate has to be probated? I have everything in joint tenancy; I have a living trust; I'm covered by insurance and other contracts. Why probate . . . darn it?"

Our position is that for any estate exceeding $1,000,000 your executor should be *prepared* for probate. He doesn't actually have to complete the process; just initiate it. There are a lot of dissidents out there who will try to disqualify your executor, if he doesn't petition for Letters **within 30 days** after your death. The term "out there" includes stalking attorneys, disgruntled heirs, activist professionals, and recalcitrant asset holders. A million dollar plum hanging from a tree is a natural target for covetous pickers. Picking at and fee-milking such a plum is a form of legalized grave robbing.

Petitioner's Name: Address: Business Hours Phone No.	*For Court Use*
SUPERIOR COURT OF __________ **COUNTY OF ____________** Address:	
Estate of ____ Decedent ____	Date of Death:
LETTERS TESTAMENTARY	Case Number:

1. ☐ *The Last Will of the above named decedent having been proved, the court appoints* __________________ ☐ Executor 2. ☐ *The court appoints* __________________ ☐ Administrator 3. ☐ *The personal representative is authorized to administer the estate under the Independent Administration of Estates Act* ☐ WITH full authority ☐ WITHOUT authority to *sell or exchange real property* OFFICIAL SEAL	4. AFFIRMATION *I solemnly affirm that I will perform the duties of personal representative according to law.* Executed on __________ At ________________ ________ /s/ ________ Personal Representative 5. CERTIFICATION *I certify that this document is a correct copy of the original on file in my office, and that the letters issued the above-appointed person have not been revoked, amended, or set aside, and are still in full force and effect.* Date: ____________ ____________, Clerk by __________, Deputy OFFICIAL SEAL

Fig. 12.1 - Near-Replica of Official Form: Letters Testamentary

So, get your executor prepared. In fact, **accompany him** to your county law library, to the superior court probate clerk, and to the legal forms publisher in your area. Get sample petition forms and pleadings. After a petition for letters case has been heard, that case's records are open to public inspection. You and your executor should inspect several such records in the probate clerk's office. Seek permission for photocopying, and pay whatever clerk's fee is necessary. The procedures and hearing on a petition for Letters Testamentary are quite perfunctory. No attorney is needed. Only if your will is contested, or your executor is charged with malfeasance of duty is an attorney required.

Overview of Part 4

Now, back to Form 706 and its Part 4: ***General Information.*** Just below this title heading is what we call: *Authorized Representative for the Executor.* Officially, the wording at this portion reads:

> *Authorization to receive confidential tax information . . ., to act as the estate's representative before the Internal Revenue Service, and to make written or oral presentations on behalf of the estate if return* [Form 706] *is prepared by an attorney, accountant, or enrolled agent for the executor.*

There follow 10 entry boxes for the name of the "tax representative," his address, state in which licensed, type of license ☐ attorney, ☐ CPA, ☐ EA (enrolled agent), ☐ CAF number (Centralized Authorization File, maintained by the IRS), phone number, and signature of the representative. This authorization is for **tax** representation only; it is not legal authorization before the Probate Court. Your executor, with Letters Testamentary, is his own legal representative. If you haven't already done so, we suggest that you and your executor shop around for a tax specialist. Our position is that a tax specialist can relieve your executor of the Form 706 tasks, without interfering with probative tasks, should the need for probate arise.

Items 1 through 5 of Part 4: General Information, are matters which relate to your occupational background, marital status, and amount of dispositional intent. Item 1 reads:

Death certificate number and issuing authority (attach a copy of the death certificate to this return).

Obviously, you have to leave item 1 blank. As to items 2, 3, 4, and 5 you can certainly fill those in.

Item 2 asks for your business or occupation, or former business or occupation. Item 3 asks for your marital status (including date of divorce and date spouse predeceased you, if applicable). Item 4 asks for your surviving spouse's name, social security number, and the amount that you have specifically bequeathed to her. Item 5 asks you to list: *Name of individual, trust, or estate receiving $5,000 or more; Identifying number; Relationship to decedent; and Amount.*

Except for the amount column, items 4 and 5 can be filled in now. The amount column displays the final amounts that each of your heirs (distributees) will receive . . . **after** expenses and taxes. You won't know what your expenses and taxes are, until after completing Part 2: Tax Computation.

General Information: Continued

Items 6 through 16 of Part 4 are quite technical and detailed. Each item requires a "Yes/No" checkbox answer. In some cases, research of the applicable tax law and extensive inquiries to your heirs, transferees, and custodians of property will be required. Somewhere in the process of answering these questions, presentation by your executor of his Letters Testamentary will be required . . . and possibly challenged. You can help to reduce any post-death discord that might arise by doing pertinent research and inquiry on your own, while alive.

We urge that you read through all of the questions yourself. Better yet, you and your executor go through them together. Skim-read them first, for orientation purposes. With Form 706 in front of you, start at the top of page 3 which is headed: ***Part 4 — General Information (Continued).***

Preprinted bold instructions to Questions 6 through 16 say—

Please check the "Yes" or "No" box for each question.

If you answer "Yes" to any of the questions, you must attach additional information as described in the instructions.

It is our belief that you'll probably answer "No" to about half the questions — maybe more than half.

The questions are too lengthy and too intensive to present them verbatim here. Besides, you should read them directly off of Form 706 yourself. The questions are trying to establish what prior-to-death transfers of property interests you may have made, or may have received. The questions refer to specific tax code sections and to specific pages of the instructions for more information.

For example, the first such question (item 6) reads—

Does the gross estate contain any section 2044 property (qualified terminable interest property (QTIP) from a prior gift or estate) (see page 6 of instructions)? ☐ *Yes,* ☐ *No.*

The referenced instructions read—

If you answered "Yes," these assets must be shown on Schedule F. Section 2044 property is property for which a previous section 2056(b)(7) election (QTIP election) has been made, or for which a similar gift tax election (section 2523) has been made. For more information, see the instructions on the back of Schedule F.

This gives you an idea of why we think you should read each of the Part 4 Continuation questions yourself, and follow up on the references as needed. As to the references to sections of the IR Code, visit your local public library or your tax professional's office, and photocopy them. While at it, you may want to consult with your tax specialist on these questions only.

Following the completion of Part 4: General Information, there is Part 5: ***Reconciliation***. The term "reconciliation" summarizes the assets in your gross estate, and the expenses and deductions allowed against your gross estate. Schedules A through I are asset schedules, whereas Schedules J through U are deduction schedules. Obviously, you can't even begin Part 5 until all of the applicable schedules are completed. Hence, skip over Part 5 for the time being.

Schedules A through U

The "heavy duty" of Form 706 is its nine asset schedules: A through I. Together, they constitute your gross estate. Your total gross estate, in turn, constitutes Step 1 in the tax computation process in Part 2 above. There is just no way around it. To know the value of your gross estate and how it is derived, you have to fill in all of those schedules which are applicable to your situation.

We are not going to repeat that which we have already presented in previous chapters. Our position is that, if you haven't heeded our earlier suggestions, you need to plow through each and every one of the nine asset schedules. The presumption is that each applies to you, unless you can establish that one or more do not apply. You won't know until you actually look at each schedule and read the IRS instructions thereto. Doing this while alive, we believe, will cause you to more fully appreciate what your executor — or some tax specialist — will have to do after your demise.

As to your deduction schedules — J through U — much is common sense. Helpful in this regard is to think in terms of two classes of deductions, namely: (a) *expense* deductions, and (b) *bequest* deductions. The expense deductions are J, K, and L. The types of expenses covered by these schedules are:

1. Funeral expenses — Sched. J, part A
2. Administration expenses — Sched. J, part B
3. Litigation expenses — Sched. J, part C
4. Debts and claims — Sched. K, part A
5. Mortgages and liens — Sched. K, part B
6. Property casualty losses — Sched. L, part A
7. Property protection expenses — Sched. L, part B

You can actually fill out Schedules J, K, and L by following two principles. For those expenses that you simply cannot avoid, make reasonable estimates of them. Talk to family and friends, and to other knowledgeable persons who have gone through the Form 706 experience. The second principle is to prejudge those allowable expenditures which can reasonably be eliminated before death. Try to hold all expenses in check, as much as you reasonably can. Whatever is paid out of the gross estate — for professional fees, expenses, debts, claims, losses, etc. — reduces what is left for distribution to your heirs.

As to the bequest schedules M through U, the official titles are:

M — ***Bequests, Etc., to Surviving Spouse***
O — ***Charitable, Public, and Similar Gifts and Bequests***
T — ***Qualified Family-Owned Business Interest Deduction***
U — ***Qualified Conservation Easement Exclusion***

Any of those schedules can reduce your death tax significantly. Schedules M and O are most useful **after** you have exhausted your exemption amount (up to $1,000,000) via ordinary bequests to your nonspousal and noncharitable heirs. Schedules T and U, where applicable, can extend the exemption amount another $300,000 to $500,000 (depending on year of death). See IR Code Sections 2031 and 2057.

The instructions to Schedule M (about 3,600 words) are preprinted directly on Form 706 itself. In contrast, the instructions to Schedule O (about 2,700 words) are found in the instruction pamphlet which accompanies Form 706. On *each* schedule, after listing the bequests of property interests and totaling the amounts, three computational lines appear. Said lines are—

a. *Federal estate taxes payable out of property interests listed* $______
b. *Other death taxes payable out of property interests listed* ______
c. *Federal and state GST taxes payable out of property interests listed* ______

When added together, a, b, and c are *subtracted* from the bequeathed amounts. This way, Schedules M and O bear their own prorata share of the total transfer tax imposed on your gross estate.

Part 5: Recapitulation Now

Previously, we suggested that you skip over Part 5: Recapitulation, until you have completed Schedules A through I (for assets in your gross estate) and Schedules J through U (for deductions against your gross estate). Now that you have completed the schedules that apply, you have the task of entering their bottom line amounts onto Part 5. For your filling-in purposes, omit the *Alternate Value* column for Schedules A through I. In edited form, we are reproducing Part 5 in Figure 12.2. As indicated, Part 5 is arranged into two portions, namely—

Gross Estate: ***Items 1 through 12***

Deductions: ***Items 13 through 23***

In the gross estate portion of the Form 706 instructions, there is a bold printed leadoff statement which reads:

You must make an entry in each of items 1 through 9.

This instruction is followed by an explanation as to why you "must make" an entry on each line. Said explanation reads—

If the gross estate does not contain any assets of the type specified by a given item, enter zero for that item. Entering zero for any of items 1 through 9 is a statement by the executor, made under penalties of perjury, that the gross estate does not contain any includible asset covered by that item.

Other instructions to Items 1 through 9 refer you back to specific questions that you answered in Part 4: General Information. If you answered "Yes" to certain questions, you must attach the relevant schedule to explain why there are no assets to report on Form 706.

The only instruction of significance regarding deduction items 13 through 23, is item 17. Here, you get into a technical matter, called: *property subject to claims*. This is property in Schedules A through I where debts outstanding, judgment liens, tax liens,

FORM 706	Part 5 - RECAPITULATION	
Item No.	**Gross Estate**	**Value at Date of Death**
1	Schedule A - Real Estate	
2	Schedule B - Stocks and Bonds	
3	Schedule C - Mortgages, Notes, and Cash	
4	Schedule D - Insurance on the Decedent's life	
5	Schedule E - Jointly Owned Property	
6	Schedule F - Other Miscellaneous Property	
7	Schedule G - Transfers During Decedent's Life	
8	Schedule H - Powers of Appointment	
9	Schedule I - Annuities	
10	Total gross estate (add items 1 through 9)	
11	Schedule U - Conservation Easement Exclusion	
12	Total Gross Estate less exclusion (subtract item 11 from item 10). Enter here and on line 1 of the Tax Computation	
Item No.	**Deductions**	**Amount**
13	Schedule J - Funeral and Administration Expenses	
14	Schedule K - Debts of the Decedent	
15	Schedule K - Mortgages and Liens	
16	Total of items 13 through 15	
17	Allowable amount of deductions from item 16	
18	Schedule L - Net Losses During Administration	
19	Schedule L - Expenses Incurred in Administering Property NOT Subject to Claims	
20	Schedule M - Bequests, etc., to Surviving Spouse	
21	Schedule O - Charitable, Public, and Similar Bequests	
22	Schedule T - Family-Owned Business Deduction	
23	Total allowable deductions (add items 17 through 22). Enter here and on line 2 of the Tax Computation	

Fig. 12.2 - The Recapitulation of Form 706 Schedules A through U

mortgage defaults, and other liability claims have not been settled at time of death. The instructions for item 17 read—

> *If the amount on item 16 is more than the value of the property subject to claims, enter* ***the greater of*** *(a) the value of the property subject to claims, or (b) the amount actually paid at the time the return is filed.*

Items 12 and 22 in Part 5 (and also in Figure 12.2) read, respectively, as—

12. ***Total gross estate less exclusion (subtract item 11 from item 10). Enter here and on line 1 of Tax Computation.***

22. ***Total allowable deductions (add items 17 through 22. Enter here and on line 2 of Tax Computation.***

As you may recall, the "Tax Computation" is Part 2, on page 1 of Form 706. We'll address Part 2 in a moment.

The GST Tax Explained

There is just one more matter pertaining to Form 706 that we have to tell you about. It has to do with the GST tax on Generation-Skipping Transfers. If your adjusted taxable estate exceeds $3,000,000 and you have made bequests by will or trust to your grandchildren or great-grandchildren, there will be a GST tax. Said tax is a modified second transfer tax. It is a tax on the privilege of skipping over your children and passing property interests down generational lines. The tax is "modified" to the extent that a $1,000,000 GST exemption applies [Section 2631].

The GST tax is imposed only on the value of property interests that are actually transferred to skip persons. If the transfer arrangement is such that there are skip persons and nonskip persons (your children or siblings, for example), there is no GST tax on property transfers to the nonskips. The reason for this is that, when the nonskip person dies, the transferred property is includible in his gross estate. There, it will be fully Form 706 taxed. For skip persons (your grandchildren and great-grandchildren), the GST tax applies only to property which is includible in your gross estate: Schedules A through I. The GST tax is added onto your regular Form 706 tax. The "add on" point takes place after your net estate tax is computed.

In Figure 12.3, we present a schematic arrangement of what may be helpful in explaining the GST concept. Complications arise when non-GST trust arrangements are used to effect the property transfers (such as QTIP trusts, charitable remainder trusts, insurance trusts, annuity trusts, life estate trusts, etc.). A GST trust is one in which the only beneficiaries are skip persons; there are no intermediate property interests. When there are no intermediate (nonskip person) property interests, the GST transfers are referred to as: *Direct Skips*.

The GST tax rate is a flat 55%. This is the same rate that applies to all Form 706 adjusted taxable estates over $3,000,000. Before the 55% GST rate effectively applies, however, there is a $1,000,000 exemption from tax. This exemption is equivalent to $1,818,182 (1,000,000 x 1/0.55) in property interests being transferred directly to your grandchildren. Adding the $3,000,000 and $1,818,182 together, it is evident that gross estates over $5,000,000 are the ones most affected by the GST tax.

Schedules R and R-1

If your Form 706 estate is subject to the GST tax, you are required to prepare Schedules R and R-1. Both schedules have the same title, namely: ***Generation-Skipping Transfer Tax***. Both schedules apply to direct skips from you to your grandchildren. Schedule R applies to direct skips from your estate (to irrevocable trusts) at time of death; Schedule R-1 applies to intervivos transfers (into revocable trusts) made prior to your death. Part 1 of Schedule R permits computation of an *inclusion ratio* for indirect skips via non-GST trusts.

There are some 4,000 words of official instructions explaining what goes on Schedule R and on Schedule R-1. Schedule R is three pages (with three parts), whereas Schedule R-1 is one page. We urge that you examine these two schedules on your own, and the

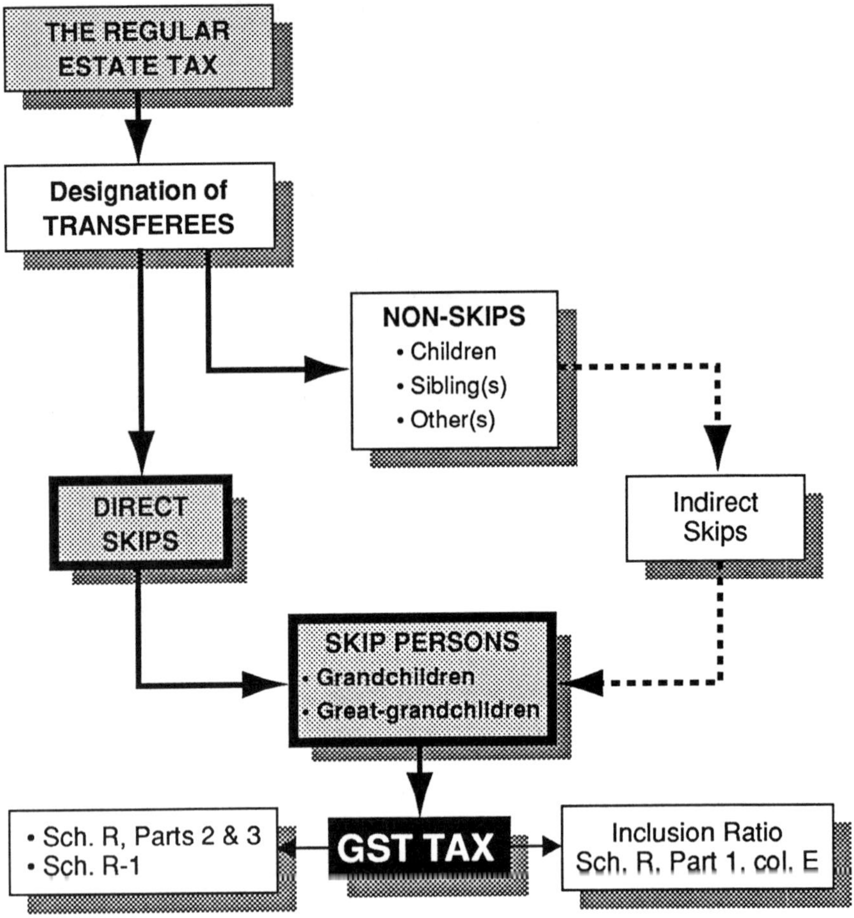

Fig. 12.3 - Representation of What Takes Place for Generational Skips

instructions thereto. Our bet is that if your gross estate exceeds $5,000,000 and you are serious about making GST transfers, you will — and should — seek competent professional assistance. In the meantime, we offer a few instructional highlights.

Part 1 of Schedule R is subtitled: ***GST Exemption Reconciliation***. The substance of the term "reconciliation" means that the $1,000,000 GST exemption can be *allocated* to any one, or combination, of six different property interest transfers. The six allocable ways are—

1. By decedent against his lifetime transfers,
2. By executor against decedent's lifetime transfers,
3. By property interests bearing the GST tax,
4. By property interests NOT bearing the GST tax,
5. By direct skips from intervivos trusts, and
6. By skip person distributions from indirect trusts.

All of these exemption allocations, when totaled, cannot exceed $1,000,000.

Part 2 of Schedule R computes the GST tax on property interests which bear the GST tax. Let us illustrate with simple numbers. Suppose you have a gross estate of $7,000,000 of which you direct by will that $3,000,000 go into a GST trust. Your entire $1,000,000 exemption is allocated to this property. Your regular net estate tax (after all deductions and credits on Form 706) is assumed to be $4,000,000. What is your GST tax?

Using simplified procedures, the computation goes as follows:

Step 1 —	Estate tax value of all property interests transferred	$3,000,000
Step 2 —	Portion of net estate tax borne by property interests (3/7 x $4,000,000)	1,714,285
Step 3 —	Tentative direct skip amount (subtract step 2 from step 1)	1,285,715
Step 4 —	Allocable GST exemption	1,000,000
Step 5 —	Amount subject to GST tax (subtract step 4 from step 3)	285,715
Step 6 —	GST tax due (*divide* step 5 by **2.818182**)	101,385

In other words, over and above the regular Form 706 tax on the $3,000,000 direct skip (at Step 2), there is added another $101,385 in GST tax. This tax is paid out of the $3,000,000. This leaves $1,184,330 [3,000,000 – 1,714,285 estate tax portion – 101,385 GST tax] to be transferred into a GST trust which is exempt from further transfer tax.

The divisional factor of 2.818182 at Step 6 is *preprinted* on Part 2 of Schedule R. It is also preprinted on Schedule R-1. It derives from the fact that direct skip property bears its portion of the estate and GST tax. Mathematically, it derives from 1 + 1/0.55 = 2.818182.

If the direct skip property does *not* bear the GST tax (Part 3, Schedule R), the same computational procedures as above apply, down through Step 5. Instead of Step 6 applying a divisional factor, a *multiplying* factor of 0.55 is used. For the same example as above, the Part 3 GST tax would be $171,145 (285,715 x 0.55).

These numbers illustrate that for direct skip bequests of $3,000,000, the GST tax is not severe. Once the full exemption is absorbed, the GST tax adds on to the regular estate tax.

Putting It All Together

Now is the time to turn back to page 1 of Form 706 and focus on its Part 2 — ***Tax Computation***. To appreciate the full 706 experience, you have to go through the computational steps yourself. We will simplify them for you. We know that all of the 28 preprinted steps will not apply in your case. The basic ones will apply, and such is the sequence we want to present. So that you'll understand the steps better, we need to make a few simplifying assumptions.

Our first assumption is that all of your prior estate planning activities — wills, trusts, life estates, annuities, taxable gifts, etc. — took place **after** October 22, 1986. This was the date of enactment of the Tax Reform Act of 1986 (P.L. 99-514), which made sweeping changes in the Internal Revenue Code. The unified gift/death credit concept was instituted then, as was the GST exemption concept.

Secondly, we are assuming that all your Schedules A through I assets are located within the U.S., and that you have inherited no property from other decedents within the past 10 years. This assumption eliminates your need for Schedule P: ***Credit for Foreign Death Taxes***, and Schedule Q: ***Credit for Tax on Prior Transfers***. Since these are credit schedules, any entry from them would help reduce your Form 706 tax.

With the above assumptions, the complete death tax computational sequence is presented in Figure 12.4. For each step, you can fill in your own numbers, using those developed from your

FORM 706	Part 2 - TAX COMPUTATION		
Step	**Description**	**Instruction**	**Amount**
1	**Total gross estate**	From line 12 Reconciliation	$5,000,000
2	**Total deductions**	From line 23 Reconciliation	365,000
3	**Taxable estate**	Subtract step 2 from step 1	4,635,000
4	**Total taxable gifts**	From latest filed Form 709	250,000
5	**Adjusted taxable estate**	Add steps 3 and 4	4,885,000
6	**TENTATIVE TAX**	From Table A Instructions	2,327,550
7	**Gift tax payable**	From latest filed Form 709	- 0 -
8	**Adjusted estate tax**	Subtract step 7 from step 6	2,327,550
9	**MAXIMUM UNIFIED CREDIT**	For year 2002 (Figure 1.1)	229,800
10	**Tentative net tax**	Subtract step 9 from step 8	2,097,750
11	**Credit for state death tax**	From Table B Instructions	350,720
12	**Net estate tax**	Subtract step 11 from step 10	1,747,030
13	**GST TAX**	From Sch. R, part 2, line 10	337,730
14	**TOTAL TRANSFER TAX**	ADD steps 12 and 13	2,084,760
Make check payable to Internal Revenue Service • Write decedent's name, SSN, and "Form 706"			

Fig. 12.4 - Basic Steps for Determining Your Death Tax With Form 706

own estate.

Simply to help step you through Figure 12.4, we are presenting example numbers of our own. As such, we are assuming that your gross estate is $5,000,000 and that you have willed $3,000,000 in direct skips to your grandchildren. We are also assuming the year 2002, when the unified credit is $229,800 (which is equivalent to a $700,000 exemption; recall Figure 1.1). Furthermore, you made $250,000 in taxable gifts during life, but you paid no actual gift tax.

Completion and Conclusion

For the numbers that we have entered in Figure 12.4, your total transfer tax turns out to be: $2,084,760. Thus, of your $5,000,000 gross estate, your heirs (nonskips and skip persons) will receive $2,550,240 [5,000,000 – 365,000 expenses – 2,084,760 tax]. Of this amount, your children (nonskips) will get $936,190; your grandchildren will get $1,614,052 [3,000,000 – 1,048,218 estate tax portion – 337,730 GST tax]. The prior $250,000 in taxable gifts, presumably were made to your children. Your children also got the benefit of your $10,000 annual gift tax exclusions.

With this information, you can now finally complete the *Amount* column for items 4 and 5 in Part 4: ***General Information***. The item 4 amount would be whatever you entered on Schedule M: Bequests to Surviving Spouse. The item 5 amounts might be:

Child A	468,095)	
Child B	468,095)	$ 936,190
Grandchild 1	403,513)	
Grandchild 2	403,513)	
Great-grandchild x	403,512)	$1,614,052
Great-grandchild y	403,512)	
	2,550,240	

With this item 5 entry in Part 4, your draft Form 706 should be as complete as you can possibly make it.

What is the conclusion that we want you to come to?

We want you to conclude that computing — estimating, really — your death tax while alive is an entirely different experience from that derived from your annual Forms 1040 that you have, or will have, filed over 35 to 50 years throughout life. Form 706 is so different that only a rare person — such as yourself — actually undergoes the experience. Therefore, our contention is that by experiencing Form 706 now, you'll develop much better insight into why simplification of your estate is so necessary.

ABOUT THE AUTHOR

Holmes F. Crouch

Born on a small farm in southern Maryland, Holmes was graduated from the U.S. Coast Guard Academy with a Bachelor's Degree in Marine Engineering. While serving on active duty, he wrote many technical articles on maritime matters. After attaining the rank of Lieutenant Commander, he resigned to pursue a career as a nuclear engineer.

Continuing his education, he earned a Master's Degree in Nuclear Engineering from the University of California. He also authored two books on nuclear propulsion. As a result of the tax write-offs associated with writing these books, the IRS audited his returns. The IRS's handling of the audit procedure so annoyed Holmes that he undertook to become as knowledgeable as possible regarding tax procedures. He became a licensed private Tax Practitioner by passing an examination administered by the IRS. Having attained this credential, he started his own tax preparation and counseling business in 1972.

In the early years of his tax practice, he was a regular talk-show guest on San Francisco's KGO Radio responding to hundreds of phone-in tax questions from listeners. He was a much sought-after guest speaker at many business seminars and taxpayer meetings. He also provided counseling on special tax problems, such as divorce matters, property exchanges, timber harvesting, mining ventures, animal breeding, independent contractors, selling businesses, and offices-at-home. Over the past 25 years, he has prepared nearly 10,000 tax returns for individuals, estates, trusts, and small businesses (in partnership and corporate form).

During the tax season of January through April, he prepares returns in a unique manner. During a single meeting, he completes the return . . . *on the spot!* The client leaves with his return signed, sealed, and in a stamped envelope. His unique approach to preparing returns and his personal interest in his clients' tax affairs have honed his professional proficiency. His expertise extends through itemized deductions, computer-matching of income sources, capital gains and losses, business expenses and cost of goods, residential rental expenses, limited and general partnership activities, closely-held corporations, to family farms and ranches.

He remembers spending 12 straight hours completing a doctor's complex return. The next year, the doctor, having moved away, utilized a large accounting firm to prepare his return. Their accountant was so impressed by the manner in which the prior return was prepared that he recommended the doctor travel the 500 miles each year to have Holmes continue doing it.

He recalls preparing a return for an unemployed welder, for which he charged no fee. Two years later the welder came back and had his return prepared. He paid the regular fee . . . and then added a $300 tip.

During the off season, he represents clients at IRS audits and appeals. In one case a shoe salesman's audit was scheduled to last three hours. However, after examining Holmes' documentation it was concluded in 15 minutes with "no change" to his return. In another instance he went to an audit of a custom jeweler that the IRS dragged out for more than six hours. But, supported by Holmes' documentation, the client's return was accepted by the IRS with "no change."

Then there was the audit of a language translator that lasted two full days. The auditor scrutinized more than $1.25 million in gross receipts, all direct costs, and operating expenses. Even though all expensed items were documented and verified, the auditor decided that more than $23,000 of expenses ought to be listed as capital items for depreciation instead. If this had been enforced it would have resulted in a significant additional amount of tax. Holmes strongly disagreed and after many hours of explanation got the amount reduced by more than 60% on behalf of his client.

He has dealt extensively with gift, death and trust tax returns. These preparations have involved him in the tax aspects of wills, estate planning, trustee duties, probate, marital and charitable bequests, gift and death exemptions, and property titling.

Although not an attorney, he prepares Petitions to the U.S. Tax Court for clients. He details the IRS errors and taxpayer facts by citing pertinent sections of tax law and regulations. In a recent case involving an attorney's ex-spouse, the IRS asserted a tax deficiency of $155,000. On behalf of his client, he petitioned the Tax Court and within six months the IRS conceded the case.

Over the years, Holmes has observed that the IRS is not the industrious, impartial, and competent federal agency that its official public imaging would have us believe.

He found that, at times, under the slightest pretext, the IRS has interpreted against a taxpayer in order to assess maximum penalties, and may even delay pending matters so as to increase interest due on additional taxes. He has confronted the IRS in his own behalf on five separate occasions, going before the U.S. Claims Court, U.S. District Court, and U.S. Tax Court. These were court actions that tested specific sections of the Internal Revenue Code which he found ambiguous, inequitable, and abusively interpreted by the IRS.

Disturbed by the conduct of the IRS and by the general lack of tax knowledge by most individuals, he began an innovative series of taxpayer-oriented Federal tax guides. To fulfill this need, he undertook the writing of a series of guidebooks that provide in-depth knowledge on one tax subject at a time. He focuses on subjects that plague taxpayers all throughout the year. Hence, his formulation of the "Allyear" Tax Guide series.

The author is indebted to his wife, Irma Jean, and daughter, Barbara MacRae, for the word processing and computer graphics that turn his experiences into the reality of these publications. Holmes welcomes comments, questions, and suggestions from his readers. He can be contacted in California at (408) 867-2628, or by writing to the publisher's address.

ALLYEAR Tax Guides

by Holmes F. Crouch

Series 100 - INDIVIDUALS AND FAMILIES

BEING SELF-EMPLOYED .... T/G 101
DEDUCTING JOB EXPENSES .... T/G 102
RESOLVING DIVORCE ISSUES .... T/G 104
CITIZENS WORKING ABROAD .... T/G 105

Series 200 - INVESTORS AND BUSINESSES

INVESTOR GAINS & LOSSES .... T/G 201
SIDE BUSINESS VENTURES..................................... T/G 202
STARTING YOUR BUSINESS .... T/G 203
MAKING PARTNERSHIPS WORK .... T/G 204

Series 300 - RETIREES AND ESTATES

DECISIONS WHEN RETIRING .... T/G 301
WRITING YOUR WILL .... T/G 302
SIMPLIFYING YOUR ESTATE .... T/G 303
YOUR EXECUTOR DUTIES .... T/G 304
YOUR TRUSTEE DUTIES .... T/G 305

Series 400 - OWNERS AND SELLERS

RENTAL REAL ESTATE .... T/G 401
OWNING NATURAL RESOURCES .... T/G 402
SELLING YOUR HOME .... T/G 404
SELLING YOUR BUSINESS .... T/G 405

Series 500 - AUDITS AND APPEALS

KEEPING GOOD RECORDS .... T/G 501
WINNING YOUR AUDIT .... T/G 502
DISAGREEING WITH THE IRS .... T/G 503
CONTESTING IRS PENALTIES .... T/G 504
GOING INTO TAX COURT .... T/G 505

For information about the above titles, and/or a free 8 page catalog, contact:

www.allyeartax.com

Phone: (408) 867-2628 Fax: (408) 867-6466